**All the Facts You Need—
From an Expert Who's Been There**

THE ULTIMATE
INSIDER'S GUIDE TO ADOPTION

"An incredibly informative, readable, and practical guide for anyone considering or pursuing adoption. At last, there is a book that successfully demystifies adoption and presents a thorough and accurate look at both domestic and international adoption."

—Ellen S. Glazer, LICSW, author of *The Long-Awaited Stork: A Guide to Parenting After Infertility*

"Thanks to Elizabeth Swire Falker for giving us this guide to what is often a long, winding road to forming one's family through adoption. Her knowledge, wit, and ability to use her own and others' personal experiences make this the Bible of the nuts and bolts of domestic and international adoption. I will recommend this to all those exploring adoption as the road to building their families."

—Phyllis Lowinger, MS, LCSW

"Finally, an adoption-savvy friend who experienced the process first-hand guides us through the logistics, emotional turmoil, legalities, and financial picture of adoption."

—Kathy Furbush, founder of www.TryingToConceive.com

"Extraordinarily comprehensive, as well as encouraging and upbeat in its approach to assisting would-be adoptive parents. The up-to-date information, insights, and resources provided are very rich and will undoubtedly help readers understand and manage the adoption maze more effectively and efficiently. I suspect that the book will also inherently enable many who are still undecided about adopting to make the leap to this wonderful family-building alternative."

—Linda Applegarth, EdD, director of psychological services,
The Center for Reproductive Medicine & Infertility,
Weill Medical College of Cornell University

THE ULTIMATE
INSIDER'S
GUIDE TO
ADOPTION

Everything You Need to Know

About Domestic and

International Adoption

ELIZABETH SWIRE FALKER

**WARNER
WELLNESS**

NEW YORK   BOSTON

If you purchase this book without a cover you should be aware that this book may have been stolen property and reported as "unsold and destroyed" to the publisher. In such case neither the author nor the publisher has received any payment for this "stripped book."

The information in this book is as up to date as possible; however, it is sold with the understanding that legal information is often subject to new and changing interpretations, government rulings, and legislation. The reader should consult with a law professional regarding specific questions.

Copyright © 2006 by Elizabeth Swire Falker

Warner Wellness

Hachette Book Group USA
1271 Avenue of the Americas
New York, NY 10020
Visit our Web site at www.HachetteBookGroupUSA.com.

Warner Wellness is an imprint of Warner Books, Inc.

Printed in the United States of America

First Edition: November 2006
10 9 8 7 6 5 4 3 2 1

Warner Wellness is a trademark of Time Warner Inc. or an affiliated company. Used under license by Hachette Book Group USA, which is not affiliated with Time Warner Inc.

Library of Congress Cataloging-in-Publication Data
Falker, Elizabeth Swire.
　　The ultimate insider's guide to adoption : everything you need to know about domestic and international adoption / Elizabeth Swire Falker.—1st ed.
　　　　p.　cm.
　　Includes index.
　　ISBN-13: 978-0-446-69730-9
　　ISBN-10: 0-446-69730-3
　　1. Adoption—United States.　2. Intercountry adoption.　3. Adoptive parents—United States.　I. Title.
　　HV875.55.F36　2006
　　362.7340973—dc22　　　　　　　　　　　　　　　　　　2006011606

Book design by Ralph Fowler

This book is lovingly dedicated
to the memory of two brave women
who enriched my life by sharing their lives with me.

Lisa Goldenberg Altman
1969–2004

Sheila Springer
1963–2005

ACKNOWLEDGMENTS

First and foremost I would like to thank my agent for her unbelievable support for this book; without Debra Goldstein (and creative culture, inc.), there would be no book. Thank you for believing in this project and refusing to give up!

To my editor at Warner Books, Natalie Kaire, thank you for contributing your brilliance and insight into ensuring that every nuance of every word contributed to the underlying message about the miracle of adoption and becoming an adoptive parent.

To my friends and colleagues at the Gladney Center for Adoption, thank you for the privilege and honor—and the amazing experience—of serving as head of the New York Tri-State Family Association. I am forever grateful for your collective and individual wisdom and support. To Andrea, Chontel, Debra, Gongzahn, Jim, Marshall, Meredith, Nonya, Sharon, Vanessa and Mike, from the bottom of my heart, thank you! (See you at the picnic!)

To the incredible staff at the Wykagyl Starbucks, thank you for making my daily delicious iced, half-caff, venti, seven-pump, skim, extra ice, double-cupped mochas (now known as an iced-half-caff-venti Liz). I would not have a functioning brain or my sanity without your coffee.

To Diane, Gretchen, Jennifer, Jill, Kate, Kathy, Kim, Laurie, Lisa, Nora, Noreen, Molly, Tara and Vickee (and all of the women who attended the GFA's Coffee Klatches), thank you for sharing your voices and experiences with me and being a part of my own process of becoming an adoptive parent.

To my amazing and brilliant office staff: my legal assistants Brenna Kaplan, J.D., and Danielle Bifulci. Your dedication to this book and attention to detail did not go unnoticed. Thank you for helping this book get to press. I am truly blessed to have such talented women working in my office.

To my husband, life partner and soul mate, for his unending patience and support while I learned to parent a toddler, run my own law practice and write a book all at the same time; thank you for continuing to help me hold the door shut!

To David, without whom I have no focus or center, thank you for being my son and bringing new richness to my life.

And to Diane,* for your bravery and honor; thank you for being our son's birth mother and being a part of our family. *Namaste.*

* Names have been changed to protect individual's privacy.

CONTENTS

Part Three
Going International

Part Four
Appendices

INTRODUCTION

CHOOSING ADOPTION

Or did it choose you?

So you're thinking about adopting? Wow! Congratulations, that's fabulous! Let me tell you, with very few exceptions, the adoptive parents I've had the privilege of meeting (and I've met many) are—in my opinion—enlightened, or at the very least, more evolved than the average parent. I know, because I've been there and faced the tough questions about how, when and why I was going to become a parent. I spent tens of thousands of dollars on assisted reproductive technologies, I endured multiple miscarriages, and it was only when I came face to face with the thought of losing my husband on September 11 that I really looked at the reality of my life and the depth of my despair (not to mention impending financial ruin) and was able to open my eyes to the beauty of adoption. I guess you could say I was a tough case at first. But let me tell you, while adoption wasn't my first choice in family building (infertility treatment came first), it was my *best* choice. And as you will read in a moment, adoption wasn't exactly the easiest experience for me. But now, as an adoptive parent, I can tell you that I've never been happier in my life. And it's what I went through to get here that makes me tell you this now—you'll never *ever* regret the decision to adopt. You'll only wonder why you didn't do it sooner!

I am proud of you for thinking outside the traditional family-building box, whatever may have brought you here (infertility, age, sexual orientation or some combination thereof). There are more babies and children in this country, let alone in the world, in need of a loving home than there are adoptive families. It is especially difficult to be considering adoption if you're going through or have gone through infertility treatment (been there, done that!). Considering other options for creating the life you've always dreamed of while letting go of fantasies about how you'd get that life isn't easy stuff. And you're facing those issues head-on if you're reading this book. You're taking charge, making a plan, and becoming a good consumer (and let's face it, you're probably going to spend a lot of money during this process, so you need to be a savvy consumer) as you work toward your dream of being a parent to one of those babies or children who need a home. So you, dear reader, are enlightened!

This book will tell you everything you'll ever need to know about becoming an adoptive parent. From talking about the types of adoption, coping with your home study, and filling out paperwork for your agency and/or U.S. Citizenship and Immigration Services (USCIS)[1] to managing the what may feel like a way-too-long wait for your beautiful family to be created, this book will help you navigate your journey and provide support and reassurance while you wait. There is a lot to learn and a lot you need to know in order to speed your journey toward parenthood, and it's hard to find the straight poop on adoption so that you can become an expert at cleaning poop off a beloved little tushie.

This book will give you the facts without telling you how you *should* adopt. Have you encountered them yet?—those exceedingly nice people who seem to think the only way to adopt is to go through a domestic open adoption in which you see the birth family every weekend? Or the people who think you're selling out if you don't schlep halfway around the world to save a child? Well, if you haven't met them yet, don't worry—you will! When I was struggling

---

1. You probably know it by its former name, the Immigration and Naturalization Service.

to become a parent, there were so many people telling me what to do and how to do it. I felt inundated with well-intentioned but completely inappropriate advice—at least it was inappropriate for me and my husband. As a result of all the "should-upon do-gooders" you'll encounter along the way, I made a decision that there will be no judgments made in these pages, no right or wrong way to adopt; just the information you need to become a parent and stay sane while you do so. Single parents, gay parents, infertile parents, not-exactly-thirtysomething-anymore parents: all are welcome in these pages. Take the information you read here, apply it to your situation, and adapt it to *your* life and needs.

There is also no right way to read this book. Please feel free to read this book in consecutive page order or to skip around. I've laid it out as best I can—chronological order in the adoption process based on the type of adoption you're pursuing—but if you're still choosing between domestic and international adoption, you might want to read more carefully the chapters that demystify these types of adoption and assess the pros and cons of each.

The first part of the book (chapters 1–3) focuses on issues that all adoptive parents must consider, from deciding where and how you'll adopt to financing your adoption and surviving your home study. The second part of the book (chapters 4–7) focuses on domestic adoption and will cover the essential aspects of adopting from the good ol' U.S. of A. We will discuss (among other things) the pros and cons of using an agency or an attorney, what you need to think about before you begin searching for a birth family, how best to market yourself, what to do and pack when you travel to get your baby, and how to cope when you get home. The third part of the book (chapters 8–10) focuses on international adoption. In Part 3 we'll talk about how to choose a country, how to find the right adoption professional to assist you, how to complete your USCIS paperwork and dossier, what to pack and what not to pack when traveling halfway around the world to get your baby, how to survive in a hotel and on the airplane home with your new little one, and how to cope once you're home.

Once you pick the type of adoption that is right for your life situation, you'll undoubtedly read every word I've written in the relevant section of the book and thus garner all the wisdom and cumulative experience I've gained from speaking with and supporting (through their adoption process) dozens upon dozens of adoptive families. We will make you an adoption pro before you even become an adoptive parent! Then, as your adoption process moves forward, you'll reread each and every word at least three times because you can't wait to make it happen!

It may have been a long haul to get here, and there's a lot still to accomplish before you actually hold your child in your arms. I want you to be excited as you read this book. Most of us—except for the unusually enlightened people who choose adoption without trying to conceive a biological child, known among adoption advocates as preferential adopters—come to adoption after an arduous journey through infertility. Once you decide to adopt, you're "expecting" just like all those people who do it the old-fashioned way, and even if no one else knows what's about to happen, you do, and you should be thrilled! There will be hard days, no doubt, but this is it: *you're about to become a parent!*

For some of us it takes a little longer and you need to do more exploration before you hit the bliss zone. Maybe you've been exploring the various ways to adopt, but nothing feels right. Birth families and relinquishment laws scare you, or the often-feared (and often baseless) lengthy wait for a domestic newborn turns you off, or traveling to Russia multiple times doesn't work for your work schedule. Don't worry if this is you; if adoption is right for you, one day you'll stumble across a seminar about adopting from Vietnam, and everything will click. Suddenly, everything in your life makes sense; it's like you've just put on a pair of glasses that bring everything into focus. Sometimes it takes even longer, and the fear and anxiety left over from years of infertility or trying to decide whether parenthood is right for you stay with you even as you pursue an adoption plan. That's okay too. For some people it takes a couple of days, weeks or even months before they realize that this is what is right for them, and then they experience the rush of rightness repeatedly (like every time your baby wakes up). I was a tough case at first, and I have to admit that more than once in the middle of the night I've started sobbing uncontrollably, holding my little boy and thanking the All-That-Is for helping me find him. It's in this moment that I realize I didn't choose adoption; it chose me.

Whichever of these paths finds you, when you decide to adopt, you experience a paradigm shift—the way you look at the world changes, and suddenly you feel more at home than you ever have before. You realize that this is what the Universe (God, Allah, the powers that be) always intended for you. There will come a day when you realize that while adoption may have been your second choice for family building, it is not—by *any* means—the second-best choice. It is in fact the *right* choice.

Although I now realize that adoption is my path and I've never been happier in my life, I first had to endure seven years of trying to conceive, six cycles of in vitro fertilization, seven miscarriages, and the donation of over $100,000 of our hard-earned money (and that of my insurance carrier) to the bank accounts of our infertility clinic. And I will admit that when we first started the process of adopting our son, I was also still trying to get pregnant (there's a confession if ever there was one!).

Our son, David, is now three and half years old, and the way he came to us has served to become a symbol to me of the destiny inherent in adoption. There were endless twists and turns in our adoption process, and because of the obstacles we faced in his adoption and the fact that he ultimately came home almost six months after his birth, there is no doubt in my mind or heart that David was always meant to be my son. He reminds me every day that our children pick us from someplace in the universe and that even if—or because—we can't or won't have biological children, they find a way to come home to us. It doesn't matter if we look the same, have the same religion, or speak the same language; our children find their way home to us. It is destiny. I know one day you will look in your child's eyes, and this knowledge will engulf and overwhelm you with a warmth and serenity that words cannot do justice.

I have learned so much from our process in adopting David and through my other adoption experiences since, and while working as an adoption advocate. I am motivated to write this book because I so wish that I had had an adoption-savvy friend guiding me through my adoption process, holding my hand, and helping me sort through emotionally and financially challenging issues without losing my sense of humor. I wish someone had told me before I started planning David's adoption everything that I know now.

In fact, it was as a result of my work as an adoption advocate for RESOLVE and as president of the Gladney Center for Adoption's New York Tri-State Family Association (the GFA), which provides support to several hundred pre- and post-adoptive families in the region, that I became dedicated to shedding light on the process of becoming an adoptive parent—demystifying and exposing the nitty-gritty truths as they are discussed by and among adoptive parents. All the "if I had only known" and the "what does this mean" conversations I've had with other adoptive parents are shared with you in this book. All the beautiful moments and experiences that I have been privileged to share with people as they become parents are shared with you in this book.

I was so moved by my experiences working with and supporting adoptive parents that not only did I seek out the opportunity to write this book (a labor of love if ever there was one) but I transitioned my career from one devoted to meaningless (to me) commercial litigation to practicing reproductive and adoption law. My understanding of adoption laws and the myriad legal issues that can be faced in domestic and international adoption gives me a unique perspective. I am not only able to help you understand the nuts and bolts of planning your adoption but I can also help you figure out when and how a particular law pertaining to consent or relinquishment of parental rights might be relevant for you, and help you understand what that law means in practical terms.

But most of all, I wrote this book because I want you to know in your heart and soul that your baby was always meant to be yours. I want you to be educated enough to know how to find the *right* birth mother. I want you to be aware of what is legal and possible in international adoptions and to choose a program that works for *your* family, not to select the popular program or agency that everyone else is using (or the only one that you think will accept you when there might have been others available) and wind up dissatisfied, frustrated and still waiting for your baby.

I want everyone to have the practical tips I have learned for traveling to get and bring home a baby or toddler (whether it's a two-hour or two-week journey home). I hope everyone at least thinks about the possibility of breast-feeding (and I know most of you still don't believe it's possible despite my assurances to the contrary), having a baby shower, planning a nursery, or hiring a doula (even if only for your hotel stay). And I want everyone to be prepared for the all-too-common depression that often follows adoption. No one talked openly to me (and I am an educated consumer and parent) about these things, and they're so important! I hope this book will help to educate and empower you, to help you find the resources you need when you need them so that you too will one day sit, rocking your child in your arms, and feel the power and love of adoption and know in your soul that this was meant to be.

PART ONE

~ ~ ~

THE ADOPTION DILEMMAS

~ 1 ~

DOMESTIC VERSUS INTERNATIONAL ADOPTION

The Pros, the Cons and All the Beautiful
Screaming Babies on Airplanes

There are a ton of misconceptions about domestic and international adoption, and I hope to dispel most of them in this chapter and help you figure out which of these two types of adoption is the right way for you to bring home your baby or child. Becoming a parent is hard enough an experience. (I'm sorry, my friend, but everyone has been right—you've got no idea until you're doing it just how tough it is to be a parent!) You owe it to yourself to make sure that you're comfortable with the type of adoption you're pursuing and that it's the right fit for your family and/or lifestyle. You will minimize the difficulties inherent in the adoption process and make the transition to parenthood smoother when you choose the right type of adoption for your family's needs. Not everyone can or should try to parent a child of a different ethnicity, or for that matter take care of a newborn. Making smart choices now can make life easier down the road.

Before you make up your mind between domestic and international adoption, you first might want to think about all the variables that go into building a beautiful family. Take the time now to think about skin color, racial features, age, finances, ignorant and enlightened family members, and political preferences (e.g., making a statement that you're making the world a better place by adopting an orphan), and then decide how and when you want to pursue adoption. One of the great things about being an adoptive parent is that you get to choose so much about how your family is going to look and be. Parents of biological children take what the universe gives them. We have the unique opportunity to say we want to parent a little girl from China, a little boy from Guatemala, a sibling set from Russia, or even a blond-haired, blue-eyed baby girl from Oklahoma. Ours is a unique situation, and for those of us who've lost all control over our reproductive lives, having the opportunity to exercise degrees of choice not common among the general population is pretty interesting and refreshing.

Let's take a moment to focus your thoughts. Take a look at the following questions, and then go through your answers with the detailed discussions that follow each topic. (There are no right or wrong answers here, so relax and have some fun fantasizing about your future family.) This exercise will help determine whether domestic or international adoption is right for you.

- **Question # 1—The Baby Age Issue:** Do you want to adopt a newborn, or are you open to adopting an older infant or child? You are going to have sleepless nights either way, but it is way, way more intense with a newborn than a two-year-old.

- **Question # 2—Birth Family Contact, Identity Issues and Relinquishment Laws:** Do you want to have a relationship with your child's birth family, or do you not want to deal with this at all? What will it be like for your family when you're helping your teen through the emotionally complex waters surrounding identity issues *and* adoption when you know little or nothing about his or her birth family, or when you can pick up the phone and call his or her birth mother? How are you going to handle the prospect that a birth mother might have days or even weeks before her relinquishment of parental rights is irrevocable and binding? Would it be easier for you to know that the baby someone is handing you has legally been declared an orphan and there isn't a birth family in the picture?

- **Question # 3—Estimated Time to Parenthood: Houston, We Have a Problem:** Do you need this to happen *yesterday*? It isn't going to. This is a long, arduous process, whether you go domestic or international. What you need to look at is whether you have the emotional and physical energy to devote to searching for a domestic newborn in need of a loving home or to traveling, perhaps multiple times, around the world to get your baby. Do you need someone who can handle everything for you? Do you need to know what is going to happen every step of the way and have a definite time line for when you will complete various steps in the adoption process, or can you go with the flow? International adoption follows a specific time line, with specific steps to follow every step of the way. Domestic adoption doesn't offer any definites about anything. You could have a baby in a few months or a few years (a lot depends on what you want and need in an adoptive situation, as we will discuss in chapter 5).

- **Question # 4—Ethnicity Issues:** Do you care whether your baby looks like you or are you open to adopting a baby or child that (quite frankly) everyone will know is adopted (and will want to know all the details about his or her "real" family)? Is your immediate and/or extended family going to be receptive to a child of a different race or with different physical characteristics? How is Great-Aunt Agatha going to react to your beautiful Asian toddler, and do you care?

- **Question # 5—Finances:** Do you have limited resources to spend on an adoption, or is the sky the limit? Does your employer offer adoption assistance? Do you have friends or family members who can loan you money if you're broke after years of expensive infertility treatment?

- **Question # 6—Medical Background and Health Information:** How much information would you like or do you need about your child's medical history? Do you want/need a detailed family history of cancer and heart disease risk, prenatal exposure to toxins and medical care, or are you okay with a physician reviewing a brief medical file and/or a video of your child to help assess physical and developmental issues (if any) that you may be facing?

- **Question # 7—Parents with "Special Needs":** Are you one of the many same-sex and/or not-thirtysomething-anymore parents trying to adopt? Are you physically challenged or recovering from a long-term or potentially life-threatening illness? You may have to adopt internationally or go through a public agency or the foster-care system. Are you okay with that? If not, are you prepared to be aggressive and proactive during each stage of the process?

Question # 1
The Baby Age Issue

When we started the adoption process, I knew that I wanted the experience of holding a tiny screaming newborn and being up all night, every night (*what* was I thinking?). Being in my midthirties at the time, sleep deprivation didn't scare me. Now, being an experienced and profoundly sleep-deprived parent, I know that adopting an older baby or child with established sleep patterns (even if temporarily disrupted by the strangeness and excitement of a new home) may be a *good* thing!

One of the most common reasons people choose to adopt domestically is because they want to parent from the first days of a baby's life. If you have your heart set on being in the delivery room (not always possible, but sometimes it does happen) and cutting the cord or taking a baby home shortly after birth, you're going to have to stick to the continental United States. I chose domestic adoption because I didn't want to miss any part of my child's life—I wanted to share his life history from day one. I also wanted to breast-feed, which is easier with a newborn adoption than an older infant adoption. Thus, Charlie and I chose a newborn, domestic adoption.

The youngest baby you can adopt internationally is *usually* about four months old. Indeed, if the age of the baby isn't important to you and you think that adopting a baby who's six or nine months old is just fine, then you have far more options. You can adopt an older infant internationally (Guatemala, however, is one country that regularly places younger infants) through a private domestic adoption, through an agency or through foster care. And if you're open to adopting a toddler, preschooler or child, then you can go just about anywhere in the world, including your hometown!

Now is the time to really think this through. Having the energy to be a good parent is hard, so maybe *not* facing the every-two-hour feeding thing is better for you. Can you really manage being kept up all night and stumbling through a fog and into office furniture during the day? Don't get me wrong, this is going to happen to you as a parent at some point, regardless of the age of your child. (One good stomach bug and no one gets any sleep for a couple of days.) But newborns basically give you about four hours of interrupted sleep in any given twenty-four-hour period. If you've got a partner who can help take a few hours at night for you, that's a big plus, but eventually even with night support, about six weeks after the baby comes home, you're going to be standing in your kitchen, crying from exhaustion at 7:15 A.M. because you have to face *another* day with a screaming, colicky newborn (one look at your baby, however, and the exhaustion is totally worth it). I have spoken with so many "older" adoptive parents who chose international adoption at least in part because they would bring home a baby who wouldn't interrupt as many nights' sleep (theoretically, at least). My friend Jenna adopted a little girl from Ethiopia because she had "been there and done that" with the sleep-deprivation thing with her three biological children. Being in their forties and deciding to add a sibling through adoption, Jenna and her husband were very clear about what would push them over the edge; for Jenna it was the sleep issue. While she recognized that there would be some initial sleep issues due to adjustment and bonding, Jenna knew that once life settled down, her new daughter would know how to sleep for eleven hours. You cannot say that for a newborn, that's for sure!

The other side of the equation, however, is that when adopting an older toddler or child, you may (not always, but certainly sometimes) have to contend with a history of abuse, child neglect, language differences, developmental delays, or illness due to a prolonged stay in an orphanage. For many caring and devoted families these are not obstacles but are instead hurdles to overcome. Early intervention, psychological care and good medical care go a very long way toward overcoming deficits and challenges presented from less than ideal living conditions early in life. And Jenna is the first to tell you that the language thing—while challenging at first—is overcome amazingly fast. Little people have a surprising (only to adults) ability to learn languages at astonishing speed.

One final note about adopting domestically or internationally—the flight home is going to be terrifying and basically one of the most trying parts of your adoption experience. (Are you surprised?) The advantage with a domestically adopted newborn—putting aside your terror that the newborn is going to be contaminated by recirculated airplane air—is that the baby will usually sleep through the flight, which is probably not more than twelve hours, inclusive of layovers. But you could also have to endure hours of high-pitched newborn squawking and the evil looks from fellow domestic travelers. International adoptive parents, on the other hand, are potentially looking at days of travel with a baby or child they barely know, can't communicate with, and who will likely scream the entire flight back to the States.

Question # 2
Birth Family Contact, Identity Issues and Relinquishment Laws

A major difference between domestic and international adoption is access to information about, and contact with, your child's birth family. Knowing specific details about your child's birth family may help your child through potential identity issues as she grows older. Some parents are unconcerned and undaunted by the thought that they will never be able to explain to their offspring anything about her birth family or why she was placed for adoption.

In contrast, some adoptive parents feel very strongly that maintaining an ongoing relationship (even if it's through sending cards and letters through an intermediary) with their child's birth family is important so that the adoptee maintains a connection with his or her biological family and can ask questions when and if necessary. Others don't find this to be important, but having met or spoken with a birth family or even just receiving a letter describing the circumstances surrounding the child's conception and placement for adoption provides much more insight and closure than that presented by sketchy details from an orphanage halfway around the world. (Many adoption support groups have programs to help offset these "disadvantages." See the Resources section for more information.) Several international countries now provide, or are attempting to provide, information about birth families. Typically, however, you get little or no information about your child's birth family when you adopt internationally.

The ability to have contact with the birth family is another of the major reasons people choose to do a domestic adoption. Whether it's limited to prebirth contact or an ongoing postadoption relationship, you have far more options to design an adoption that enables you to have knowledge of your child's background and help your child understand where he or she comes from, biologically speaking. This is

An Unforeseen and Unexpected Perspective

My good friend Julia, who is one of the most educated and aware adoptive parents I've ever met, confided something to me the other day. Julia and her partner adopted a little girl from China a few years ago. They had gone to China on their honeymoon and had fallen in love with the culture and the people. When they discovered they were infertile, they didn't even think twice: they would adopt from China! And they loved the idea that they would be helping to make the world a better place for a child.

Julia, however, never considered the fact that she would never be able to explain to Hannah (their daughter) why her birth mother abandoned her (Julia and her partner know that Hannah was left at an orphanage when she was about a week old) or anything about her birth family. Julia never realized this might be important information to Hannah, or indeed that it was important to know for Julia's own peace of mind.

It actually was *Julia's* reaction to not having contact with the birth family that was more startling to both of us. Indeed, Julia carries a heavy weight around with her every day, trying to resolve her feelings of sorrow and worry about Hannah's birth mother. Julia wishes there was some way she could reassure Hannah's birth mother that Hannah is well, thriving, and is the light of her adoptive parents' lives. My educated, adoption-advocate friend Julia didn't realize the grief she and Hannah would face from not knowing any details about Hannah's background, her birth family and their decision to leave Hannah one night on an orphanage doorstep.

As Julia and her partner consider building their family again, they are going back to China to adopt. Julia says she will be much more proactive in trying to get information about the circumstances surrounding their next offspring's birth history. They also plan to take trips to China and to the orphanage where Hannah spent her early months so that Hannah may feel some connection to, and understanding of, her birth history.

something you can "negotiate" before the baby is born, and you can define the degree of anonymity or contact you wish to maintain with the birth family.

Domestic adoptive parents who establish relationships with the birth family prior to birth also may have the option to begin to bond with the baby prior to birth. This can be very risky and traumatic if the birth mother or father chooses to parent before placement of the baby with the adoptive parents, but when it works out, it is a wonderful experience. I have known adoptive parents who attended OB visits, sonograms and the baby's delivery with their birth mother. One of my good friends not only coached her daughter's birth mother through delivery, she cut the cord and then started breast-feeding her daughter within minutes of her birth.

Some people, however, just cannot handle the concept of having contact with a birth family, whether prebirth or postadoption. If it is overwhelming to you to consider having to talk to birth parents or deal with the possibility of a failed match or placement, you might want to seriously consider international adoption. You get your baby or child with a clean slate and no immediate emotional baggage regarding sending cards and letters to someone forever connected to your child (which, even to those of us who happily do it, can feel very threatening). If, however, you might want the option to have contact or even an ongoing relationship with your child's birth family, international adoption may not be the best choice for you.

I spoke recently with one adoptive mother who chose to go international because she couldn't deal with the fact that she felt prospective birth mothers would be "interviewing" her or that she would have prebirth contact with a birth mother who ultimately would choose to parent. I speak from experience; it can be very difficult to talk to a birth mother—sometimes on multiple occasions and for long periods of time—who chooses to work with another adoptive family or who chooses to parent the baby herself. There are ways to manage this risk, but there's no getting around the major downside of domestic adoption: *birth parents maintain their right to parent and may choose to parent at any time up until relinquishment papers have been signed, and even for a period of time thereafter in some states.* (See the Appendix for a breakdown and analysis of state adoption laws.) It is very risky to put yourself out there and not have a baby come home.

Question # 3
Estimated Time to Parenthood:
Houston, We Have a Problem

"Liz, tell me honestly, how long is this going to take?" I hear this question all the time from prospective adoptive parents. I overhear prospective adoptive parents discussing that domestic adoption is too expensive and takes too long and that international adoption is much faster and much less expensive. They are all wrong! There are no rules, and I cannot tell you exactly how long your adoption will take. I can tell you that there will be numerous setbacks and hurdles, many sleepless nights worrying about one thing or another, and a moment of pure and utter joy when you look into your child's eyes and know that every moment of the wait was worth it.

For some domestic adoptive parents the wait can be very long and very hard. Just a few years ago the wait for a domestic adoption of a Caucasian newborn averaged three years. But recent changes in how domestic adoption takes place (for example, birth families now choose adoptive parents, and many adoptive parents post their adoptive-parent profiles on the Internet to reach a greater pool of birth parents) generally have served to speed the average wait time for a domestic adoption.

These days most reputable attorneys and agencies will tell you the average wait for a healthy newborn adopted domestically is twelve to eighteen months, and the cost will be around $15,000. Indeed, if you're savvy and do your research, it doesn't have to be super-expensive or present a long wait. In comparison, most international adoptions take between nine and eighteen months and cost around $20,000.

Some domestic adoptive parents will receive placement of a newborn very quickly (one couple I know waited only four months for their son from the time their home study was completed), and 95 percent of all domestic adoptive parents receive placement within approximately two years. Sure, there are people who wait more than two years to adopt a baby, and I have news for them (and some of them are my good friends)—there are things they could've done to speed up the process. Many of them didn't want to take a proactive and savvy approach to finding a birth family and were prepared for the wait; others were resigned to the fact that they knew they needed a particular situation, and finding the right match with a birth family was going to slow the process down.

The twelve to eighteen months is merely a national average and doesn't consider how open and flexible you are to different birth-family situations, which can have a significant impact on how long you'll wait to bring a baby home. However, whether you wait three months or two years, it is the plain truth that with domestic adoption, you're going have to let go and let the process unfold before you, even when you take an aggressive approach to finding a birth family. You can be proactive and aggressive about finding your baby or sit back and let an agency do everything for you, but either way, you will have to let go of all your expectations about adoption and how long it will take you to become a parent. This is truly one of the defining characteristics of domestic adoption: *you don't know when it will happen.* You could get a phone call tomorrow that there's a baby waiting for you in Texas. Or you could wait and wait and wait and *wait.*

Domestic adoption is a very unpredictable and challenging adoption path. It is up to you to decide whether you can handle the potential feelings of helplessness (and if you're infertile, this is a tough thing to do, as you've already lost control over your reproductive abilities; losing control to some random woman in Kansas who is deciding between you and three other adoptive families may not be so much fun) in exchange for possibly being able to be present when your baby is born, cut the cord and all that good (but bloody) stuff. Indeed, one of the hardest things for adoptive parents to handle about the process of domestic adoption is the powerlessness they often feel while waiting to be picked by a birth family or advised of the availability of a baby for adoption. Once you start the process of domestic adoption, there is a lot of waiting involved with little or no power over time frames, and it can be really tough.

But the flip side of the fear and powerlessness you may feel during a domestic adoption is the control that you can exercise in a domestic adoption. Certainly, you will be there from the early days of life and can help minimize adjustment, attachment and bonding issues that many international adoptive parents struggle with. You may also wind up with a beautiful healthy baby who—despite the fact that you didn't care what race or ethnicity your baby is, you just wanted a newborn—strangely looks exactly like Great-Aunt Agatha!

The great advantage of international adoption is its predictability. The reliability of the international adoption process goes something along these lines: Fill out forms A to Z, have a home study, get fingerprinted, send forms A to Z along with dossier (which may also contain forms A to Z) to agency and government(s) for approval, wait for referral, receive referral, wait x number of weeks to travel to get baby. Domestic adoption has no milestones or markers to help you tick off the time. If you choose domestic adoption, while you may wait the same period of time for a baby as someone adopting from China, you may sit on your thumbs for much of the time, while the parents adopting from China have milestones that tick off the wait to receive the referral of their baby. With international adoption there is no guesswork or worry about whether the baby is

This Is All Part of the Parenting Experience

Hassles and setbacks of all kinds happen with adoptions. From complications with processing fingerprints, foreign red tape, and birth parents who choose to parent, it can be overwhelming at times. Remember, however, that biological parents experience difficult pregnancies too. At least we don't have to go on bed rest for three months while we're waiting to become a parent!

Find a good support group and seek comfort from those who know what you're experiencing. And remember one very important and often overlooked fact: *the worry and stress you feel now is all part of the experience of being a parent.* You are just going to be trading one batch of worries (over your fingerprints or home study) for another (over earaches, teething pain or how early or late your little person is walking).

This too is part of being a parent; consider it your version of pregnancy angst and misery. Frankly, I am beginning to really appreciate the whole notion that we get to be pregnant with impending parenthood without the belly and weight gain that come with pregnancy.

Becoming a parent is tough no matter how you do it. There are just different stories to tell, but it is all part of becoming a parent. Consider the time you spend planning your adoption your parenting boot camp!

really coming home. There is no worrying about a birth mother who chooses to parent. The baby you receive a referral for is already classified as an orphan; the birth parents are out of the picture. Once you get your international adoption referral, that baby is coming home!

But that isn't to say that things always go smoothly with international adoptions. There are instances—rare instances—when things go awry. I know one woman who got her referral to adopt a baby girl from Guatemala and then, due to unforeseen and incomprehensible paperwork, waited four months longer than the average to travel to get her baby. Also, international adoption laws can change with no warning. Recently (in 2005), the Ukraine closed itself to adoptions by United States families. The U.S. government is working hard to reopen adoptions from the Ukraine (as of the date of this writing, it was reported that families who were waiting to travel to the Ukraine would be able to do so imminently). However, the likelihood that this will happen to you is small compared to the number of domestic adoptions that don't result in a placement.

Depending on whether you go the independent route or work with an agency, the success or placement rate of domestic adoption varies dramatically. Most reliable statistics indicate that as many as 60 percent of independent adoptions result in a placement (meaning 60 percent of adoptive parents receive placement of a baby with the first birth family with whom they match or choose to work with exclusively), whereas some agencies report statistics as high as 75 percent for successful placements (meaning 75 percent of the parents adopting receive a placement with their first birth family).

Whatever type of adoption you choose, you must remember that adoption is *guaranteed* as long as you follow through and keep working toward an adoption. As long as you don't give up, your baby *will* find his or her way to you. If you ever speak with parents whose first adoption didn't work out, they will undoubtedly tell you that the baby who didn't come home wasn't their baby, and it wasn't meant to be.

Question # 4
Ethnicity Issues

I was really honest with myself when the process began. And while it isn't flattering to admit, I knew I had so much on my plate being a first-time parent that I wasn't going to be able to be a good parent to a baby that didn't look like me. That's the ugly and honest truth. Now that I've been a mom for a while and am confident in my parenting skills, I am not in the least bit intimidated about having a child with different skin color and having to respond to the intrusive, stupid and sometimes nasty questions from strangers in the supermarket (or even worse, insensitive comments from ignorant family members). But I wasn't ready for that experience as a first-time adoptive parent. One of the features of domestic adoption is that you can specify that you want to adopt a child who looks like you (or somewhat like you). You even can tell your adoption professional that you want to adopt a blond-haired, blue-eyed baby boy. You may have to wait longer when you're this specific (for example, most birth mothers don't know the gender of the child they're carrying, at least not until they receive some form of health care), but if you want a baby who looks exactly like your husband and you want a little boy, you can delineate these requirements as part of your domestic adoption.

I've known adoptive parents who feel very, very strongly that there are too many children in need of good homes to choose to adopt from this country, where the competition for a newborn is high. These parents were committed not only to building their families but to helping make things better in our world community. They knew they could handle all the insensitive comments from relatives, whereas I knew I couldn't.

One of my best friends in the whole entire world has two beautiful little boys who were born in Korea. She was educated and prepared, but even she will admit that she was dumbfounded, horrified and infuriated the first and the one hundredth time someone asked a question such as "Are they really brothers?"; "Where are their real mothers from?"; or her personal favorite "They're so lucky you saved them!" It took her a while to learn to just walk away or to come up with a smart-ass response. Parents who adopt babies with similar racial features will get these comments too when people learn that they've adopted, but they happen all too frequently to parents who've adopted children who don't resemble them. By all means, fire away with a nasty comeback. But better yet, correct the misconception, change the negative language and help educate that person in the supermarket aisle. Adoptive parents everywhere will salute you!

Please also remember that parenting a child who is adopted, regardless of ethnicity, will require a greater degree of awareness and sensitivity as your child ages. School projects for which you have to create a family tree can pose difficult issues for adopted kids. It doesn't matter if your child looks like you or not—being a child who was adopted presents unique issues. But those issues definitely come up faster and are often more powerful when you and your child don't share skin color or eye shape. Are you going to be able to help her (and yourself) deal with this?

Question # 5
Finances

Believe it or not, as I noted above, domestic and international adoptions can sometimes cost about the same, but international adoptions tend to be more expensive. This is largely due to the costs incurred in traveling to get your baby. There's nothing like having to live in another country for three or more weeks to drive up the cost of your adoption! Some international programs cost less than the more expensive domestic adoptions, but a recent survey conducted by *Adoptive Families Magazine* revealed that the vast majority of domestic adoptive parents spent between $10,000 and $15,000 (inclusive of travel expenses) for their adoption.[1] That certainly isn't pennies, but it's far from the $28,500 I spent on my first adoption (we chose to work with a full-service agency, which tends to be more expensive than an independent adoption).

What is harder to gauge ahead of time is how much a domestic adoption will cost. International adoptions have more clearly de-

1. See *Adoptive Families Magazine*, February 2006, vol. 39, no. 1.

fined costs than domestic adoptions and tend to be more expensive. According to the survey in *Adoptive Families Magazine,* most international adoptive parents spent over $20,000 on their adoptions.

Informal 2002 and 2005 polls in *Adoptive Families Magazine* (see the Resources section for more information on these polls) showed that between 25 and 35 percent of domestic adoptive parents responding to both polls paid between $10,000 and $15,000. Of those domestic adoptive parents responding to the 2002 poll, 70 percent waited less than one year (data on wait times was not included in the 2005 poll). Of the international adoptive parents who responded to the 2002 poll, 31 percent paid between $15,000 and $20,000 and 28 percent spent between $20,000 and $25,000; 66 percent waited less than one year, and 31 percent waited one to two years. The 2005 poll, however, shows increasing costs for international adoptive families. By 2005, of those responding to the poll, the vast majority (61 percent) of international adoptive parents paid more than $20,000. According to these polls, domestic adoption appears to be faster and less expensive than international adoption.

If you need to know for sure how much it's going to cost every step of the way, you need to use a full-service agency. Agencies have set fees and guidelines for you to anticipate cost. And if you're doing a domestic adoption, using an agency can help absorb some of the risk of a domestic adoption gone wrong. (For one set agency fee, you usually can have several adoptions fall through. If, however, your first match with a birth family results in a permanent placement, you may have spent more than if you had chosen to work with an attorney.) An independent adoption—one that takes place using an attorney or facilitator or some combination thereof—will have more hidden and unanticipated costs. You could luck out and have an adoption that costs less than $10,000, or you could wind up shelling out larger sums of money if you have an adoption fall through and have to start from scratch.

If you want to control costs and go for a lower-cost adoption, domestic adoption may be the way to go, especially if you are open to adopting a special-needs baby or a child from the foster-care system or can undertake a lot of the legwork to locate a birth family yourself. There are also ways to make adoption more affordable, but if you need to know ahead of time exactly how much you will be spending, you need to consider working with an adoption agency (domestic or international) that presents a predetermined fee schedule.

Question # 6
Medical Background
and Health Information

A major reason people choose domestic adoption is that they get more information about a child's birth family's medical history. You usually also receive information about prenatal care (if your baby's birth mother received any) and anything that occurred during delivery that might impact your child's development or help you assess developmental issues later on (for example, low birth weight, poor Apgar scores or even oxygen deprivation). Indeed, more reputable domestic adoption agencies and attorneys make it their practice to take detailed medical and lifestyle histories from birth families, and you can thus learn everything from "Great-Uncle Bernie's" heart disease or diabetes (both of which may be genetic conditions) to whether your birth mother likes the color blue. International adoptions rarely offer the same amount of medical information that is available in a domestic adoption and hardly ever offer information about the child's birth family (although some countries, such as China and Korea, are making efforts to change this; in some cases you now can receive information from and maintain relationships with the foster family that cared for your baby).

Indeed, in the domestic arena you can hold out until you find a birth family that has a genetic, medical or psychological history that meets your requirements, and also a situation in which there is a degree of prenatal care and/or exposure to medications, drugs, or cigarette smoke with which you are comfortable. I have known adoptive parents who have chosen not to adopt when they didn't feel comfortable with a birth mother. In fact, one of my friends was so troubled by her introductory conversation with a birth mother that she alerted the agency with whom she was working that she was concerned this birth mother had psychiatric problems. The agency did some more investigation and learned that the birth mother did in fact have an extensive history of mental illness, which allowed them to place the baby with an adoptive family that was receptive to the birth mother's personal issues and the possibility that the child had inherited one of her psychiatric conditions.

International adoptive parents don't have those luxuries. They receive a referral of a baby or child and often have very little medical information about the baby's life thus far and no information about prenatal exposure to alcohol or drugs, prenatal care, or the birth family's medical and genetic background. Fortunately, there now are a bunch of highly trained pediatricians that specialize in helping adoptive parents assess the medical information they receive on an international adoption referral and will review pictures and videotapes. These specialists are also experts at identifying mysterious illnesses and symptoms when your child comes home. But the reality remains that, absent a visible deformity like a cleft palate or clubfoot, most international adoptive parents are in the dark about their child's medical condition until they bring their beloved new baby girl home and spend some time with her. International adoptive parents can choose to wait for another referral if they are uncomfortable with the medical background of the child for whom they receive a referral. However, most parents adopting internationally could care less about this stuff. While they may make an effort to preassess potential medical issues, they just want to bring their child home to a healthier, more loving environment with better medical care. They are prepared for the worst and hoping for the best—and the vast majority of the time, it is the best!

Domestic adoptive parents can also back out of a planned adoption if a child is born with a medical condition they are not prepared to deal with, but 98 percent of the time the adoptive parents are aware of most medical and genetic details of the baby's birth family and gestation and may even be aware of a cleft palate before birth. Serious medical issues in the neonate or newborn usually place the baby in a special-needs category. Adoptive parents interested in adopting a baby with special needs (commonly fetal alcohol syndrome or drug exposure) will have lower adoption costs, so if you're open to the possibility of parenting a special-needs baby, this is a more affordable way to adopt domestically.

Question # 7
Parents with "Special Needs"

There are a few more, albeit superficial, factors that shouldn't be overlooked when considering domestic versus international adoption, including your age and/or sexual orientation and physical abilities. Let's deal with the ultimate in superficiality—the beauty contest aspect of domestic adoption. It has been my experience (and my disgust) that a lot about domestic adoption comes down to marketing. Come on, let's face it: many birth families choose younger, more attractive adoptive parents. This is life and why I will talk a great deal about how to market yourself competitively if you choose domestic adoption. Indeed, some private adoption agencies have age cutoffs and won't even consider working with first-time domestic adoptive parents over the age of forty-two (which, between you and me, is ridiculous). If this is you, consider working independently with an attorney or a public agency (that may not discriminate against you because of your age) or going the international route.

Another ugly truth about domestic adoption is that it can be harder to adopt domestically if you are single or gay. It is not impossible to adopt domestically as a single or gay parent; it's just usually *harder*. You will have to choose your agency or attorney very carefully and may have to be very proactive in your search for a birth family. No one ever said anything about adoption was fair, and I will be absolutely blunt with you (it's why you bought the book)—gay and/or single adoption, whether domestic or international, is a challenging path. That said, Rosie O'Donnell and Sharon Stone are just two examples (and exemplary ones at that) of gay or single parents who've adopted domestically. They did it, and so can you! If you are gay, single or some combination thereof, don't immediately rule out domestic adoption. Read on in this book about working independently, marketing yourself and being aggressive about making adoption happen, and you too can be sitting watching the Home Shopping Network or reruns of *Gilligan's Island* at 3 A.M. with a hungry infant. But basically speaking, if you're on the older end of the parent spectrum, single and/or gay, international adoptions may be a more clearly defined path for you, because countries specify age requirements (usually much higher than for a domestic agency adoption) and whether they will accept single applicants. (Some countries specify that they won't accept applicants from gay individuals or couples). China, for example, has annual quotas for adoptions by single parents (we'll discuss age restrictions and other criteria for international adoptions in greater detail later in the book). And of course, foster-care and special-needs adoption is always an option for you (unless you live in a super-conservative state like Florida, which prohibits gay individuals from adopting, period).

One last category of special-needs parents are those who are physically challenged or recovering from a major illness such as cancer. As with the categories of special-need parents I discussed above, there is no reason that you can't try to adopt. You will have added pressure during your home study to demonstrate to your social worker that you're capable of taking care of a child and that your illness is conquered (to the degree that medical science can determine that). For example, someone who is a breast cancer survivor, and has gone more than seven years without a recurrence, and has a letter from an oncologist stating that the cancer is (presumably and we pray) permanently in remission has a good chance of being approved. Apart from the home study you may have a harder time finding an agency or an attorney who will work with you. The same goes for you as for all other special-needs parents—do your homework, be proactive, and you will find an adoption professional willing to help you adopt.

So let's review for a moment (in no particular order): Why would you choose domestic or international adoption?

Features of the Adoption	Domestic	International
Access to and control over medical and genetic information	Yes	Usually not
Access to information concerning the birth family's decision to make an adoption plan	Yes	Usually not
Possibility of being present at or before birth	Yes	No
Ability to parent from time of birth or shortly thereafter	Yes	No
Ability to choose or exclude racial or ethnic characteristics	Yes	Yes
Ability to have and control the type and extent of contact with the birth family after birth	Yes	No
Flexibility for designing an adoption that meets your financial needs	Yes	Yes

Features of the Adoption	Domestic	International
Flexibility in the system for older, single, gay or disabled adoptive parents	Sometimes; it depends on where and how you choose to adopt	Sometimes; it depends on where and how you choose to adopt
Making the difference in the life of an orphan	Yes	Yes
Ability to adopt an older child	Yes	Yes
Ability to adopt a child with special needs	Yes	Yes
Predictable system and process with milestones and established timeframes	No	Yes
High placement or success rate	Sometimes; nothing is guaranteed	Yes
Not having to deal with birth-family contact at any point in time	No	Yes
Ability to predetermine costs of adoption	Not unless you use a full-service adoption agency	Yes
Cost of adoption may be less than $15,000	Yes	Probably not

❧ 2 ❧

AFFORDING ADOPTION

A Little Creativity Goes a Long Way
Toward Making Your Dreams a Reality

T here is no doubt about it—adoption is expensive. We talked a little bit about the financial side of adoption in chapter 1, but now let's talk about it in great detail. Chances are you're among the vast majority of adoptive parents who don't have great sums of money on hand to pay for an adoption and you need to figure out how to come up with the necessary funds. You may also be basing your decision on where and how to adopt in part on how much various programs cost.

Surprising as it may be, as we've discussed, domestic adoption is generally less expensive than international adoption. According to a 2005 *Adoptive Families Magazine* cost survey, the most common price of any adoption (before tax credits and employer benefits are applied) is between $20,000 and $25,000.[1] However, almost 36 percent of the domestic adoptive families responding to the survey paid between $10,000 and $15,000, compared to 52.6 percent of those responding who paid $20,000 to $30,000 for an international adoption,

---

1. *Adoptive Families Magazine,* February 2006, vol. 39, no. 1, p. 33 (and breaking down cost by country for international adoptions)

with another 28.4 percent paying over $30,000 for an international adoption. According to the magazine, it broke down as follows:

Cost Incurred*	Domestic	International
$5,000–$10,000	9.7%	1.1%
$10,000–$15,000	35.5%	3.2%
$15,000–$20,000	19.4%	14.7%
$20,000–$25,000	16.1%	26.3%
$25,000–$30,000	9.7%	26.3%
Above $30,000	9.7%	28.4%

* Cost incurred before employee benefits or tax credits were taken

We're going to assume—for the purposes of this chapter—that you're going to need $20,000 to adopt your baby. Got that much cash sitting in the bank? I didn't think so. So let's figure out how you're going to pay for all this.

Show Me the Money!

First, and perhaps most important, you'll be happy to know that you probably won't need to come up with $20,000 all at one time. Whether you're going domestic or international, working with an attorney or an agency, you'll likely pay in installments as you go along. For example, your first payment might be a $2,500 retainer to your adoption attorney or a $300 application fee to your agency. Two notable exceptions will be for international adoptions, where you pay the bulk of money when you travel to get your baby (but in this scenario, you have enough advance notice to build up your financial resources) and when you work with a full-service, expensive agency that may require two or three large installments (close to $10,000 at three different points in time). Most adoptive parents, however, likely will be able to pay smaller increments over a period of six months to one year and thus may be able to save slowly and/or borrow from different sources to have money available on a rolling basis. I have included a link in the Resources section to a budgeting spreadsheet prepared by *Adoptive Families Magazine* that is very useful in helping to estimate your costs for both domestic and international adoptions and when you'll incur them.

Flexibility and creativity are going to be the name of this financing game. I don't care how debt- or risk-adverse you are—unless you've got tens of thousands of dollars in cash in the bank, you're going to need to make some hard choices and call in a few favors (even those with major strings attached). If you own your own home, you need to seriously consider leveraging this asset. If you'd consider obtaining a home equity line of credit (HELOC) to renovate your kitchen or bathroom, then why won't you think about doing the same to build your family? It is an easy source of money (provided you haven't already leveraged yourself to the hilt to afford infertility treatment), and it might even be tax deductible. (Check with your accountant about whether the interest on a HELOC is tax deductible.) If you can refinance your mortgage to reduce your monthly payments so that you have more money to save or to put in the bank right away, *do it!* If you can take a second mortgage, *do it!* Build a kitchen, build a family? New Viking range versus new viking baby? (Okay, so you can't adopt from Norway, but you get my point!) It seems like a no-brainer to me!

Other creative ways to finance your adoption are credit cards (check out some of those low-interest, or even better, zero-percent interest offers you're always getting in the mail) and loans from retirement plans like your 401(k) (although this might come with a penalty; at least you're paying yourself back and not some nameless, faceless bank). And let's not overlook the obvious but unpleasant—family members are always a good place to go for low- or no-interest loans. Heck, some family members will even give you money as a gift to help finance your adoption. Both my parents and my in-laws provided tax-free monetary gifts to help us afford our adoption(s). In fact, mom and dad and your mother-in-law and father-in-law (if you have such folks in your life) can each give about $10,000 per year, tax free, to both of you (that's $40,000 total if you're a couple and each of you has parents with cash to gift to you). If you feel super-guilty about taking money from family members, offer to pay them back out of your tax credit (which we'll get to in a moment) or over time.

But frankly, you need to start sucking it up! Whether it's your in-laws, mortgage or a credit card, you're going to have to find the cash and just accept the fact that unlike the vast majority of the parenting population who don't have to pay for this stuff, we do, and we have to make financial sacrifices. (All parents make financial sacrifices. Ours just come earlier than expected and usually exceed the norm.) You can console yourself by feeling morally superior to all those "got-pregnant-by-accident-again" (doh!) people and know that you're doing something truly magnificent by building your family through adoption. Seriously, I come from an anti-debt household (Charlie and I abhor all forms of debt, even mortgage debt—so realistic a world we live in!), and we're looking into credit cards to finance our next adoption. You gotta do what you gotta do!

Other ways to raise money to finance your adoption include (but aren't limited to):

- selling stock or investment properties

- refinancing car loans

- selling a second car

- raising your deductibles on your insurance policies to save money on premiums

- taking an extra job

- obtaining less expensive phone and Internet service plans (get rid of AOL for a few months and get a free Yahoo! account!)

- having a garage sale or selling stuff on eBay

- asking for donations from your church or temple (offer to babysit or perform community service in exchange for the support from your community)

- cutting coupons

- brown-bagging lunches

- eating in instead of going out to dinner (ouch—okay, one dinner out per month, but only one and keep it *cheap*!)

- subscribing to movie rental services like Netflix and Blockbuster that don't have late fees, and stop going out to the movies

- buying food in bulk

- cooking in bulk (check out cookbooks on once-a-month cooking; it's an investment in time over one weekend that saves money and means you've got prepared food in the freezer for a month)

- using up *everything* in your pantry before you go shopping again

- switching from name-brand to store-brand products

- exercising at home with videos (borrow them from the library or go to Wal-Mart, Target or Collage Video) instead of frequenting an expensive gym

- choosing not to buy coffee at Starbucks (oh my God—did I just say that?? But seriously, did you know you can save about $5,000 a year this way if you have a daily habit?)

- borrowing books and magazines from the library instead of buying them

- collecting your change in a jar at the end of every day and taking it to a Coinstar machine once a month

- looking at your balances on frequent-flier accounts and hotel rewards programs, as you may be able to use these toward travel expenses and deduct the cost of airfare or hotels from the dollar amount you're saving toward.

I know some of this seems like it is only going to add pennies to your savings account and isn't worth the hassle and stress it would cause your life and relationships, but if you ask adoptive parents who've done stuff like this, they will tell you it really *did* help!

Grants, Loans, Your Boss and Uncle Sam to the Rescue

There are also some grant and loan programs available to adoptive parents that you might be able to utilize to help raise money. Some employers offer adoption benefits where they *help* you pay for your adoption. (I'm constantly shocked by this; it just seems so progressive and cool to me.) These benefits are even tax free (subject to certain income limits), meaning you don't have to pay taxes on the money your company gives you toward your adoption. The trick is finding an employer who has an adoption benefit program in place and then getting hired. Check with your employee benefits department (or human resources) to see if your current company has adoption assistance, and if it doesn't, ask HR to consider it. Many people have successfully lobbied for their employer to create an adoption assistance program, arguing that they're very rarely used and look great in promotional material about the company. (I have provided a URL in the Resources section for how to go about lobbying your employer for these benefits). Check the Resources section for a link to an up-to-date listing of adoption-friendly workplaces.

There are several companies that offer grants and loans to people seeking to adopt. The criteria for receiving an adoption grant vary tremendously. Some of the grant programs are only available to low income families who are willing to adopt from foster care or accept a special-needs baby. Others just consider your income. I have provided a list of some grant programs in the Resources section. Do some research and see if you qualify for one or more of them, and then apply even if you think you don't meet all the criteria. It never hurts to try!

Low-interest loan programs exist for adoption too. I am, however, skeptical about these loans. When I was researching them for this book, so many of them were promoted alongside loans for cars that I really wondered if they were legitimate loans. I called around and got the runaround. I am sure some of these loans are legitimate (the ones that seemed "for real" are listed in the Resources section, but don't be limited to the information I provided. Do your own Internet search and see what you can find!), but I have to say I'd personally rather use a low-interest credit card than take a loan that has repayment terms and higher interest rates. The nice thing about credit card debt is that if you manage your credit well and have a good credit score, you can keep rolling it over from one zero-percent- or low-interest card to another. You cannot do that with a loan that has a contract and repayment terms. And watch out—some of these adoption loans have balloon payments, meaning that while you have low initial payments, you have a huge payment at the end of the term. As with everything else we savvy consumers must do, read the fine print!

One place you definitely need to read the fine print but don't need to be scared about is the Federal Adoption Tax Credit. Whether you adopt domestically or internationally, Uncle Sam will give you a dollar-for-dollar credit, up to $10,630 (as of 2005), for monies expended in connection with an adoption. Now what you get to expense and when depends on whether you adopt domestically or internationally and what your income level is. You may even be eligible for additional state and/or federal assistance if you adopt a special-needs child or a child from foster care. The Federal Adoption Tax Credit, however, is the subject of much consternation and confusion. Let us take a moment to examine this important aspect of adoption financing.

Oversimplified, if your adjusted gross income is less than $150,000, you're entitled to a tax credit of $10,630—meaning you get every dollar you spent, up to $10,630, back as a refund (as of

2005). If you earn more than $190,000, forget even applying for the credit; and if you earn between $150,000 and $190,000, the credit phases out, depending on your income level. There are little quirks about this law that confound even the most sophisticated accountant, so let's look at the following chart. This shows you some things you may need to tell your accountant and things you need to know when filing your tax return.

Domestic Adoption

When the Credit May Be Taken	For domestic adoptions you may take the credit in the year the expense was incurred, regardless of whether your adoption was finalized in that year. So if you start paying adoption expenses in 2005 for a baby who is born in 2006, you should start applying monies toward your tax credit on your 2005 return. (There are some exceptions, but generally you take the credit in the year in which the adoption expense was incurred.) This credit applies even if the adoption never takes place, the baby goes back to a birth mother, or the adoption is finalized in the following year.
How Much of a Credit You're Entitled to Take	The tax credit is per child. If you adopt 2 children in the same year, you're entitled to take the credit twice. Adoption expenses must be documented by receipts, and not all (but most) expenses are allowable.
What If I Can't Take the Entire Credit in One Tax Year?	If your tax liability in a given year is less than the amount you can take as a credit in a given year, you may carry forward a balance for up to 5 tax years until you have claimed a credit for the full $10,630. So let's say you can only claim a credit of $5,630 in 2005 for reasons that I

won't ever begin to understand (mercifully one of the degrees I didn't earn is that of CPA), you can claim the balance of $5,000 as a credit on your 2006 tax return.

The ability to carry forward the tax credit, however, does not mean that if you paid $30,630 dollars for your adoption that you may carry forward the $10,000 credit each year for 3 years until you've been reimbursed the $30,630 you paid for your adoption expenses. The maximum amount of the credit, per child, is $10,630.

International Adoption

When the Credit May Be Taken

For international adoptions, you usually may take the credit *only* in the year your adoption is finalized in the United States. If you start paying monies toward your adoption in 2005 but don't travel to get your baby until 2006 or don't receive her status as a U.S. citizen until 2006, you cannot take the credit until you're filing your tax return for the year 2006.

You may also only take the credit for an adoption that is finalized. If your adoption falls through and you wind up pursuing an adoption through another agency, country or program, you cannot apply the monies for the first international adoption toward the tax credit as you can for a domestic adoption.

Please have your accountant or CPA check the rules as they apply to your international adoption situation; there are circumstances in which an adoption is finalized in the country of birth that might qualify you for the credit prior to the year in which your child obtains U.S. citizenship.

International Adoption, continued

How Much of a Credit You're Entitled to Take	The tax credit is per child. If you adopt 2 children in the same year, you're entitled to take the credit twice.

Adoption expenses must be documented by receipts, and not all (but most) expenses are allowable. |
| **What If I Can't Take the Entire Credit in One Tax Year?** | If your tax liability in a given year is less than the amount you can take as a credit in a given year, you may carry forward a balance for up to 5 tax years until you have claimed a credit for the full $10,630. |

Special-Needs or Foster-Care Adoption

When the Credit May Be Taken	Special-needs and foster-care adoptions have different rules. For special-needs adoption you get a flat credit regardless of the actual documented expenses incurred. Foster-care adoptions are also eligible for adoption benefits from the Federal Title IV-E Adoption Assistance Program (see the Resources section for more information).

A child who is adopted internationally cannot qualify for the special-needs adoption credit, as the child must first be deemed a citizen or resident of the United States, and it must be documented that the adoption would not have taken place without financial assistance.

Check with your accountant for exceptions that may apply to your situation. |

How Much of a Credit You're Entitled to Take	The full credit applies even if your expenses do not come to the full $10,630.
	Additional state subsidies may be available to you (see the Resources section for more information).
What If I Can't Take the Entire Credit in One Tax Year?	The full credit applies even if your expenses do not come to the full $10,630.

When doing your taxes for the years surrounding your adoption, please consider the following tips:

- Make sure you've got an accountant experienced with this provision of the IRS Code (it changes frequently), as it is complicated and you need someone who understands the differences between domestic and international adoptions.

- If you do your own taxes (my recommendation is to get professional help on a tax credit of this nature), you will need to file **IRS Form 8839** and attach it to Form 1040 or 1040A and report the credit on line 50 of form 1040 or line 34 of 1040A (based on the 2004 forms). These forms are subject to change, so please check the instructions or go to the IRS Web site (www.irs.gov/taxtopics).

- You also will need the following forms, depending on where you are in your adoption process:

  — Form SS-5 to apply for a social security number for your child

  — Form W-7A to apply for an Adoption Taxpayer ID Number (ATIN) if you're in the process of adopting a baby domestically and it has not yet been finalized, and thus the child is not eligible for a social security number

— Form W-7 to apply for an Individual Taxpayer ID Number (ITIN) if your child is a legal resident or nonresident alien who doesn't qualify for a social security number

Please check the Resources section for a list of Web sites and other information on the Adoption Tax Credit and forms you need to file to receive the credit.

Adoption Insurance: Is it Really Worth it?

Several companies now offer adoption insurance. Depending on your situation and policy, if you have a domestic adoption that falls through, the insurance company will repay all or a part of the expenses incurred in connection with that adoption. It sounds like a great idea, except the premiums tend to be high and the circumstances under which you receive money back are stringent (for example, you might only get back monies contributed to the birth mother's living expenses). You may not qualify for the policy at all if you're adopting internationally. And as with all insurance (especially health insurance), you often have to fight for what you're entitled to.

If you're working with an adoption agency toward a domestic adoption, it definitely isn't worth your money to buy an insurance policy, and yet adoption insurance carriers often require you to be working with an agency to be able to qualify for a policy. Because the agency *should* have a system in place in which you don't expend additional financial resources if you have a failed adoption and need to work with another birth family, there *shouldn't* be a need to have insurance for a failed adoption or placement. This type of insurance might be worth considering if you're going the independent route, but as most families only lose about $5,000 on a failed independent adoption[2] and you get that money back on your taxes (under most circumstances), why spend even more money on a policy that may

2. *Adoptive Families Magazine,* February 2006, vol. 39, no. 1, p. 33 ("68.6% of failed adoptions cost the family less than $5,000").

or may not pay you anything? Check the Resources section if you want to do more research, but I encourage you to think long and hard before spending money on an adoption insurance policy.

Still Having a Hard Time Coming Up with Cold Hard Cash?

If you're still having a hard time coming up with enough money to adopt domestically or internationally, my next suggestion is to take a look at foster-adopt programs and special-needs adoption. I find it somewhat distasteful to be discussing these programs under finances, but I also realize that we all need to be realistic. If you're open to diverse adoption situations (discussed in greater detail in chapters 1 and 4) and you're low on cash, I urge you to consider adopting through your states foster-care system or accepting a special-needs baby or child.

These types of adoption are not right for everyone. You should *not* consider foster-adopt programs or special-needs adoption unless you're open to the risks and challenges inherent in these situations. First of all, you will have to go through extra hurdles (usually, at the very least, you're required to take some type of parenting class) on top of your home study to become a licensed foster parent. And you need to be prepared that, as a foster parent, the child you're seeking to adopt may not be freed for adoption (according to some studies 59 percent of foster children return to their biological parents and are not placed for adoption with their foster families[3]). That is the inherent risk in the foster-adopt system. Although it is often a wonderful way to build your family, many foster parents struggle through difficult situations before receiving final placement of a child in their home.

If an agency or social worker knows you're looking for a permanent placement, they may be more likely to try to match the baby or

---

3. Source: Evan B. Donaldson Adoption Institute, "Foster Care Facts" (http://www.adoptioninstitute.org/FactOverview/foster_print.html, January 9, 2006).

child placed in your home with a birth family that is less likely to receive permanent custody or that is not interested in parenting, thereby reducing your risk of heartbreak. There are also babies and children who are already available for adoption. Many states have Web sites on which you can start considering the children currently waiting for homes (see the Resources section).

Special-needs adoption is another great way to adopt, and when you consider the state subsidies and tax incentives, it's often free. But you need to do your homework and decide what you can and cannot handle as a parent of a special-needs baby or child before you consider this as a means of building your family. Some older children are categorized as "special needs" simply because of their age. Others are newborns who were born drug exposed or young children who were abused. If you're interested in considering this as a way to build your family, call the social worker who did your home study to get some references to agencies, both state and private, with whom you could discuss potential adoption situations.

Whatever avenue you choose to become adoptive parents, there's no doubt that you will incur additional financial burdens above and beyond what other families experience. Be creative and flexible, be diligent, and do your homework, and you'll find a way to pay for it. I have yet to meet a family that let its finances stand in the way of an adoption. And as a wise friend told me one day, "No matter how rich you are, you'll never have enough money to be a parent, because it's not about the riches; it's about what's in your heart."

~ 3 ~

THE INFAMOUS AND ANXIETY-PROVOKING HOME STUDY

One of the first things you'll be doing on the path to adoptive parenthood is getting a home study completed. I fondly refer to this step toward parenthood as getting your license to be a parent. This is the process by which you receive approval from the state in which you live to become an adoptive parent. You cannot adopt without it.

Whether you adopt domestically or internationally, use an agency or an attorney, you will need to have a home study conducted and probably updated. (If you do not complete your adoption within one year of the initial home study visit, you'll need to have it updated, and then it gets updated every six months until you're a parent.)

Avoiding the Home Study from Hell

Your home study will be one of the biggest stresses in your process, second only to completing your dossier and waiting for the referral of a baby for an international adoption or for a baby to be born and your birth family to sign relinquishment papers if you're adopting domestically. Many adoptive parents who were *preparing* for their home study told me there wasn't enough Valium on the planet to get them through the process.

The reality, however, is that as important as a home study is, it really isn't that big a deal. This is an important part of your adoption process but also one that is way overhyped. I think every adoptive parent I've spoken with about their home study realized *afterward* what a waste of energy all that obsessing was!

Before you have your first interview with a social worker and/or have your first home inspection (most of the time these occur at the same time; sometimes, however, they are separate steps), talk to people who've gone through a home study and/or go to online bulletin boards to get some sense of what other people have experienced (see the Resources section for a list of some online discussion boards). Depending on whether you're using an agency or an attorney, you may have to provide your social worker with copies of your income tax returns, an essay on why you want to adopt, letters of reference from friends (at least a few of whom should hold semi-impressive jobs and all of whom should understand that this reference is serious business; this is not the time to play practical jokes or be sarcastic or witty), *and* you will get fingerprinted and have a criminal background check performed. If you're working with an agency, you likely will provide copies of this information to the agency, which will then share copies with the social worker.

Once you've provided all the documentation and had your fingers inked up or scanned into a computer in support of your application to adopt, you will meet face to face with a social worker. Keep in mind that you'll likely have updates on your home study after your initial home visit, and there likely will be one visit after the baby has been placed in your home. Your social worker may become your best friend. It is, however, the first home visit or interview with your social worker that will send you (if you're like everyone else) to the edge of reason. (Once it is over, you'll wonder why you were so nervous; I promise!)

Our home study was pretty straightforward. A social worker came to our house and sat with us over coffee at our dining room table. She asked us questions about why we were making an adoption plan, why we chose adoption over pursuing more infertility treatment or surrogacy, which one of us (Charlie) first broached the subject of adoption and how the other partner (me) responded to the topic (I needed more time). She asked us about our childhoods and how that might or might not impact our child-rearing styles (I found this to be a surprisingly difficult question). She also asked us questions about our personalities, relationship, anger management styles, how we fight and resolve problems, and whether we'd ever been in therapy. She seemed to accept as normal the fact that we had both been therapied to death, taken antidepressants, and basically felt that we are neurotic but normal.

I have learned over the past several years that depression and anxiety are nothing to worry about when it comes to a home study, and most social workers do expect one or both partners to have experienced some kind of therapy at some point in their lives, especially if they went through infertility treatment. What does concern a social worker performing a home study is the failure to disclose this information or a severe mental illness that recurs or is not adequately controlled by medication. If you suffer from a major personality disorder, or take an antipsychotic drug (and I don't include antidepressants in any list of antipsychotic meds), or have attempted suicide more than once, it may be prudent to get a letter from your psychiatrist and/or therapist describing your treatment history and current status to alleviate any concerns that your social worker may have about your ability to parent. I did disclose the fact that I had suffered from severe depression accompanied by a four-year battle with anorexia nervosa. Our social worker didn't even blink an eye.

We also encountered questions about how our family reacted to our decision to adopt and whether they were supportive. We discussed our plans for returning to work and child care, managing household chores (and man, was she right to get us thinking about how we'd handle this stuff when we would have another family member taking up our time, as doing the dishes or a load of laundry can become a major source of tension when you're strung out and sleep-deprived), and how we were planning on paying bills on a reduced income. She asked to meet with each of us for a few minutes privately, mostly to make sure we presented consistent stories and history and felt comfortable sharing feelings honestly (sometimes when your partner isn't there, you will share things that you might hold back if he's sitting next to you). If you haven't guessed, most of the questions are geared toward helping the social worker determine whether you can provide an emotionally and financially stable home and are prepared for the challenges of parenthood.

If you're planning a transracial adoption (domestic or international), you can expect to spend a decent portion of your home study going over your decision to adopt a child outside your own ethnicity. The social worker likely will ask about your family's reaction to your decision, what your personal community of friends is like and how receptive they're likely to be to a child of a different race, and what if anything you've done to educate yourself about your child's racial or ethnic background. If you're adopting from China or Korea, there are extensive networks of family support groups that you can utilize both pre- and postadoption to help with your transition to parenthood and racial issues you may face as you raise your child. I recommend reaching out to these support groups (see the Resources section for a list of adoption-support organizations) before your home study and getting some orientation information from them (they often have great tip sheets and things like that) or even making some friends. Your proactiveness will only help allay any concerns your social worker may have about your preparedness to parent a child of a different ethnicity or race.

If you're single, you can expect your social worker to ask you questions about who's available in your life to help you in an emergency and what resources you've lined up to help you manage the stress of being a new parent. It is helpful to tell your social worker about your extensive network of supportive friends, the local drop-off child care center you've visited, and how anxious your mother or Great-Aunt

Agatha is to come help take care of the baby. Most social workers have interviewed multiple single-parent prospective adoptive parents (unless they are newbies or you live in a rural area) and are merely looking for evidence that you have thought through this decision and have a plan for taking care of your baby and yourself.

If you're gay (single or part of a couple), you may face some questions about how accepting your family is of your lifestyle and whether they are supportive of your decision to become a parent (heterosexuals get this question too, remember?). Your social worker is not—and should not be—judging you or your lifestyle. Some social workers are up-front that they won't do home studies for same-sex couples or gay singles who are adopting, so you might want to point out your sexual orientation and/or marital status when arranging for your home study. It's better not to schedule a home study with a narrow-minded, disapproving adoption professional and harm your chances of moving forward with an adoption plan!

We gave the social worker a tour of our home, and she asked to see smoke detectors, fire extinguishers, emergency ladders, and baby-proofing paraphernalia. I had not yet installed any locks on my kitchen cabinets or put in outlet covers, but we had them, and she was impressed that we were preparing ahead of time. I think she made note of the fact that our home was clean (but not immaculate) and that I had made an effort to begin to clean out the room that would later become a nursery. Like I said before, she is looking for evidence of a loving, stable home and parent(s) who are realistic and prepared for the task before them. You need not be thoroughly baby-proofed or have a nursery completed. You should be aware of the things that need to be baby-proofed (especially if you're adopting a toddler) and begin to make a physical space ready for a baby.

So, what can cause problems in your home study?

Lying

Not being completely honest or not disclosing whatever fact may be relevant to your social worker's questions is a huge red flag. There is nothing worse than not telling your social worker about that arrest for drunk driving when you were eighteen and having it show up when she gets your criminal background check. She will be mighty concerned about what else you haven't disclosed and why you felt this wasn't important enough to share with her. When in doubt, disclose!

Felony- or Child Abuse–Related Arrests

The federal government, in the Adoption and Safe Families Act[1], has specified what types of crimes states should screen for when evaluating you for your parenting license. Each state has its own list of what will disqualify you from becoming an adoptive parent. I am not talking about one arrest for disorderly conduct when you were nineteen. I am talking about an arrest for child abuse or neglect, rape or sexual assault, spousal abuse, possession of or selling drugs, physical assault or battery—you get the idea. Being arrested *and* convicted for a crime against a child will preclude you from becoming an adoptive parent. A conviction in the other categories of felonies also will make it almost impossible to adopt unless the arrest occurred a *very* long time ago.

If you or your partner has an arrest but not a conviction like this in your distant past (if it's in your recent past, within the past five years, it will be very difficult to convince your social worker that you'll be a fit parent), disclose it to the social worker and talk about what if anything has occurred since then to "rehabilitate" you and why it would not affect your ability to parent today. But you need to face the reality now that you're going to have an uphill battle convincing her that you are a good choice for a parent.

Recent Drug Addiction

Recent battles with drug addiction also can be problematic. The term "recent" is somewhat vague, I know. Being sober for a year is an amazing accomplishment but may not be enough to demonstrate to your social worker that you've got your addiction under control.

1. Adoption and Safe Families Act of 1997, Pub. L. No. 105-89, 11 Stat. 2115, § 106 (1997), (Criminal Record Check for Prospective Foster and Adoptive Parents).

A WORD TO THE WISE

When in Doubt, Disclose!

My friend Jenna called me rather panicked one day. She was preparing for her home study and someone had just told her they were going to do a criminal background check on her and her husband. Her husband Ian had been arrested—but not convicted—of scalping tickets to a New York Rangers hockey game. Was this going to stop their adoption? In a word, no. But I did let Jenna know she should tell her social worker about it so she wasn't shocked or concerned that Jenna and Ian had withheld a "criminal record." Jenna and Ian adopted a beautiful little girl from Ethiopia eight months later.

When Charlie and I were at our orientation for the agency and our caseworker was describing the home study process, a gentleman across the table from me got very agitated. Eventually our caseworker picked up on the fact that he looked like he was going to have a heart attack. Turns out the man had been arrested for drunk driving a few years earlier and had a series of bar fights on his record. He explained he had been stupid and had needed help for an alcohol problem. Since participating in a (court-mandated) alcohol treatment program, he hadn't had an arrest. Our caseworker wasn't in the least bit fazed (although the poor man's wife was rather perturbed to be disclosing this to a table full of strangers) and told him to make sure he discussed it openly and honestly with the social worker conducting their home study. Moreover, she said he should comply with any request she made of him, if she made any, regarding his sobriety. They adopted a baby girl eleven months later.

Being able to demonstrate active involvement and regular atten-
dance in a twelve-step program or other addiction-support organization will certainly be persuasive, but the reality is that many social
workers will be concerned that the stress of new parenthood may
cause you to relapse. If she has concerns about your ability to stay
sober, talk about it with her and see if she is willing to talk to your
sponsor or other therapist. Explain what it is that helps you get
through each day still sober and why you don't think that personal
stress would cause you to relapse. Recidivism or resuming your drug
use more than once and/or multiple stays in rehab will also cause
your social worker great pause. Of course, if it's been ten years since
your last relapse, it may not be such a big deal.

Finances and Marital Status

Less troubling but still of concern to your social worker will be a history of multiple divorces, bankruptcy filing(s), or being in arrears
with child support (as in not paying it in a timely manner). Of more
concern will be excessive consumer debt without compensating income. If you've got $30,000 of credit card debt and only make
$30,000 a year, don't own your own home and are about to spend
money to adopt a child (not to mention increase your monthly "nut"
with diapers and formula), your social worker is going to ask you
some unpleasant questions. Plan ahead for this and be able to tell her
about your medical insurance, your debt-reduction plan (create one
if you don't already have one), parental or other support you can rely
on in a pinch, or anything else that might help alleviate her fears that
you cannot provide for this child. I am not saying this will stand in
your way of getting approved, but it's going to cause some legitimate
concern. You want your social worker to see that you are a fiscally
responsible future parent.

Parents with Special Issues

Similarly, people with disabilities or those recovering from major illnesses may have additional hurdles to overcome during their home
study. However, with a little diligence and open dialogue and aggres-

siveness on your part, your social worker should be willing and able to help you get your parenting license. Go online and search through adoption bulletin boards (see the Resources section for chapter 1) to see what if anything people in your situation—or one similar to it— have used to help them convince their social worker that despite a physical disability or battle with cancer, they could and would be good parents. Get letters from doctors testifying to your current health status, and if need be, consult an attorney who specializes in disability laws about your rights as a prospective adoptive parent not to be discriminated against because of your disability. The fact that you cannot hear or cannot walk doesn't mean that you won't be a good parent. You may have to fight, but you won't be the first disabled person or cancer survivor to become an adoptive parent!

The bottom line is that as long as you can sincerely and honestly demonstrate your maturity and responsibility as a future parent, your social worker will be willing to help you overcome obstacles in your home study. If she has concerns, ask her what you could do to help demonstrate your commitment to becoming a parent. The more you're willing to demonstrate your level of responsibility and commitment, the more she should be willing to help you try make it work.

Aside from major issues with drug addiction or serious arrests, I promise your home study is truly not a big deal. It is an opportunity for someone from your agency, attorney's office and/or home state to come in and make sure you understand the myriad issues you'll face as an adoptive parent, that you've thought through the process and the potential problems you may be facing, and that you're prepared, mature and responsible. Is it fair that educated, mature, hardworking people have to prove their worth or merit to become parents when far too many irresponsible, neglectful, drug-addicted and abusive people get to bring children into this world with little or no oversight? Absolutely not! But think about it from the perspective of your child's birth family and even your child. It must be extremely reassuring to them to know that the people who will be caring for this baby have demonstrated to an educated, independent third party that you will do everything in your power to give this child a stable and loving home.

Many people want to prepare their homes before their home study. You don't have to have an immaculate home that is completely baby-proofed in order to "pass" your home study. But if you're like most of us, you will want to do as much as possible to prepare and make a good impression on your social worker. Here is what I encourage you to do and buy before that first visit to your home:

The Essential Home Study Checklist

- ☐ Smoke detectors. If possible, follow the recommendations for placement on the package or contact your local fire department for assistance with how many you need and where they should go. Manufacturers of smoke detectors also provide maps and suggested locations on their Web sites; refer to them if you need help figuring out where to put your smoke detectors.

- ☐ Fire extinguishers. One in the kitchen near the stove and at least one per floor, as centrally located as possible.

- ☐ An emergency fire ladder if you live in a house, or easy access to a working fire escape if you live in an apartment building.

- ☐ Baby-proofing paraphernalia. You can a buy a kit at your local baby store that will have the basics in it. You don't have to put them all out or use them all right away (although you certainly could get used to having them around), but definitely make sure you have opened the box and are familiar with the contents and what each piece does and why. Selectively choose a few pieces that evidence your commitment to safety (electrical outlet guards and cabinet safety locks are a good choice to start with). Remove all potentially hazardous chemicals, including dishwasher detergent and cleaning supplies, from floor-level cabinets and place them somewhere that would be out of reach to a small child. Lock any cabinets that contain glass or hazardous products in your kitchen, bathroom and laundry room.

☐ There should be gates or metal guards on apartment windows (they are also required by most building codes, so make sure that your building is in compliance).

☐ Make sure all windows and doors open and close properly (sticking doors can present a hazard by accidentally locking a child or parent in a room away from the other).

☐ Clean and vacuum your entire place. You don't need to go crazy here; a couple of dust bunnies under the bed (if she even checks) will make you look human.

I promise that your home study won't be too big a deal. Don't get too worked up about it. Take it seriously and answer all questions openly and honestly. Before you know it, you'll be obsessing about birth mothers or dossiers.

PART TWO

~ ~ ~

GOING DOMESTIC

Jetta or Jet Blue, Jetting to Baby

❦ 4 ❧

BEGINNING A
DOMESTIC ADOPTION

Agencies and Attorneys Demystified
for the Soon-to-Be Sleep-Deprived

This chapter is devoted to telling you how to decide how to do a domestic adoption, whether you're going to use an attorney or an agency, and how to get the ball rolling. Before we begin addressing one of the nuts-and-bolts topics of adoption—how to do it—I want to apologize. I am a humorous person and I think one of the most important things you need to have when you're attempting to adopt is a sense of humor (a really good one, too, because you're going to need to see the funny stuff when you're having a really bad day). Alas, there isn't a lot of funny stuff to convey at this stage of the process. I will try to lighten things up where I can, but let's face it, you need this information rather badly, and you need it in no-nonsense language. I therefore am taking the funny bone out of my "gorgeous" post–infertility treatment, breast-feeding body and will sit as I would across from you at a table at Starbucks and tell you *what you need to know*.

There are far too many pesky little details that we need to discuss before you can really make the decision about how to do a domestic adoption. So go grab a cup of java, and let's discuss the stupid and not-so-stupid little reasons why going the independent or agency route—the first decision you'll need to make in the process—might be better for you.

The options are quite varied, from expensive, one-stop we-do-it-all-for-you agencies to attorneys who do everything to doing it all yourself to some hybrid of all these options. (Please note that whatever route you pick to parenthood, you will always need an attorney to complete the adoption and make it legal and final.) Much of your decision here will come down to your financial position and how much time you've got to devote to the process of adopting. I know you just want a baby today (okay, you wanted him *yesterday*!), but I'm going to ask you to take some time before starting your domestic-adoption process to think about some stuff.

Before you pick an agency or attorney, you need to do some homework. Do not—I repeat do not—default into doing what everyone at your fertility clinic recommends (like I did) or listening to what your mom's friend's sister said was the way her best friend Vera's daughter got a baby in *three* months. Let me tell you an embarrassing secret I've learned from working with adoptive parents: most people do more research on car seats and strollers than they do on ways to complete a successful domestic adoption. If you're going to research car seats and strollers, you'd better spend some time selecting your adoption attorney, facilitator (you definitely must research facilitators) or agency, because it's *way* more important. Not to mention the fact that you've got much more money at stake! Besides which, without your agency, attorney or whomever else you work with toward becoming a parent, you ain't gonna be buying that Bugaboo Frog stroller and Britax Marathon car seat.

I'm going to give you a quiz to help you define where your needs and interests lie and how they impact whom you choose as your adoption professionals, and then we're going to talk a little bit about the factors that go into determining whether you need an agency involved or whether an attorney is the right way to go. Then we're going to talk about how to pick and hire your adoption professionals.

Type-A Personalities and the "New York Minute" versus Southern Personalities and the Laid-Back Style

I have had so many discussions with families in New York working with various agencies located in the South or Midwest who expect things to be done in the proverbial "New York Minute." Southerners are more laid back and don't understand the urgency with which most things get done in the Big Apple. I've even had conversations with some California super-type-A couples who've expressed similar issues working with more laid-back California agencies or attorneys. More than one adoption professional has caused an adoptive parent unexpected angst or anger by not returning a phone call for a day or even several days. These adoptive parents have had to understand the different paradigms and styles by which business is conducted to be able to effectively manage the process. You need to find an agency or attorney that works on the same time frame and the same way you do.

Make smart choices and exercise the skills you've learned from years of savvy consumer shopping, and your experience will be better for it. Research, research, research, and then do some more research! Think, think, think, and then do some more thinking! Let's begin with the essential questions.

How needy are you right now?

I want you to think about what your needs are and how needy you are right now. Don't underestimate your emotional state or that of

A WORD TO THE WISE

Know Your Neediness Number, Speak Up, and Choose Your Words Carefully

Adoption is an exceptionally emotionally charged process. Most adoption professionals are aware of this and are great at adapting their style to meet your needs. If you can go with the flow, they'll go with the flow (Neediness Number 1). If you need to have your hand held every day, they'll call you regularly and check in to see how you're doing (Neediness Number 10). If you don't know your Neediness Number ahead of time, you can get yourself into serious trouble. Occasionally adoptive parents and the adoption professionals assigned to them are like oil and water. I worked with one couple, Andrew and Angie, who did not get along with their social worker. Andrew and Angie were open to adopting a baby of almost any ethnic background and even one with special needs, so their agency had assigned them to a special program for prospective adoptive parents like them. Unfortunately, however, there was only one social worker staffed to this program, who had a very particular communication style. They tried really hard to express their needs to their social worker as soon as they realized they had different communication styles and needed more hand-holding, but by then, it had escalated to the point where things were pretty ugly. It got to the point where no one was being civil. Ultimately Andrew and Angie and the agency they had retained agreed to part ways. The agency lost their fee and got some negative media attention. Andrew and Angie had to start the process all over again, *from scratch,* with a new adoption professional. It really sucked for them!

I think that Andrew and Angie are like 90 percent of prospective adoptive parents, who don't assess their Neediness Number ahead of time and communicate that up front to whomever they would be working with. Andrew and Angie were able to do that with their new adoption professional, and things are going much more smoothly now. Fingers and toes crossed for them—at the time of this writing, they have a baby coming home pretty soon!

Take it from me—it is far better to express your needs and your communication style at the beginning of the relationship than to have to fire someone, ask for a new staff assignment, or alienate the person you're depending on to complete your adoption process. Be up-front and honest in the beginning to make sure you get the right people on your team, always be diplomatic and friendly (and ask the same from your professional), and you'll save yourself a nightmare or two!

your partner. Even if you go the high-end route and have an agency do everything for you, you need to make sure that you select the right agency for your family needs and that the caseworkers who will be assigned to assist you through this process are going to be responsive to your personality.

On a scale of 1 to 10, 10 being "I need someone to hold my hand through this entire process" and 1 being "I can probably handle just about anything without needing any support from anyone at any point in time" (more power to you; I wish I was like that!), how much attention are you going to need? This is your Neediness Number. We will use this number as we discuss the professionals involved in different types of adoptions and as you interview attorneys and agencies and go through the process of selecting your adoption professional. There is no judgment here. I will tell you right now, I am a Neediness Number 10. You don't get higher maintenance than me!

Domestic adoptions can be very challenging, and you really want to have the right people supporting you through the process. There is nothing worse than firing your agency or attorney halfway through the process or even asking to be reassigned to a new caseworker because someone is making your life more difficult or is making you cry after a phone call. Knowing your Neediness Number will help you make the right agency or attorney match.

How much money do you have right now?

I hate asking you to do this, because I know that if you're like most post–infertility treatment families or even just among the vast majority of human beings, this is an unpleasant task, but I want you to take a good hard look at your checkbook. How much cash do you have on hand to put toward your adoption process?

Next, think about friends and family members who can help you pay for this, and find out whether you have employer adoption assistance. Also consider whether you can take out a home equity loan or an adoption loan. If you don't know how much money you might be able to contribute to your adoption process, skip back and read in chapter 2 about ways to make this more manageable.

Considering all the various sources of revenue available to you, how much can you spend on your adoption? If you have zero financial resources right now, you need to consider adopting through a state agency or foster-care system, as these are the least expensive options available for building your family through adoption. If you can allocate somewhere in the neighborhood of $10,000 to $15,000 toward your adoption, you can probably do an independent adoption with an attorney or even use some agencies. If you have in excess of $20,000 to throw at this process, you can retain an adoption agency to do absolutely everything for you.

But your first order of business is to *set your budget* and figure out how you're going to pay for it. Because how much moola you have will impact your decision on who you use to bring your baby home, no doubt about it!

Do you live in a state that requires an agency to be involved in your adoption process?

Please check the Appendix to determine whether the state in which you reside requires an agency to be involved in your adoption process. This doesn't mean you have to use the agency for all aspects of the adoption process, it simply means you're going to need an agency to process and finalize your adoption.

Now you should have two numbers sitting next to you on a piece of paper. One indicates the degree of hand-holding you'll require throughout this process, and the other the amount of money you can throw at the process of becoming an adoptive parent. You should also have the words "agency required" or "no agency required," which will help you decide how you're going to adopt.

∽ ∽ ∽

Let's talk for a few pages about the various people who will be involved in your adoption and who can do what for you and why you'd want them—or not want them—involved. I want to give you background about the various adoption players, because you need to understand what they do and how they do it before you can decide how *you* want to do it and with whom you want to do it. Bear with me here; this is important stuff. Remember Andrew and Angie? They not only needed to know their Neediness Number, they needed to read this before they hired that agency!

Agencies

One major advantage of using an agency is that it's one-stop shopping. The agency usually arranges and handles *everything* for you, and you don't need to do anything yourself except maybe talk to a

birth mother and pick up a baby. I am overstating things a little—
you still have to collect your birth certificate(s) and marriage license
(if any), get fingerprinted, and write a birth mother letter or prepare
an adoptive-parent profile (we'll get to these in a few pages), but
other than that, the agency does everything. They will, in a nutshell,
find your birth mother for you and handle all the pesky little details,
like getting her Medicaid if she doesn't have insurance, making sure
she has food and clothing, and taking care of all the legal paperwork
for you. You have no worries about placing advertisements in news-
papers (the agency does this) or screening birth mothers who might
be scammers (the agency does this). Another advantage of working
with an agency is that agencies often have birth mothers with whom
they are already working and have extensive networks for locating
other birth families seeking to make an adoption plan.

Agencies vary on how much they do, but most agencies will take
care of the stuff I just outlined so you don't have to. Some agencies
offer a hybrid of the independent/full-service adoption in which you
do a lot of the marketing and screening and searching yourself in exchange for a lower agency fee. With the full-service type of agency-
assisted adoption, you pay a premium (sometimes upwards of $25,000,
usually based on your income), but you get access to the agency's
network, including birth mothers who are already working with it
and are looking for adoptive parents. The agency takes care of all aspects of your adoption, from taking care of the birth mother and her
medical and financial needs to finalizing the adoption. You don't
have to sweat the small stuff (and not-so-small stuff, like locating a
counselor for your birth mother)—you just sit back and hope that
everything goes well and you will be bringing home a beautiful little
baby in a very short time. A hybrid system might cost more in the
range of $15,000 (including legal fees), but again you have more leg-
work to do than with a full-service system.

There are two types of adoption agencies: public agencies, like
state child-welfare organizations, and private agencies, like Spence-
Chapin in New York City, New York, and the Gladney Center for
Adoption in Fort Worth, Texas (see the Resources section for a more

---

A WORD TO THE WISE

Are Agencies Really Better than Attorneys?

Are Attorneys Really Better than Agencies?

I have been on both sides of this issue. I have adopted using a full-service agency and I have worked with an attorney to complete a newborn adoption. It's my humble and informed opinion that if you're going to do all the work yourself (that hybrid system I talked about) anyway, you're better off working with an attorney. You will probably save time and money. But if you're the post–infertility treatment variety of adoptive parent who works full time, is patient, and has the moola available, going with a full-service agency may be your best bet.

---

comprehensive list of agencies). Public agencies can help you find a baby, but more often than not you cannot adopt a newborn through a public agency unless he or she is a special-needs baby. Public agencies are great places to go for foster-care adoption and to adopt an older child. Private agencies—of which there are many, both reputable and disreputable—can do everything for you or provide assistance and guidance but put the onus on you to locate your birth family.

Some states (see the Resources section for a breakdown) will require that you use an agency to finalize your adoption. This does not mean that you need to hire an agency in your state or use an agency for everything connected with your adoption. You can still use an attorney to help you find a birth mother or do the search all by yourself.

You'll just need an agency to finalize your adoption. And whether or not your state requires an agency, remember that you're not limited to hiring an agency located in the state where you live. You may choose to use an agency located in another state, provided the agency is licensed in the state where you live.

Attorneys

Attorneys *have* to be involved in your adoption. Whether you work with an agency, a facilitator or find your birth mother yourself, you will still need an attorney to finalize the adoption (to make it legal). Most agencies have an attorney on staff or a network of attorneys to help finalize your adoption. (Sometimes you will need to use an attorney in a state in which your agency is not licensed. In that event the agency will have someone it can refer you to for finalization.) If you go the independent route and find a birth family yourself (we'll discuss finding birth families in a moment), you will need to find an attorney to complete and finalize the adoption. However, you can also use an attorney to help you find a birth family, although not every state will permit an attorney to do this directly (see the Appendix for a breakdown of states that require you to use an agency or permit you to use an agency and/or attorney and/or facilitator). If attorneys in your state are precluded by law from helping you locate a birth family, they can tell you how you can do it yourself and help you manage all aspects of the process along the way, and then finalize the adoption for you.

Attorneys can and should be able to do *everything* that an agency does for you in connection with an adoption (subject to restrictions set by state law, like locating a birth mother). Each attorney, however, will set different parameters for how much he or she is willing to perform on your behalf and how much those services cost. You need to check carefully when hiring an attorney to be sure you know exactly what the attorney will and won't do for you or how much legwork your attorney will require that you do in connection with your adoption.

Although we will discuss the details of hiring an attorney in a moment, let me say that working with an attorney usually provides more flexibility for creating the type of adoption that is right for you, provides a more personal experience, and can be much faster—especially if you're willing to be proactive about finding a birth family—and less expensive than using an agency. It has been my experience that most attorneys are more service-oriented than are agencies. Thus they are more flexible in working with you to plan an adoption that meets your requirements without imposing rules or judgments about lifestyles, as many agencies do. Now there are exceptions—there are attorneys who will not work with single or gay adoptive parents, and there are agencies that are extremely flexible. But finding an attorney willing to work on your terms is easier than finding a flexible agency.

The average cost, from start to finish, including all aspects of the adoption process when using an attorney, is approximately $10,000 to $15,000. Many attorneys provide the same degree of service as an agency, with lower fees and better service. But you have to choose your attorney wisely, and we'll talk about that in a moment.

Facilitators

A facilitator is a third party who is not an attorney and who is paid to find you a baby. (This is someone you hire in addition to working with an attorney and maybe even an agency.) Frankly, facilitators scare the poop out of me, and most states agree with me on this (facilitators are illegal in most states). There is nothing that raises that black-market adoption flag for me faster than hearing that someone worked with a facilitator. Facilitators can be great if they are located in a state where they are licensed and regulated, like California (the only state that, as of this writing, licenses facilitators).

Most states, however, prohibit the use of a facilitator to find a baby unless that facilitator is unpaid. This type of facilitator is usually a clergyperson, a teacher in a school, a social worker or nurse at a hospital, or some neutral and independent third-party intermediary. Frankly, I don't even call these people facilitators; they're your best adoptive friends and are doing something for truly altruistic reasons.

A true adoption facilitator (or consultant, as they now like to be called) is someone who is not a social worker or an attorney (and thus is not licensed and responsible to a licensing and governing body) who will—for a fee—help locate a baby for you. Facilitators may help you write advertisements, teach you how to talk to birth parents, and help you write your adoptive-parent profile or birth mother letter. But more often than not, they will tell you that if you pay them a sum of money, they will go out and find a baby for you. The more money you pay some of them—the disreputable ones— the faster they claim they will be able to locate a baby for you. A reputable facilitator will offer you a detailed contract that spells out what he or she will do for you, how much it will cost, and what your rights and remedies are in the event that he or she does not locate a baby for you within a reasonable and defined time frame. Good luck finding a facilitator who offers a contract like this (getting a contract like this is not optional; you must have one).

Now, if you know of an adoption facilitator who comes highly recommended to you by friends, has great recommendations, offers you a detailed contract, and is located in California, I say go for it! But if you are in New York (a state that does not permit the use of adoption facilitators) or are talking to someone who doesn't offer a contract and promises you a baby in three months, *run*—do not walk—*away!* I do not want to see you on the end of an illegal or questionably legal adoption, and this person may be leading you in that direction.

The following chart shows the characteristics of each type of adoption professional, and what they have to offer:

	Agency	Attorney	Facilitator
Cost	Usually $25,000 or more	Usually $10,000 to $15,000, depending on birth mother expenses	No reliable statistics are available. The less they charge, the better.
Time to Baby	On average, 12 to 18 months; some agencies quote lower wait times; in reality most wait times are closer to 18 months unless you're very flexible.	On average, 12 to 18 months; many attorneys accurately report faster wait times. Again, a lot will come down to your flexibility.	No reliable statistics are available. As long as the amount of money you pay the facilitator is not tied to the wait time, you should be able to rely on whatever statistics he or she provides (check references).
Offers Flexibility to Adoptive Parents	Usually not much. Agencies have their set ways of doing things and may not be willing to change when you want them to (semi-open versus open adoptions are one notable place adoptive parents often differ in perspective with their agency).	Usually very flexible and will work with you toward an adoption that is right for you.	Usually very flexible. However, some less-reputable facilitators may represent facts to meet your criteria that are not accurate based on the birth family's medical records.

	Agency	Attorney	Facilitator
Services Offered	Tons. A full-service agency should do everything for you except fill out your paperwork for your home study and help you prepare your adoptive-parent profile or birth mother letter.	Depends on the state you reside in. In some states the attorney cannot locate a birth mother for you, and thus you will bear a greater burden because you have to do all your own advertising and marketing. However, your attorney will be able to guide you and direct you toward reputable means of locating a birth family.	Usually limited to locating a birth family, although more reputable facilitators may also be able to assist you in locating services to help support your birth mother. Read your contract carefully to see what services are offered as part of the fee.

Hiring Your Adoption Professional

Now you know the adoption players you can utilize in connection with a domestic adoption and some of the basic issues that go into your adoption. You know your Neediness Score, how much money you have to play with, and whether you live in a state that is going to require you to have an agency involved in your adoption. I am going to assume that you will want some form of licensed professional helping find you your birth family (although some of you may choose to find your birth mother yourself), so I've included questions and issues you need to address as you look for a professional to assess how quickly he or she will find your baby for you. If you're going über-independent on me and are going to find that baby all by yourself (you've got more guts than I do, that's for sure!), just skim over what isn't relevant to you. You still need to read this to find the right professional to finalize your adoption.

This is where you get some of the scoop that Andrew and Angie needed, that I needed, and that you bought this book for. I am going to tell it to you like it is, no holds barred. You want the dirt on hiring a professional and how it really works (or how you should make it work). Here it is.

Hiring an Agency

You can locate reputable agencies through RESOLVE or by going online (see the Resources section for a list of some agencies and references for obtaining a more exhaustive list of public and private agencies). There are both state (public) and private agencies (for-profit and not-for-profit) to choose from. Either way, public or private, almost all agencies have well-established practices and requirements that you need to research before you choose to work with them. Some agencies work only with couples married for more than five years with diagnosed and medically verified infertility. Other agencies are very flexible. An agency may prefer working with Christian couples but will consider a family with mixed religions or even Buddhists. (Are you shocked that this might be an issue?) A surprising number of agencies won't work with gay families or single parents, although there are some out there that will. (Check out the Resources section for a list of adoptive-parent support groups that can steer you in the right direction if you fall into one or both of these categories of "special-needs" parents.)

Find out where each agency you're considering working with comes down on the religion, marriage and sexual orientation factors. An agency is not necessarily going to tell you the truth about this. This is a business, and at least some of them will do anything and say anything to attract your business. Check with local adoptive-parent support groups or go online to get as many unbiased opinions as possible about an agency's policies with respect to these factors.

For example, an agency may represent that it will work with a conservative Jewish family but not disclose that the wait for a baby will be longer, because most of the birth families who place babies through this agency want Christian families. Similarly, an agency may say it will place a biracial (half African American) baby or full African American baby in a Caucasian home, but the reality is the agency prefers placing African American babies in a home with at least one African American parent (state agencies may have similar reverse-racist policies) and will give priority to those families over a fully Caucasian adoptive family. These policies and preferences are not usually disclosed to you, the prospective adoptive parent with loads of money in your wallet.

Other things you need to consider when selecting an agency is whether the agency will only do semi-open or open adoptions. In an open adoption you share more personal information with the birth family and may even choose to have ongoing contact after placement of the baby in your home. In a semi-open adoption things are more anonymous and more restricted, with postadoption contact usually taking place through your agency or attorney. Some agencies will do both, depending on the needs and desires of the adoptive and birth parents. You may want the option to do the opposite of what one agency recommends as the "ideal" type of adoption, while another agency may offer a system that would permit you to do what is right for you and your birth family. You may be able to negotiate with the agency to have a different type of adoption, but many adoptive parents find going against an agency's policies to be a very difficult experience. (One adoptive family described its experience trying to do a semi-open adoption with an agency that promotes openness as like swimming against a riptide. Virtually impossible and exhausting!) As we will discuss later in the book, sometimes the best postadoption relationships are those that are permitted to evolve naturally over time, with no preconceived rules over who may contact whom and how often. Some agencies tend to be very narrow-minded about how an adoption "should" be conducted, both before and after placement of the baby in your home.

For example, some agencies are very traditional and prefer to place babies in homes with a stay-at-home mom. Well, not all of us can afford to be stay-at-home moms, and not all of us want to be. Even more, many birth mothers don't care about whether you're going to be a stay-at-home mom, and yet your agency may stress the fact that you're a working parent as a negative to the birth mother. This is called prescreening, and it isn't exactly fair (not all agencies do it, either). Some agencies will only do semi-open adoptions or open adoptions, and yet the birth mother who wants to work with you wants the type of adoption that the agency doesn't regularly engage in. Thus, depending on the agency's practices and policies, pursuing an independent adoption or finding a more open-minded agency might be in your best interest. An agency that lets you choose the type of adoption that is best for you and the birth family, or at least gives you input in the process, is the ideal, and it may be very hard to find.

You also want to find out how long the wait for a baby is at your agency. And again, I wouldn't trust what the agency tells you. Wait times vary from situation to situation and month to month at each agency. And they can vary significantly from agency to agency. This is going to be one of the biggest factors in your selection of an agency—you did want that baby yesterday, right?

So here is the straight poop—no matter what an agency tells you, *it cannot predict exactly how long you will wait.* No one can. Too much goes into each match between a birth and adoptive family, and since most birth mothers now select the adoptive parents, an agency usually has *absolutely no control* over how long you're going to be waiting, because it cannot control when a birth mother will pick you. No matter what an agency tells you about its average wait time, you need to consider that when a birth mother is choosing the adoptive parent (as also is the case with independent adoptions—see the Glossary in the Appendix for clarification of the terms), the agency *cannot* control when a birth mother will select you. The agency's average wait time is merely that, an average of how long *all of its parents* have waited to get a baby, and it usually recalculates that average every month to reflect recent placements (one month it will represent an average wait time of ten months, and another month it will be sixteen months).

An agency that represents a much shorter wait than the typical twelve to eighteen months—unless it is explained to you that the wait time is shorter for your family because of your flexibility and openness to various birth-family situations—probably isn't telling you the truth. An agency that represents its wait at longer than two years is doing something wrong in locating birth families—unless it is explained that the wait time is longer for your family because you seek a specific adoption situation (such as a specific gender baby).

To help you determine how long your wait may be at a particular agency, ask the agency how it makes a match between adoptive parents and birth families. The agency will either provide the birth mother access to its entire adoptive-parent applicant pool, or it will preselect several adoptive parents (especially if the birth mother is asking for adoptive parents of a particular religion or who already have children) and present her with adoptive-parent profiles or birth mother letters (discussed in a moment) specific to her needs or requests. Certain factors—like your flexibility and openness—make it more likely that you will have a shorter wait than another family who is more restrictive, but the agency cannot guarantee you that a birth mother will select you tomorrow, next week or next year.

While flexibility and openness can certainly speed up your wait time, you'd be surprised what might slow your process down. As we discussed, some agencies are predisposed to believe that an adopted child should be placed in a home with one full-time parent. Thus, if you have a career or satisfying job and are planning on going back to work after a brief maternity leave, you may wind up waiting longer than someone who is planning on being a stay-at-home mom. Or it may simply come down to the fact that the birth mothers with whom the agency commonly works want "traditional" homes for their babies, and they consider two working parents to be untraditional. Discrimination comes in all forms. Again, ask around at different agencies about their wait times and what, if anything, impacts how long you will wait. If you doubt the answer the agency gives you, check with other adoptive parents who've placed with this agency. Most agencies can provide a list of references of other adoptive parents in your area. You also can go online to various Yahoo! user groups or adoption bulletin boards and ask people what they have heard or personally experienced. However, never rely on one person's experience; try to get a sampling of responses and see what the average comes to by doing your own math.

The only way an agency can actually control how long your wait time will be is when the agency makes the match between you and the birth family (as in selects the adoptive parents for a particular birth mother). In this case, usually a first-come, first-matched system, the agency knows that couples at the top of its list are soon to have a baby. A hybrid of this system is when an agency has a "list" based on when you join its prospective adoptive-parent pool and presents profiles to birth families based on who is at the top of the list. Again, there are always exceptions to these systems (you may have just joined the applicant pool, but a birth mother selects you off the Internet and agrees to work with the agency toward placing her baby in your home), but a list or ordered system guarantees you more accuracy in gauging how long your wait will be, especially if you know where you are on the list! Most agencies won't openly admit to having a list, but if you push them—or ask other parents who have adopted through the agency—they will acknowledge having some type of list-based system. If you know that the agency you're working with has a list-based system, you may be able to find out where you are on that list. Some agencies even have lists of their top-ten longest-waiting families or families who've had failed matches or placements. These families usually get priority over other families and get more exposure to birth mothers than does a family that just signed up with the agency.

Agency Fees

Most agencies are expensive (upwards of $25,000), but given the amount of work they do for you and the services they provide to both you and the birth family, the fees are usually justifiable. A full-service agency will locate a birth mother for you (many have birth mothers already registered and admitted to their programs who are actively looking for adoptive parents) and make sure your birth mother has a place to live (some agencies even have residence facilities for birth mothers), a doctor to go to (even if that means getting her Medicaid), counseling if needed, clothing on her back and food in her fridge. (These expenses are usually limited by state law. See the Appendix for information on how long and/or how much money can be allocated to such expenses.) The agency should also handle all of the legal work for you (not necessarily as part of its fee, but usually) and arrange for all legal relinquishment papers to be signed. If you go the independent route, these are all things you will pay for (depending on state law; see the Appendix for information on what each state allows you to pay in birth mother expenses) on top of your attorney's fees.

Look for an agency with a fee structure that is tied to your income; some type of "percentage of your income" fee structure is the most appropriate (in my experience) and fairest to prospective adoptive parents. Many agencies set a sliding scale (not based on a percentage of your income), and their fees are based on incomes in the region in which they are located, but do not consider the needs of people in other areas of the country, where money may not go as far. When considering fee structures, one thing most people don't consider is *where* they live in relation to the fee structure being presented to them to determine whether the fee is really fair in comparison to that charged by other agencies.

I have spoken with so many adoptive parents in the Northeast or northern California who find a fee structure scaled to a national income average to have a disproportionate impact on them, compared with parents living in the Midwest or Southeast. For example, an agency fee of $30,000 that is scaled to an income of $150,000 per year may be much more difficult to pay for someone living in San Francisco, where $150,000 doesn't go very far; whereas someone in

Austin, Texas, or Phoenix, Arizona, earning $150,000 is living the big life, and a $30,000 agency fee is small change.

I have a really hard time rationalizing agency fees that are based on a sliding scale related to your income. When you're evaluating agency fees, please consider the fact that a $150,000 income where the agency is based may be the equivalent of a $337,000 income in the New York metropolitan area. A $150,000 income in the New York metro area may be equivalent to a $66,000 income in the city where the agency is based. Thus, asking a New Yorker making $150,000 to pay $30,000 in an agency fee is a little different than asking a regional adoptive parent making $150,000 to pay $30,000. These fees are fair to local families (local to the agency) but not to families living in big cities where the cost of living is dramatically higher.

In contrast, some agencies scale their fees based on a percentage of your annual income, so that wherever you live, your fee is 10 or 15 percent of your annual income. For a couple in northern California earning $150,000, a percentage agency fee of 10 percent means that they are only paying $15,000 for their adoption instead of $30,000 at an agency with a scaled system. It therefore becomes much more affordable to adopt with a percentage system! It is even more affordable for the adoptive parents in Phoenix who have an entirely different cost of living than someone living in San Francisco. The services may be exactly the same between the agencies, but the fee structure is much more equitable.

An agency that ties its fees to how fast you will get the baby concerns me. I have heard of agencies that say the more you pay them, the faster they get the baby to you. Pay the agency $30,000, and wait six to nine months. Pay it $10,000, and wait two years. An agency may rationalize to you that the more money you pay it, the more services it can offer the birth mother, and thus the easier it is for it to find a birth mother who is willing or able to place her baby through it. This argument makes no sense to me. A birth mother honestly and legitimately interested in making an adoption plan doesn't consider— at least initially—how many services she will receive. In fact, a birth mother who is overly concerned with financial arrangements may be less likely to place her baby for adoption (because she's not concerned with the well-being of her child but her own financial gain; this *might* be a sign she's scamming you).

In fact, spending more money than someone else to get a baby before they do sounds to me like you are either buying a place at the top of the adoptive-parent pool (you get first dibs, so to speak), or the agency is doing something less than legal. (Is the agency paying a birth mother more than the law legally permits in order to get her to place the baby with you?)

If you are in fact paying more money to provide this birth mother with "extra" services, what happens to your fee with this agency if the birth mother chooses to parent after you've paid her expenses? Most agencies will apply your fee to another adoption and not ask for additional monies from you. Can this agency do that when you have (theoretically) paid more birth mother expenses than another couple in exchange for a shorter wait time? And what happens if your birth mother lives in a state where the agency must break down the birth mother expenses and agency fees for a judge to review (see the Appendix)? How does the agency justify the $30,000 or more you may have paid when the state doesn't authorize that level of financial expenditure on behalf of a birth parent?

A reputable agency should be able to provide a detailed breakdown of your birth mother's reasonable, necessary and legal expenses. The agency should also be able to offset the cost of your birth mother's expenses relative to those of other birth mothers with whom it is working so that you don't pay more money in the event that your birth mother chooses to parent. Indeed, you should make sure the agency has some kind of system where part of your fee is used to make some kind of contribution that will be pooled and used collectively with all the other contributions to help pay all birth mother expenses.

This leads me to another important question about agency fees. If your first (and/or second) birth mother chooses to parent, find out how the agency handles your fee. Again, most agencies don't ask for more money; your fee applies to as many prospective adoption situations as you pursue with them until finally receiving placement of an infant in your home. This is the insurance factor of working with an agency and one of the biggest reasons people choose an agency over an attorney. Independent adoptions are pay-as-you-go situations. If your birth mother chooses to parent, you're (usually) out the money you spent on her living and medical expenses. This may depend somewhat on state law, but most attorneys will tell you to write the expenses off as part of the process on your income taxes (see chapter 2) and start again with another birth mother. With an agency you have the ability to go back into the adoptive-parent pool and wait for another match with a birth mother without incurring additional expense. If you receive placement from the first birth mother with whom you match, you may pay more for your adoption than someone who has several failed matches or placements. Either way, all of the adoptive parents working with the agency are ensured that whatever happens, they will only spend a specified sum of money.

You *must* do the research and talk to other adoptive parents about their experience working with a particular agency. This is the time to go online and to support group meetings to discover what people really think about the agency you are considering using. More than one prospective adoptive parent I've spoken to has wisely chosen to work with a different agency (and been very *happy* as a result) after speaking with adoptive parents who've used one or more of the agencies they've been interviewing and regretted it! Listen and learn from those who have been through the process with the agencies you're interviewing. Certainly, other adoptive parents who have worked with an agency will be able to enlighten you about the matching process at the agency. Last, it never hurts to check with the Better Business Bureau where you live and where the agency is located (if they are different) to see if any complaints have been lodged against the agency.

* * *

Here is a list of questions for you to ask an agency to help assess whether it is the right agency for you to work with:

- Do you provide a contract that establishes our respective rights and obligations?

- How do you determine adoptive parent eligibility or acceptance into your program(s)?

- If I am not approved, will I be able to find out why?

- Do you provide a breakdown of fees and expenses and when they are due and to whom?

- Who does your home study? Is this part of your fee or in addition to your agency fee?

- What costs aren't covered by your fee(s)?

- What services are included in your fee?

- What services do you offer to birth mothers?

- How do you determine your fee?

- What is the process like once I have been accepted?

- How does your system for matching work? Does the birth mother select the adoptive parent? Do you prescreen for particular criteria requested by the birth mother? Do you make the match (choose the adoptive parents) for the birth mother?

- Do you recommend that the birth mother and adoptive parents meet before the baby is born?

- Do you permit or recommend that adoptive parents be present at the birth or waiting in the hospital?

- What happens with your fee if I have a failed placement or match?

- What support do you provide to me if I have a failed match or placement?

- Do you provide any preferential treatment to adoptive parents who've experienced a failed placement or match?

- Who will handle my adoption at your agency?

- What is the average time frame from acceptance into your program to placement of a baby?

- What support do you provide postplacement?

- What type of postplacement relationship is most common for your adoptive and birth families (open, semi-open or closed)?

I know reading all this information on selecting an agency may have made it seem really discouraging. If your head is spinning right now, sit down and look at the piece of paper you created after the initial questions in the beginning of this chapter. If you have a high Neediness Number and/or work full time and/or have a lot of money and/or live in a state that requires an agency to be involved, you've automatically narrowed the field. You know you're probably going to have a better experience (without incurring financial ruin) using an agency. Then talk to other adoptive parents, especially those who've adopted more than one child. Find out their thoughts on various agencies. Then go with your gut. And if it isn't working out with an agency, don't freak out. If you truly don't think your agency is doing a good job for you, talk to the agency about what it can do differently to better serve you. What's the old adage—the squeaky wheel gets the grease?

Hiring an Attorney

Your attorney should charge a flat fee (ranging between $4,000 and $7,000) for his or her services. Those services may vary dramatically between attorneys, in part because of state regulations governing what attorneys can and cannot do on your behalf when looking for a birth mother. At the very least your attorney should be giving you guidance on how to locate a birth mother; making sure your birth mother has a place to live, a doctor to go to, clothing on her back and food in her fridge; and handling all the legal aspects of the adoption. You may have to pay for the clothing on her back, for her medical expenses, and for her rent (depending on what the state permits you to pay; see the Appendix), and that may be on top of your attorney's fees. This is why working with an attorney provides less predictability regarding how much your adoption is going to cost. Many of your adoption expenses will be dependent on the birthfamily situations you pursue and how many of them you pursue.

Attorney's Fees

The average legal fee for a domestic adoption with a reputable attorney is (at the time of this writing) around $5,000. More complicated adoptions will cost more. For example, if the birth father has to be located using private investigators or he contests the adoption, you're going to pay more. Some attorneys charge hourly rates. This is perfectly legal but can make your adoption way more expensive (hourly charges add up quickly!). Make sure you ask an attorney who charges hourly how much time he or she spends on an average adoption to help you gauge your expenses. You also need to know if your attorney includes something called "disbursements" in his or her fee. Disbursements usually include charges for phone calls, overnight mailings, postage, and facsimile charges.

Get a detailed list from your attorney of what is and is not included in the fee or hourly rate. If he or she doesn't have a written breakdown to provide you, take this is a warning sign. A reputable attorney should know how much his or her clients will be charged, given average expenses.

Last, make sure you clearly understand how much money is due and when. Some attorneys (like agencies) require a large retainer, while others offer a payment schedule. If your attorney doesn't have a retainer agreement that spells out what monies are owed and when you must pay them, ask him or her to create one or otherwise put the terms of payment in writing for you. That way you will never have an argument with your attorney or his or her billing person about the fact that you supposedly owe money. Retainer agreements that spell out what you're responsible for financially and when you're responsible for making those payments are extremely helpful and a sign of a good attorney.

In addition to talking about your attorney's legal fees, you need to discuss how your attorney handles birth mother expenses. It is often very hard to gauge how much you're going to spend on your birth mother until you've found her. (State laws vary significantly on how much you can pay to help a birth mother with her living and medical expenses. See the Appendix for a breakdown.) However, you can find out how your attorney likes to handle things and what he or she does in the event that you've paid birth mother expenses and she chooses to parent.

Most attorneys have some kind of escrow account or trust account that they use to pay birth mother expenses. Oftentimes an attorney recommends planning to set aside approximately $5,000 in an escrow account for anticipated expenses. What you can pay for on behalf of a birth mother varies from state to state, and what types of expenses she will have will vary from situation to situation. It will likely come down to whether she has a stable living situation, health insurance, a job, etc. For example, if your birth mother doesn't have health insurance, your attorney should be able to help her obtain Medicaid (provided she qualifies for it) to help offset her medical expenses. If she doesn't qualify for Medicaid and doesn't have insurance, you probably are going to be responsible for all her medical expenses, which, even without a C-section, could be several thousands of dollars (*yikes,* I know!).

And regardless of her insurance status, it may also be a good idea to get her some counseling from a reputable therapist (who may or may not take Medicaid or her insurance). Those therapy expenses can add up quickly but may be some of the best dollars you've ever spent to help ensure that your birth mother gets the support she needs during such a profoundly emotional time. Knowing that you have set aside money that is sitting in an escrow account to be paid out by your attorney for things like delivery expenses or therapy takes a lot of pressure off you to come up with cash throughout the process.

You also should make sure you understand how your attorney's office works. Will you be speaking directly with your attorney, or will a paralegal call you with updates? Some offices are staffed by very few people, and you get highly personalized service. Some offices are much larger, and you get equally attentive service, but not necessarily from the same person every time. Other questions to ask are what hours your attorney is available to answer questions directly (some have hours during which they return client calls) and whether he or she has e-mail access. Last, ask what the turnaround time is on phone calls. If you call at 9:15 A.M. with an emergency, you want to know that call will be returned by 11:00 A.M. If the office can't promise that someone will return the call during same-day office hours, I'd recommend finding another attorney. Too many times you really do have an emergency question (like when your birth mother goes into premature labor), and you do *not* want to be waiting all day for a return call from a paralegal with whom you have never spoken! Remember your Neediness Number as you evaluate how the office operates.

The process of interviewing attorneys shouldn't take long. If you have to wait weeks to get in to see an attorney for an initial consult, take heed! This attorney may be too busy to take on new clients unless he or she has a very busy office. Many attorneys try to leave room in their schedules every week to meet with new clients. If they don't get a call to fill a new consultation appointment, they use the time to provide extra service to existing clients. If the consult slots are filling up too quickly, many attorneys will take a break from accepting new clients.

My recommendation is to speak with at least two adoption attorneys before you decide on one. Compare their fee structures and the services they provide, the degree of support or empathy they provide (most adoption attorneys are like me and are adoptive parents—we should be understanding of where you are emotionally!) and their experience. Talk to people who've used them, and then go on to research other ways to do a domestic adoption. Once you've spoken to attorneys and an agency or two (and maybe even a facilitator) and you've decided on using an attorney, you'll know which of the attorneys you've spoken to (or neither of them) is a good fit for you.

The following is a list of questions to help you interview attorneys:

- Do you provide a contract that establishes our respective rights and obligations?

- Are there any circumstances under which you would decline to represent an adoptive parent(s)?

- Do you provide a breakdown of fees and expenses and when they are due and to whom?

- Who does your home study? Is this part of your fee or in addition to your fee?

- What costs aren't covered by your fee(s)?

- What services are included in your fee?

- Who will assist me in locating a birth mother?

- What is the process like once I have found a birth mother?

- What happens with your fee if I have a failed match or placement?

- Who will handle my adoption in your office? Will I speak to you, one of your associates, or a paralegal (otherwise known as a legal assistant)?

- Whom do I call if I have an emergency?

- What type of birth mother screening do you provide when a birth mother is interested in working with me? What questions will you be asking birth mothers interested in working with me?

- What type of documentation do you request from birth mothers?

- What types of expenses should I expect to pay for on behalf of a birth mother?

- How does the process work in general?

- What is the average time frame from retaining you to placement of a child?

- What support do you provide postplacement?

The risk of using an attorney for a domestic adoption is that he or she cannot anticipate every eventuality that may come up during your adoption process. Your attorney is going along for the ride with you. Do not have unrealistic expectations of your attorney. While he or she may be able to give you excellent advice about the legal risks posed by a particular adoption situation, the attorney cannot tell you how it will resolve. The attorney can tell you the various ways it might resolve and what he or she will do if one thing happens versus another. A good attorney will be prepared to help you through almost any situation—even if it means referring you to more specialized counsel (like someone who specializes in adoptions involving the Indian Child Welfare Act (ICWA). See the Glossary in the Appendix for more information).

Adoptions present unique situations; every single adoption is different. You need a skilled and experienced attorney to help you, but the attorney cannot foresee the uniqueness of your adoption until you're all knee deep in it. If you've taken the time to think and do research, you've chosen your attorney wisely, and you understand the law as it pertains to your adoption, then the particular facts of your adoption shouldn't present a problem for anyone involved in your adoption plan, most especially *you*.

If you need help locating a reputable adoption attorney, contact your local chapter of RESOLVE, the American Academy of Adoption Attorneys (AAAA), or attend a local adoption support group and ask people who they like (and don't like). Remember, what is right or wrong for others may not be right for you, so take their advice with a grain of salt, and do your own research. There is contact information for RESOLVE and the AAAA in the Resources section; RESOLVE can also help you locate a support group (although there are also some listed in the Resources section).

One last thought, provided it's not excluded by your contract with your professional and you can afford to do it: There is absolutely no reason you couldn't work with both an attorney and an agency or work independently and with an attorney or an agency. The advantage of doing this is that you're essentially searching the earth looking for your birth family. By not relying on only one person or source to locate a birth mother, you create more opportunities for yourself to find a good situation. However, the downside is that it is extremely expensive and time-consuming. I usually recommend this course of action to families who've been waiting a long time (more than a year) to find a birth family. If you have a lot of money and time or your frustration level is very high with whatever (thus far fruitless) steps you've taken to find a birth family, I recommend considering this as an option. Be as aggressive as you can afford to be!

Know the Law

I don't care whether you do an agency-assisted or independent adoption using an attorney—I want you to know the law as it applies to your situation. By the time you finish this book and have read the Appendix, you will know enough to troubleshoot your own adoption situations. Because you may have the option to choose between state laws as they pertain to an adoption situation and utilize the laws that are most favorable, you should take time to get familiar with—at the very least—the laws in the state where you reside and those states where birth mothers you're interested in working with reside. Although not all agencies will give you input into the legal steps involved in finalizing your adoption, knowing that (hypothetically) New York law is more favorable to your adoption than is Pennsylvania law may lead to a productive conversation with your attorney in which you both agree which state's laws you will use to finalize. There are myriad factors that will go into making this final decision about which state law will apply to your adoption, and you won't be able to make the decision until you have a specific situation and know the details about when and how the child will be born. It can also help you in defining those states in which you choose to look for a birth family. You can choose to advertise or work with birth families only in certain adoption-friendly states. I leave it up to you to decide what adoption-friendly means, as everyone defines it differently. Some people care a great deal about relinquishment waiting periods, while others care about whether the birth mother has to appear in court (which can be very intimidating to a birth mother). I cannot make this decision for you, nor should I attempt to impose my judgment of what adoption-friendly means.

Let's talk about why knowing a little bit about the individual state laws might be important for you. Let's say you live in Texas and are working with a Texas-based agency or attorney, but your birth mother is located in Colorado. You will need to know the law as it applies to adoption in both Texas and Colorado. I want you to know what your agency (or you) can and cannot pay for with respect to your birth mother's expenses in Colorado and know what the relinquishment and consent laws are in both states. You will be able to have more input in the process and know when your agency or attorney is making good and not-so-good recommendations on behalf of your birth mother. Why is this important? Why should you care? Let me share with you the experience of my friends Tom and Lisa.

Tom and Lisa used a reputable, well-known adoption agency that has tons of experience doing domestic adoptions. The problem Tom and Lisa encountered with the agency was that the birth mother with whom they were working had conceived a child with a man of Native American heritage. While this birth father had signed his relinquishment papers and was supportive of the adoption plan, the agency felt it was necessary to comply with the Indian Child Welfare Act (ICWA) and obtain tribe approval for the adoption (see the

Glossary and the Appendix for more information on ICWA). This was no doubt a good instinct on the part of the agency, but tribes can create sticky situations for adoptive parents. ICWA gives Native American tribes an opportunity to express independent approval of the adoption, separate and distinct from any other state requirements.

Frequently, in an adoption subject to ICWA, the baby must be placed in foster care for a period of days or weeks while the tribe determines whether it will consent to the adoption. You think it's hard to live through the process of obtaining the birth parents' consent to the adoption? It's a thousand times harder to live through the process when "your" child is in foster care and an independent and insular third party is determining whether your adoption can be finalized. Adoptive parents make little or no impact on the tribe's decision, no matter how much the birth parents may love you or how wonderful you are as a person. You could be Mother Teresa, and the tribe wouldn't care. This is their kin, and they can be very (appropriately) protective.

Now please don't get me wrong. I fully believe that Native American tribes should and must be informed of adoptions that fall within the purview of ICWA. And oftentimes the tribe does consent to the adoption. But the process of complying with ICWA can be very complicated and trying for adoptive parents. Tom and Lisa—being savvy prospective adoptive parents—weren't certain that ICWA applied to their adoption situation and consulted an independent attorney who specialized in Native American adoptions to confirm whether the tribe had to be notified of the pending adoption.

After consulting this attorney, Tom and Lisa learned that because the birth father *and* his father had never resided on the reservation or been involved with tribe activities, and because the birth father's mother and the baby's mother were both Caucasian (I am oversimplifying; ICWA is very specific about the circumstances under which you must obtain the consent of the tribe), the tribe had no jurisdiction over the adoption. Tom and Lisa then went back to their adoption agency and reviewed the appropriate section of the statute with its attorney, referred the agency to their attorney for further discussion, and ultimately they all agreed that ICWA did not apply to the adoption. Tom and Lisa thus spared themselves a potentially agonizing and unnecessary procedure with the tribe that could have disrupted their adoption process had they blindly listened to their agency. Be like Tom and Lisa. Learn the laws that apply to your adoption, even if you have to retain another attorney, and be smart. This is no time to go brain-dead (no matter how much you may need or want to). Do the research!

So are you ready to start planning to adopt your baby? And more important, are you ready for the sleep deprivation that will soon follow?

～ 5 ～

MANAGING A
DOMESTIC ADOPTION

Adoptive-Parent Profiles, Birth Families,
Cell Phones and Sudden Terror Attacks

his is the exciting part—getting ready for your adoption and
pursuing your adoption plan! Once again we're in the midst of
super-important but sometimes dry information. I will try to
lighten things up when I can, but just to be forewarned, make sure
you've had a good dose of caffeine before you sit down and go over
managing the process of the baby hunt. This stuff is too important
to zone out on.

Filling Out Your Placement Profile

Once you've completed—and passed—your home study, you will
be faced with the prospect of filling out a form that describes your
preferences and tolerance levels for various adoption or placement
situations. Some agencies call this form a placement request. Some
attorneys get a sense for your ideal placement situation after speaking with you and taking extensive notes but without providing you
with a form to complete. Frankly, I think filling out the form is very

useful, as it gives you time to think about options and possibilities. Whether you get a form or have a conversation, I am going to refer to the process as creating a placement profile (not to be confused with your adoptive-parent profile), as it is the profile of what you will and won't accept in an adoption situation.

Your placement profile outlines whether (among many other things) you're willing to work with a birth mother whose family has a history of heart disease or cancer, and/or who smokes, and/or does not know who the birth father is, and/or whether you are willing to adopt a child of a different racial background. These are only a few of the items you will cover with your agency or attorney. Most placement profile forms are several pages long and go into great detail about potential adoptive situations and what is and isn't acceptable to you, or what you may be willing to consider but are not certain you would agree to (for example, you might need more medical information to fully evaluate whether a situation is right for you).

Understanding Placement Profiles and Birth Family Situations

Your adoption professional will ask you to consider various racial characteristics and whether you would adopt a baby who is full Caucasian, Hispanic or part Hispanic, African American or part African American, Asian or part Asian—you get the idea. This comes down to how much you want or need your baby to look like you. There are babies of all colors and races available for adoption. We discussed this in chapter 1. Are you open to parenting a child who isn't the spitting image of you or a reasonable facsimile thereof?

Many people wrongly feel they have to express a preference or openness for a baby of a different ethnicity because there aren't enough full-Caucasian newborns available for adoption. It is somewhat of a myth that full-Caucasian infants are harder to adopt than are Hispanic or African American infants. What makes it hard to adopt a newborn is not whether that newborn is Caucasian but what you put on your placement profile about that newborn's medical or family background.

You could be receptive to adopting a baby of a different ethnicity or an open adoption (both of which reduce the time you may wait for placement), but because you want the birth mother to have received prenatal care and not consumed alcohol, smoked or taken any illicit drugs, you're limiting the pool of adoptive situations you are eligible to be considered for. Similarly, if you want to adopt only a baby who has curly blond hair and blue eyes, and maybe even is of a specific gender, you will be lengthening your wait by placing such restrictive criteria on your placement profile. Besides which, I never know how anyone can guarantee that the baby will have these characteristics, as all it takes is one dominant brown-eye gene in a grandparent to cause your little Amanda or Adam to develop brown eyes about eight weeks after he or she comes home. And unless absolutely everyone in your family—for generations and generations—has those facial features and no others, even *you* can't guarantee yourself a biological boy with curly blond hair and blue eyes.

This brings me to another point: selecting gender. This is a surprisingly heated area of debate in the adoption community. Should adoptive parents be able to specify the gender of their adopted child? Proponents of gender selection in adoption say that adoptive parents usually have lost all control over their reproductive lives and should be able to exert this little bit of control. It is one of the so-called perks of adoption. Opponents say that if you cannot select the gender of a biological child, you shouldn't be able to do so in an adoption setting, either. I find both of these arguments persuasive, and I refuse to take sides. The only major comment I have on this score is to say that specifying a gender may slow your process down substantially, as most birth mothers do not know what gender child they are carrying. If your adoption professional doesn't know the gender of the child a particular birth mother is carrying when you have specified that you only want to adopt a girl, your adoption professional likely will not present you with that birth mother's situation. Your adoption professional will only present you with situations that meet your criteria—in this case only birth mothers who know they are carrying a girl.

The one piece of advice I can give you is this: if you don't want to slow down the process and want a specific-gender child, go international. This is an easy way to adopt a child of a specific gender within a reasonable time frame, especially if you choose to adopt from a country that places a disproportionate number of children of one gender over the other (for example, China places predominantly girls for adoption, and South Korea places boys). Even if you choose to adopt from a country such as Guatemala that places children of each gender in roughly equal numbers, it should not slow down your process one bit, as the orphanage or agency from which your child will be placed knows exactly how many boys and girls it has available to place with U.S. families. If your heart is set on a *newborn* baby girl, however, just be prepared that you may be facing a longer than normal wait for your baby to come home.

Evaluating Prospective Situations: What Matters, What You Need to Know

I have mentioned that there are ways to speed up your adoption process. One of the most important ways you can do this is by being flexible and open-minded when completing your placement profile. Now, before we talk about being open and flexible, I want you to know that I do believe it is perfectly okay to ask your adoption professional to consider you only for situations in which a birth mother took amazing care of herself: never smoked, drank, or took any medication; did take prenatal vitamins; got prenatal care; and exercised under medical supervision for her entire pregnancy. If this is what you need and want in an adoptive situation, you're fully entitled to ask for it. You must, however, accept in the beginning of your baby hunt that this will significantly lengthen your wait for a baby.

Smoking

Most birth mothers smoke; in fact, according to some statistics, as many as 60 percent (or more) of birth mothers smoke. If you say you won't work with a birth mother who smokes, you've just cut yourself off from being considered as adoptive parents by 60 percent of birth mothers considering making an adoption plan.

What I think is a good idea for everyone is to do some research when you're creating your placement profile. What are the true risks of having a birth mother who smokes? You should talk to a pediatrician or other medical professional, but one major risk is low birth weight. Low birth weight, however, can be overcome with good medical care, love and attention; and it's worth noting that many low-birth-weight babies are also born to nonsmoking women. Another risk factor is that smoking during pregnancy increases the risk of sudden infant death syndrome (SIDS), as much as three times the normal rate. This is a wee bit scary to most parents, but knowing the recommendations for preventing SIDS cuts down that risk substantially, as does being aware of the fact that your child may be at risk. The bottom line is that the vast majority of babies born to smokers (and heck, both Charlie and I had moms who smoked while pregnant) do just fine, if not excel. It is up to you to decide where your tolerance level is, but being open to a birth mother who smokes exposes you (pardon the pun) to a larger pool of birth mothers.

Drug Use

If smoking concerns you, take some time to think about some of the other more serious types of in utero exposure you may be presented with. What about a birth mother who has exposed the baby to cocaine, or marijuana, or alcohol, or prescription and nonprescription drugs? Again, do your research and talk to a pediatrician or family practitioner. Charlie and I did this and learned that marijuana exposure during pregnancy causes low birth weight but usually not much else unless it is consumed in large quantities, and even then research isn't clear whether there are permanent consequences from the exposure. In contrast, almost any amount of alcohol consumed at any point during pregnancy (not just the first trimester) can result in fetal alcohol syndrome. Cocaine exposure can cause premature birth, low birth weight, an increased risk of SIDS, and neurological problems—

or nothing at all. Certain prescription drugs are perfectly safe, while others can be extremely damaging. Prescription drugs are classified according to the likelihood that they will cause injury to a fetus. Some drugs cause substantial fetal injury (such as Accutane) and are classified as such (Class C and Class D drugs are *not* recommended for use during pregnancy unless the benefit to the mother clearly outweighs the risk to the fetus). Other medications, such as acetominophen (Tylenol), are Class A drugs that pose little or no risk.

You need to know how much was taken, what class of drug it is, and why it was taken. (Sometimes these medications are prescribed and used under the supervision of a physician). Indeed, with respect to all potential toxic exposure, knowing how much was taken, when, and perhaps why can help you measure the risks to the fetus. Once you have this information, you can discuss the potential harm to the baby with a medical professional and make a more informed decision.

If instead you say that you are only willing to consider a situation in which absolutely no medications or illicit drugs were taken, you are eliminating almost every birth mother before you know she only took a couple of Tylenol and an antibiotic that is considered safe during pregnancy and was prescribed by an obstetrician. There are also situations in which a birth mother did take (either medically supervised or not) prescription medication that can cause fetal injury, but the agency or attorney either has arranged or can arrange for advanced ultrasound testing to hopefully identify or rule out developmental defects. Knowing that your birth mother took a drug that is known to cause a cleft palate or defects to developing feet and hands and that an ultrasound shows that there is normal facial bone structure and are ten normal-appearing fingers and toes can go a long way toward giving you the comfort you need to pursue this situation. Neurological injuries are much more difficult to assess, but things like an ultrasound measurement of the baby's head can help assess the degree of exposure, as smaller-than-normal head measurements are strongly correlated with significant drug exposure. Similarly, knowing how much of what drug was taken and when it was taken can help you determine whether the risks to the fetus are too great for you to consider adopting from this situation. (International adoptive parents will never have the birth mother's medical background to know what, if anything, their child was exposed to in utero.)

And please, please, please keep in mind that many problems caused by drug or nicotine intake during pregnancy usually can be overcome with appropriate early intervention. One of the more common consequences of drug exposure is speech development delays, which are almost always completely resolved by working with a speech pathologist (paid for by your state). Indeed, research consistently shows that children born to drug-addicted mothers who receive appropriate early-childhood intervention usually catch up and do as well as (sometimes even better than) their peers who were not exposed to toxins in the uterus. A little love and extra care go a long way toward correcting and compensating for drug and nicotine exposure in utero. Again, if you tell your adoption professional that you're not willing to discuss a situation in which the birth mother took medication, drugs or alcohol, an otherwise potentially viable match with a baby with few, if any, issues may not be presented to you.

Mental Health Issues

You also will likely be presented with questions concerning psychiatric or mental health problems in the birth family. My first comment here is not to run screaming in the other direction at the thought of adopting a child who comes from a birth mother with a background of mental illness. Let me first point out that not all mental health issues are genetic; many are caused by trauma or environmental factors.

If you're willing to consider a birth family with a history of mental illness, find out what the diagnosis is and then do some research. Certain mental health issues are genetic and are carried by a dominant gene. Thus, if your birth mother and her birth mother both suffer from the disease, the baby is likely to be affected as well (he or she will certainly be a carrier). It is also important to know that there are specific diagnostic criteria for identifying most illnesses, and

Is the Birth Mother Telling You the Truth?

One rather significant caveat to the entire discussion of doing research and assessing each potential adoptive situation on a case-by-case basis is that you are assuming the birth mother is telling the truth. No one can guarantee you that the birth mother is being honest about what she is (or isn't) disclosing. Finding out after a baby is born that the birth mother wasn't telling the truth about drug or alcohol exposure can be sticky.

I know a couple, Jim and Lauren, who were very flexible about this placement profile stuff. They had matched with a birth mother who claimed to have smoked on and off during her pregnancy (fine by them) but claimed only to have had one drink (in her life) before the baby was born. Jim and Lauren were skeptical that this birth mother had only had one drink, but they agreed to work with her anyway. After the baby, a girl, was born Jim and Lauren got a phone call from their attorney that the baby had tested positive for drugs, including cocaine.

The attorney wanted to know how they felt about proceeding with the adoption plan. Jim and Lauren weren't troubled about the drug exposure; they felt they could handle whatever might be wrong with the baby as a result of the birth mother's drug use. However, they were very troubled by the fact that the birth mother had lied so blatantly about using drugs and alcohol.

If she had lied about this, what else had she lied about? Ultimately, they felt they couldn't work with this birth mother because they couldn't trust what she said and any information she had shared about her background. They walked away from this situation feeling horrible about their decision, but that it was the right choice for them. The baby was adopted by another family.

And three weeks later Jim and Lauren adopted a different baby girl. Happy ending!

Let what they experienced be a valuable lesson to all prospective adoptive parents. You need to take what you hear about your birth mother with the proverbial grain of salt. The vast majority of birth mothers are completely honest (especially those who are very forthcoming about their medical history). If it sounds too good to be true or something doesn't entirely add up, my advice is to trust your instincts! You can always ask follow-up questions or ask for additional medical testing (you may have to pay for it, of course), and you can always walk away from a situation that isn't right, even after the baby is born. Just do everyone a favor before the baby is born by being honest about what would cause you to *not* take the baby home.

many illnesses are misdiagnosed and don't really meet the relevant diagnostic criteria. If you're interested in a situation in which a birth mother has a diagnosed mental illness, ask questions to find out the circumstances surrounding the diagnosis, and then run them by a psychiatrist or mental health professional.

Charlie and I were presented with two situations involving birth mothers with mental health issues; one was diagnosed with bipolar disorder and the other with a personality disorder. Initially we felt comfortable pursuing the situation with the birth mother with the personality disorder but were wary of the birth mother with bipolar disorder. We spoke with a psychiatrist, a genetics counselor and a therapist about each situation. After discussing them with professionals, we learned that it didn't sound like the birth mother with bipolar disorder had been properly diagnosed, and there was no evidence of bipolar disorder in her family (it is a genetic condition). All the medical professionals felt that it was a fairly safe conclusion that, while this birth mother clearly had emotional issues, she did not suffer from true bipolar disorder. In contrast, the birth mother with a personality disorder had been through so many traumas in her young life and had such a severe case, we were advised not to pursue an adoption plan with her, as she was not considered stable enough to pursue an open adoption (which is what we wanted). It was interesting to us that the medical professionals with whom we consulted did not agree with us regarding the situation we would have considered pursuing (the personality disorder) and the one we shied away from (the bipolar case). This is why I say you should do your research and talk to professionals.

Another reason to be open-minded about birth-family histories is that every family, *including yours,* has someone with a mental illness and/or seriously dysfunctional relatives (and I am not referring to your partner's mother!). It behooves you to consider your own family background before you begin to disqualify birth families with a history of mental illness or other life instability. If you can accept and love members of your family who have experienced battles with alcoholism, illegal behavior, an inability to hold a job, multiple divorces or relationship failures, then how can you possibly exclude or judge a birth family with a similar history? If you love cousin John, who is an active alcoholic, has been in and out of rehab more times than you can count, has problems with depression and anxiety, dropped out of high school, and can't hold a job, then can't you begin to accept that in a birth mother's background? Indeed, you're going to be hearing some very complicated and troubling stories about potential birth families.

Other Issues

You need to prepare yourself for the fact that birth mothers are in crisis, and the stories they present are sometimes very sad, and oftentimes overwhelming. In the course of my own adoption experience I heard some unbelievably disturbing stories. I couldn't even begin to understand where these women were coming from or how they were coping. Their lives seemed so out of control and alien to me. I may have had your reasonably typical dysfunctional childhood, but compared with some of these birth mothers, I don't know squat about life! I have no right to judge someone living in circumstances I cannot begin to understand, and the very fact that this person is trying to do something positive—make an adoption plan—is a tremendous credit to her.

Talking about messy and sad life experiences, some babies are being placed for adoption who were conceived as a result of a rape. This is a tough one for many adoptive parents and presents a situation with which they cannot work. How do you explain to your child when he asks you why his birth mother placed him for adoption that his birth mother was raped? Most professionals will tell you that you need to be able to share your child's adoption story in a positive, loving light. Charlie says he needs to be able to tell his children a story that makes adoption a "good" thing, a positive aspect of our lives. It is hard, no doubt, to put a positive spin on the rape scenario. There are, however, ways to handle this issue gracefully, and I encourage you to read books and articles on raising adopted children and responding to the "Why was I adopted?" question. My personal take on it is that any woman who is raped and chooses not to abort the pregnancy, and instead faces the fact that she was raped every day of her pregnancy and values the life growing inside her more than the violent act that gave rise to that life is an incredibly brave and strong human being. How much better or good does it get to be able to tell your child that her birth mother so valued her life and wanted her to have a good life that she was willing to face and deal with her trauma on a daily basis? Finding a way to present a "good" story is truly just a matter of educating yourself and being prepared. As I said, life is messy; the very fact that your child is adopted is going to create questions and issues for her. The fact that her birth mother was raped is just another layer of complexity for you to deal with.

These are very tough issues, which is why I urge you to think them through before you're actively talking to birth mothers. You shouldn't be trying to sort out how you feel about this stuff when you are on the phone with a birth mother, sending her mixed messages. Nor should you destroy yourself trying to accommodate situations that aren't right for your family. Rape is a tough issue, and if you can't handle it, you're not doing something wrong by choosing not to work with a birth mother who was raped. People have to find their own tolerance levels and do what is right for *them*. You may not be able to handle a rape conception but may be fine with cocaine exposure or a birth mother who is in jail, whereas someone else may not be okay working with a birth mother who exposed the baby to drugs or is in jail but is fine with rape in the birth-family history.

Many of the adoptive parents I know ultimately made the choice to work with a birth family—or not work with one—based not on how complicated the situation was but rather on whether they felt a connection to the birth mother and whether they felt they could trust her.

This brings me to another valuable lesson I've learned: the "messier" the situation the birth mother describes to you and your adoption professional, the more honest she (likely) is being. I am always troubled when I hear of a birth mother's background that sounds too much like fantasy (like Jim and Lauren's birth mother, who supposedly never drank but gave birth to a drug-addicted baby). Birth mothers are in crisis; otherwise they would not be placing their children for adoption. Crisis happens to everyone, including what my mom would call "good souls." I happen to think that the people who are honest and disclose to you the full extent of their own and their family's dysfunction in all its glory are well-intentioned, brave, good souls. I am more likely to want to work toward an adoption with someone who errs on the disclosure side than someone trying to hide the fact that her life isn't perfect. If her life were perfect, she probably wouldn't be making an adoption plan.

As you make your placement profile, consider your own family in all its glory. You are not perfect, your family is not perfect, and if you expect perfection from your birth family, you may wait forever to be a forever family. And even when you get a remarkably clean background on a birth family, you cannot be guaranteed a "perfect" baby. Far too many times we forget that even when we grow a baby in our own bellies, we cannot control every possible variable of birth or life. It is the same with a birth mother. Whether or not you are open to raising a child with any degree of special needs (from the temporary to the very devastating and permanent), you need to be aware that bad things can and do happen to even the most careful and cautious adoptive parents.

Most of us have heard of at least one story of adoptive parents filing a lawsuit against an agency or attorney for not disclosing facts relevant to the child's future medical or mental status. There also are stories in which all parties were honest, and still the baby suffers from a devastating illness or disability. I know one wonderful adoptive family that waited and waited and waited for that "perfect" match with a birth mother who didn't smoke or drink and had received prenatal care. After more than two years they finally got the call and flew across the country to pick up a beautiful and apparently healthy three-day-old baby girl. A year later, after tests and more tests, they learned that their daughter suffered from a permanent, random neurological injury that probably occurred sometime during the birth mother's pregnancy and could not have been discovered or prevented. They are a loving and wonderful family, and I never cease to be amazed at how they handle their child's profound disabilities. It is a caution to all of us, however, whether we have biological or adopted children that you can never be guaranteed a "perfect" child.

Understanding Closed, Semi-Open and Open Adoptions

Another facet of your placement profile is the type of adoption relationship you wish to have; that is, whether you want a closed, semi-open or open adoption.

Closed Adoptions

Closed adoptions were the norm twenty years ago but today are very rare. A closed adoption occurs when you do not know the name or location of your child's birth family, and they know nothing about you, and you have very little, if any, postadoption contact (and always through a third party). In a closed adoption you're less likely to have a complete medical history or background on the birth family. These adoptions now most commonly take place when a baby is born at a hospital and the birth mother—who used an alias when being admitted—leaves the hospital without the baby, or when a baby is dropped off at a hospital or other safe location after he or she is born. Some birth families do seek out closed adoptions, but again, this is a rare occurrence. If you want to pursue a closed adoption, make sure to be clear about what you mean (no names, no pre- or postadoption contact, or perhaps some very limited postadoption contact through a third party while maintaining complete anonymity), and be prepared to wait.

Some adoptive parents feel this is the easiest type of adoption to manage, but many adoption advocates stress that the lack of information and knowledge of a child's birth history does tremendous damage to the adoptee (see the groundbreaking book *Adoption Nation* by Adam Pertman, Basic Books, 2000). Most birth families do not want a closed adoption. They want some degree of knowledge about how the baby is doing after placement in the adoptive home, and that is not possible in a closed adoption.

Semi-Open Adoptions

In contrast, a semi-open adoption provides for some contact both before and after birth between the adoptive and birth families. In this case you may meet or speak with the birth family, share first names and some personal information, but not disclose addresses or agree to have a long-term relationship. In a semi-open adoption you likely will share cards and letters for a period of time through an intermediary, and you will know enough about your child's birth history to be able to answer difficult questions. It also isn't unusual for the birth mother to send letters to the baby for him or her to read later in life to help the person make sense of the decision to place him or her for adoption or even to leave the possibility open of meeting the birth family later in life. The focus here is that while there is some contact between the birth and adoptive families, it is limited. A degree of anonymity is maintained, and the relationship is usually under the control or protection of a neutral third party.

Open Adoptions

An open adoption is hard to define, as every family who enters into one will likely describe a different type or degree of openness. The most open of these relationships will involve a lifelong relationship involving regular visits between the birth and adoptive families. The television program *20/20* profiled a relationship like this a few years ago, in which the birth mother visited the adoptive family almost weekly! That is, in all honesty, a little more open than the average open adoption. Most of the people I know who have an open adoption have met their birth family at least once before birth and hope to do so again after placement of the baby in the adoptive home. They have shared all identifying information, including names, addresses and phone numbers, and they speak or otherwise communicate directly with each other (no third party) and do so regularly. There is a wide variety and degree of openness in open-adoption relationships, and most adoption professionals will recommend that you take it slowly and let the relationship progress naturally.

That said, open adoption is now often the subject of a contractual relationship in which the birth and adoptive parents specifically state the expectations they have for communication and visitation in a written document. Some states recognize and enforce these contracts (see the Appendix), but most do not; and state law varies as to whom these agreements will be enforced against (see the Appendix). Some states enforce them against the adoptive parents and others against the birth parents, but not necessarily both. I am not a fan of defining the terms of an open adoption in a legal contract. The basis of an open adoption is that the birth and adoptive families see themselves as extended family and base their relationship on trust. It doesn't really strike me as a trusting thing to do to require the terms of the relationship be spelled out in a legal document. But life does change, and sometimes having an agreement that protects you in a difficult situation—like when adoptive or birth parents suddenly cease contacting the other—makes sense. At the very least the agreement could serve as the basis for a meaningful discussion about everybody's expectations.

Legal agreements governing the open-adoption relationship aside, the vast majority of birth families today want some type of long-term contact with the adoptive parents. When adoptive parents become educated about open adoption from doing research and speaking with adoptive parents, many discover that it isn't as scary a relationship as they initially thought (open adoption doesn't mean coparenting) and are inclined to pursue some degree of openness with their birth family. As most birth families are interested in having ongoing contact, being open and flexible about open adoption in your placement profile can speed up your adoption process.

However, you should *not* represent that you are more open than you really are. If you don't want to visit your child's birth father after placement, do *not* say that you will. It is better to limit the relationship in the beginning and then as trust and security—and sometimes even love—between the families develop, you can attempt to have more contact.

As wonderful and positive as open adoption can be, I strongly encourage you to be careful when pursuing it. In the right situation open adoption is a gift to everyone in the adoption relationship, especially the adoptee! But with a birth family that is not stable or becomes unstable, it is far more difficult to establish boundaries and limitations when originally there were to be none.

The most typical form an open adoption takes is that which Charlie and I have with our son's birth mother or which our good friends Mary and Bob have with their daughter's birth family. In Mary and Bob's case they have shared names and addresses with their daughter Carrie's birth mother, and they communicate regularly—although not often—through e-mail and the phone. Approximately once a year Mary, Bob and Carrie travel to visit Carrie's birth family for a weekend. In contrast, Charlie and I maintain regular communication with David's birth mother, Diane, through e-mails and letters. We send presents at holidays and birthdays and share pictures all the time. We have not yet visited, although I expect and hope that one day we will see Diane and David's half-sister again! In both situations Mary and Bob and Charlie and I expressed our desire

A WORD TO THE WISE

Never Enter Into a Completely Open Adoption with an Unstable Birth Mother

I provided support to one couple, Caitlyn and Don, who entered into an open adoption (they shared full names and addresses) with a birth mother with a history of mental illness who seemed to go more than a little crazy after the baby was placed in their home. On at least one occasion she made a comment that she was "coming for a visit," uninvited and in violation of their open-adoption agreement, which provided for mutually agreed upon visits in a location to be determined by the adoptive parents. When Caitlyn and Don reminded her of their agreement, the birth mother became verbally abusive and threatened suicide if she wasn't permitted to see the baby.

Caitlyn and Don had a very frightening conversation with their adoption agency in New York about how to protect themselves and their child from a woman who had become clearly destructive and potentially violent. They were actually advised to change their names and move to protect their child. This is an extreme and very unusual situation, but something that does inform all adoptive parents who consider or enter into open adoptions. Open adoptions are wonderful when they work. *But it is easier to make the relationship more open over time as your relationship develops than it is to restrict it later on.*

and commitment to having an ongoing relationship with our child's birth family, but we are allowing that relationship to evolve naturally over time. In the beginning any contact I had with Diane made me nervous, and I felt threatened by her biological connection to David and what it might mean to him as he grows up. As time has gone on, I have grown to respect and appreciate the decision Diane made for David's future and have become more comfortable communicating with her on an increasingly frequent basis. Recently, Mary and Bob invited Carrie's birth mother to visit them where they live. While they were a little nervous at first, they are happy that Carrie's birth mother got to see how and where Carrie lives. Every open adoption is unique, but the best of them are flexible and start carefully and slowly, developing as the trust and love between the families grow.

So now we've discussed the major points of your placement profile. You know to do research, stay open-minded about as many different aspects and types of the adoption process and relationship as feels comfortable for you, and remain as flexible as possible.

Never assume that what you initially decide to put in your placement profile must stay in the profile throughout the entire process. You may discover after waiting and working with various potential situations that you can be more flexible than you originally believed possible in certain areas and/or that you need to be more restrictive in others. This is totally okay, and I recommend it. Go with the flow! As you become more savvy and knowledgeable, let your adoption professional know where your head is. Who knows—that flash of insight you had after hearing about a particular situation (or even hearing about a situation a friend was presented with) will totally remake your own adoption process, and the next thing you know, you'll have your baby!

Finding a Baby and Becoming a Marketing Expert

Let's talk for a minute about the marketing you will do to locate a birth family. The amount of selling you will do on your own behalf in connection with the baby hunt is truly mind-boggling. And with all due respect, the more savvy your marketing and spin technique, the better off you will be! Regardless of whether you're using an attorney or an agency, you want to get down and dirty about presenting yourself in the most ideal light to a complete stranger you know nothing about.

I do not mean taking pictures of some McMansion in your town and representing that as your home. Nor should you say that you travel the world when the most exciting place you've been in the last five years is Albany, New York. That is lying, and while some adoptive parents have done it and gotten away with it (in very few instances, I might add), unless you're an extremely skilled liar and know every detail about that McMansion, you will trip yourself up, reveal yourself to be the shameless liar you are, and blow your chance at an adoption with the birth mother who is reviewing your profile.

I do mean taking your life, your dreams, and your personalities and spinning them to meet the realistic and unrealistic expectations of your prospective birth mother. We go through the details of creating an adoptive-parent profile (or birth mother letter, or video) in a moment. The bottom line here is that you are competing against several other amazingly qualified adoptive parents, and you need to spend time, money and energy creating the most kick-ass profile for your family.

I kid you not, you're going to become spin doctors when designing that profile. You will take pictures of your home, use pictures from vacations, and gather every extended-family picture you have to give this stranger a glimpse of what your family and your life are like. You will do this with care and skill and while sparing no expense, because this is the meet-and-greet of your most important job interview ever—the job of parent!

Designing Adoptive-Parent Profiles: The Most Surreal Marketing Campaign—Selling You

Your adoption professional will advise you as to the type of profile you need to create. Some only want a letter and a few well-chosen pictures to submit to prospective birth parents. Others will recommend that you make a spiral-bound and laminated album of pictures accompanied by a letter that helps explain the pictures and your lifestyle. (Relax, you can hire someone to help you make it. See the Resources section for more information on making adoptive-parent profiles.) Even more sophisticated is the new wave of video profiles for which you record both live footage of you talking and living your life (like a home movie) interspersed with still photographs and music. Somewhat like a wedding video or a video history shown of the happy couple, these video profiles can be quite fun (and expensive) to produce.

Whatever your adoption professional recommends you do to help represent who you are to potential birth families, I recommend that you take the process of creating it *very* seriously. I have seen many, many adoptive-parent profiles. Some are homemade and look it, some are homemade and you would never guess, and some are made by a professional (and these run the gamut from beautifully done to really poor quality). Most of the good ones (and I don't necessarily mean professional ones) bring tears to my eyes. They are so lovingly written, compassionate and *real* that I just want to hug the adoptive mom and dad and tell them I will give them my son (especially after a temper tantrum!).

Whether you make it yourself or have someone do it for you, this is going to take a significant amount of time, thought and effort on your part. I kid you not when I say that a well-done profile can really make the difference for a birth mother. Birth mothers see many profiles and letters in the course of their search for adoptive parents. They quickly learn who took time with their profile and really cared about how they presented themselves. The half-assed profiles, the ones that look like homework your dog has eaten, do not go over well. Not doing a thoughtful and thorough job on your profile really sends a message—if you don't care enough to make a good first impression through your profile, do you really want to be a parent?

You want to look like a fun, life-loving, happy-go-lucky couple that can offer a stable, loving home to a child. Yes, that may well be an oxymoron! If you're like most of the women I know, you work twelve or more hours a day, sleep all weekend trying to catch up from the week's exhaustion, and are still fighting to get all the weight off from the infertility drugs. Fun, life-loving and happy-go-lucky don't exactly define most thirty- or fortysomethings these days!

Before you read about how to create your profile, I want you to go online (see the Resources section) and read letters people have written to birth mothers, and look at the pictures they have included. Choose a few different couples and take notes on what appeals to you about their profiles. Go to waiting adoptive-parent bulletin boards and talk to people about what they put or didn't put in their profiles. Go to support-group meetings and ask questions about what people put in their profiles. Find a Web site that lists profiles (see the Resources section), and watch to see how long some couples stay on the site waiting for an adoption and how quickly others say "We're adopting!" While you cannot know how flexible or open they may be, there is bound to be something in each of these profiles that differentiates one adoptive family from the rest and explains why it matched so quickly. Is there something in that profile that you can adapt to your own?

Many a birth mother has told an adoption professional and/or adoptive parent that she ultimately chose her child's forever family because she could see herself (and by extension her baby) as a member of that family. If she feels comfortable with you and your lifestyle, she will feel comfortable placing her baby in your home forever. Keep that in mind when you're designing your profile. Put yourself in a birth mother's shoes, and look at your profile objectively. Would you feel comfortable with this family? Do they seem relaxed, happy, carefree and financially stable? Or do they seem snooty and stuck up?

Think back—way back—to when you lived a more carefree existence, and imagine what would have been important to you if you were considering placing a baby for adoption. This is a strange task, I know, but as I've learned, most people design their birth mother letters or adoptive-parent profiles thinking about what qualities they think are good from their perspective as fortysomething prospective adopters. Chances are you're not going to have a fortysomething prospective birth mother reviewing your profile. Think young and fun, with a good dose of financial stability and love thrown in for good measure!

There are a thousand recommendations I could make for preparing your profile, and for every recommendation I could make, someone would say "No, no, no!" And they're right! You need to prepare your own adoptive-parent profile from *your* heart. If it feels right to you to include pictures from your wedding even though someone else tells you not to, *do it!* If it feels right to include pictures of you and your partner from ten years ago when your hair was miles longer, and someone is telling you to include recent pictures only, include the old hairdo shots! My hair was about five different lengths in our profile, and that reflects the fact that I am constantly changing my look. To find pictures of me with all the same length hair is virtually impossible.

Here are a few tips and ideas for self-promotion:

- If you have dogs and cats, you will need to *use* them. If you don't have pets but will someday, go borrow someone's dog and take a picture with it so birth mothers know you're animal lovers. If you aren't animal lovers, don't misrepresent yourself by including a picture with your brother-in-law's golden retriever. But if you want to have a dog someday, by all means borrow that pooch for a photo shoot!

- If you're outdoorsy folks, play it up and include pictures from your favorite camping trip. If you like the beach, find a reasonably flattering picture of you and your partner at the beach (as if you're going to find a picture you like of yourself in a bathing suit!).

- If you have to hire a professional photographer to get a flattering picture of you, do it!

- Use only the best photographs you have from vacations, parties, and outings to include in the profile.

- If you live in an apartment, take pictures of the interior but include photographs of vacations or trips to the great outdoors or of family members with houses. You don't want to misrepresent that you don't live in the concrete jungle, but you also don't want to limit yourself by implying that you never leave the Big Apple or the hills and trolley cars of San Francisco when a birth mother may be from a rural community and a little leery of big-city life!

- Wear your favorite clothes in at least one picture that you will consider putting on the cover or will use as your first image. First of all, you will be more comfortable in this outfit than any other. Feeling relaxed will help the pictures come out better. Second, birth mothers will be seeing you exactly as you are every day. Sometimes what you love to wear, someone else will love too. I inadvertently wore my favorite leather jacket that has a lot of fringe. It was colder than I expected on the day we were taking pictures for our profile, and I grabbed it out of the closet (the way I do almost every day). The picture we put on the front of our adoptive-parent profile wound up being one with that jacket—not because of the jacket but because it was the only really nice picture of the two of us— and almost every birth mother I spoke with commented on that jacket. The jacket was even used by one birth mother to refer to us when she spoke to a caseworker; she couldn't remember our first names, but she remembered that jacket!

Some definite don'ts, however, include:

- Don't include pictures of you or your partner at a vastly different weight without explaining the weight loss or weight gain. I promise you that the right birth mother will not care whether you are significantly overweight or underweight. What she won't understand are pictures of you weighing 100 pounds less than you do now and skiing down some ultra-glamorous ski slope (fifteen years ago), and meeting you now, looking very different. She may not care that you've gained weight and no longer ski, but she might feel surprised and a little duped. Do not be ashamed of your appearance; be honest about what you look like! The right birth mother will not care about your hair, weight, or lack of six-pack abs. She *will* care about you misrepresenting yourself and your lifestyle.

- Do not include a picture of yourself sitting at the beach under an SPF-blocking sun tent. While you may well appreciate the precautions you take against getting skin cancer (as do I), a seventeen-year-old beachgoing teen may look at the picture and think that her baby is going to be doomed to a life with overprotective, boring parents.

- Don't include photographs of other people's homes because you think yours is inadequate. This is lying. Birth mothers do not like liars (who does?). By all means include pictures of family members' homes and vacation homes, even friends' homes if you live in an apartment or a house that is in the middle of a massive renovation.

- Don't include too many black-and-white pictures. These tend to be very formal or perceived as too artsy. Many people don't "get" black-and-white pictures. If you have an amazing black-and-white picture, by all means include it, but try to limit it to just one.

- If you make your own profile, when designing the pages, don't include cutsie cutouts of pacifiers or teddy bears. Using scrapbook decorators of flowers and non-baby-related decorations is perfectly acceptable, but stay away from baby stuff. This profile is about *you,* not the baby!

- I think you should be able to include as many pictures as you want and use as many pages as you want. I have seen plenty of recommendations that you stick to only three images per page, but I don't see why that has to be the case. My rule of thumb is that each page should be clean, uncluttered and easy to read. Pictures, however, should not be duplicative (you don't need fifty images of you and your partner!), but a few representative shots of each aspect of your life is a good idea.

- Have a friend proofread it before you print all the copies. Make sure your friend knows to be brutally honest. She should be able to tell you that you've included unflattering photographs, used poor grammar, and/or that the pages are too busy or even ugly!

And then you need to relax! Most birth mothers choose adoptive parents for reasons beyond our control. I have heard a birth mother say that the adoptive dad was wearing a Red Sox baseball hat, and her best friend was a huge Sox fan, and so she felt more comfortable with that adoptive family. Another might choose you because you have the kind of couch she grew up with, or because you are (or aren't) avid skiers. It is rare that a birth mother chooses you to parent her child because you promise to take the baby around the world before she is five years old, will send him to private school (although a college education likely will be important to her), or live in the largest house this side of Beverly Hills. She will be looking for some aspect of your life that makes her feel like she *knows you.* Like I said, you want her to feel comfortable with your lifestyle and values, not to mention that baseball cap.

Last, if you wind up waiting a long time, lose 100 pounds, buy a new house or pet or take a great vacation, consider redoing your profile to bring it up to date.

Talking to Birth Mothers: And You Thought Meeting Your In-Laws Was Scary!

The next step in the baby hunt is getting your adoptive-parent profile into a birth mother's hands so she can call you to see if you are the right forever parent(s) for the baby she is carrying. Now, I won't talk about how to get your profile into a birth mother's hands. That topic could be the subject of its own book and as such is beyond the scope of this not-so-little tome. I chose not to include it because you—in all likelihood—have taken my excellent advice and retained an adoption professional to assist you with this aspect of the baby hunt. I would rather devote time to what other people don't talk about, and that is the head trip of speaking to potential birth mothers. And quite a head trip it is, for both of you!

That First Frightening Contact

One day your adoption professional is going to tell you that it's time to get that infamous cell phone on which a birth mother or two (or three . . .) will call you. The cell phone will have a blind toll-free number (meaning your name will not come up on caller ID) that the birth mother may call at any time of day or night. Therefore, you will be advised to keep the cell phone with you at all times. I too recommend that you keep it with you at all times, but you don't need to take it to the potty with you or leave it on the bathroom sink while you shower (unless you're expecting a phone call from a birth mother, in which case I will instruct you to put your greasy hair in a ponytail or otherwise ignore it until after the phone call is over). Birth mother cell phones are the stuff of many an adoptive-parent story.

This phone will be your best friend and it will cause you much embarrassment. The thing about the cell phone is that you can't take it too seriously, but at the same time you really can't risk not answering it. A birth mother isn't likely to leave you a voicemail. You also don't necessarily know who will be calling and what time she will call. This can make you feel very jumpy, somewhat paranoid and definitely powerless.

Before your profile goes out to birth families, take some time one afternoon (grab a strong cup of coffee or a glass of wine), to make a list of every question you can think of that you might want to know about a birth mother. Your adoption professional may have a sample list of questions for you to use to help get you started. Then, take a pen and cross off every question—or create a second list of questions—that has to do with anything medical or baby-related.

Always Keep Your Cell Phone Handy, No Matter How Long You've Had It!

My friend Karen had a deathly silent cell phone. For months she had this thing with her wherever she went, and it *never* rang. She became paranoid that it didn't work, to the point that she repeatedly and annoyingly called Verizon to make sure that the service hadn't been unknowingly disconnected *and* called me every day to ask me if I could call her to make sure the phone would ring! Eventually she became rather blasé about the phone and decided it was just one more needless expense on her journey to parenthood (kind of like all the money she had paid to her infertility clinic).

Then one day during an important business meeting Karen heard an unfamiliar noise from her tote bag. At first she ignored the noise, so convinced had she become that the cell phone would never ring. The ringing, however, persisted until she—and everyone else at the meeting—realized that it was Karen's phone. Only Karen realized that it wasn't any old cell phone, it was *the* cell phone!

She immediately started digging through her cavernous tote bag to grab the phone and answer it. Imagine—here is Karen, this super-professional female partner in a powerhouse New York law firm, dressed up in her best don't-mess-with-me-or-you'll-regret-it business suit, the only woman at a table filled with about ten male lawyers and another half dozen men who had traveled from Japan, Australia and the UK to discuss a new merger her law firm's client was pursuing, breaking a sweat and causing a few raised eyebrows while she's trying to find a tiny phone that no one else understands is connected to her future happiness.

For the life of her she couldn't find the phone in the bag. In one desperate moment of adoptive-mom paranoia (that the birth mother would give up and *never* call back), she upended the entire contents of the bag onto the conference room table. As she described it later—laughing hysterically over an apple martini— her multiple lipsticks went rolling toward the businessman from Japan, her resume (she was interviewing for a new job because of her fear that the merger would interfere with new parenthood) landed on the floor next to her boss's chair, two Playtex super-plus tampons landed in the lap of the very uptight older gentleman from London, but she found the phone! After rapidly collecting her belongings, she excused herself from the meeting. Karen used the funny story of upending the bag onto the table as a way to explain why she took so long to answer the phone and to break the ice at the beginning of the phone call. Shrewd woman, my friend Karen, because she knew the first rule of the frightening first contact: the birth mother dialing your phone (or asking a friend to dial) is more nervous and scared than you are. She doesn't know what to say and neither will you (unless you're as quick-thinking as Karen). And there is stuff you definitely should *not* say in that first phone call!

- **Topics to Avoid:** You should never ever discuss medical stuff or the baby with a birth mother during your first phone call unless she brings it up first (then go for it!). I don't care how badly you want to know whether she's had prenatal care, smoked or drank, or anything else. I have seen lists in other books that suggest you ask background questions during your first phone call about why the birth mother is pursuing an adoption plan. But those questions, in my opinion, need to be asked by an adoption professional or be addressed in a subsequent conversation between the two of you.

  Nor do you want to ask if the birth father is involved in her life, has signed relinquishment papers, or is sitting next to her. Your agency, attorney or facilitator should be the one to ask the tough questions early on in the relationship. (They may have already asked some of these questions, and you may already have some background when you get that first fateful phone call.)

Generally speaking, talking about the baby, medical stuff or birth fathers may mean you won't get a second chance to talk with her. Let the serious topics come up naturally and be initiated by the birth mother or your adoption professional. This first conversation is a get-to-know-you chat, and you want this birth mother to hang up the phone knowing that you genuinely care about *her,* not just her baby.

- **Topics It's Okay to Cover:** Basically anything she wants to talk about or volunteers is okay to discuss. In fact, another good rule of thumb is to let her dictate where the conversation goes. If she wants to talk about something, by all means talk about it, even if she brings up the baby and the circumstances of her pregnancy. However, don't ask follow-up questions that involve medical information or seek to elicit more personal information about the baby, his or her conception or the pregnancy. Instead, listen politely and make gentle and supportive comments that are appropriate to the context of the conversation and are sincere (such as "That must be really hard!" or "You must be really strong!"). If there are lags in the conversation, go back to your list of questions and see if there is a question on your list that might flow well. Or check out this list of icebreakers:

- **Great Icebreakers:**

  — Tell her how nervous *you* are. You will be shocked to discover that most birth mothers don't think you're nervous; to them you've got your stuff together and have nothing to be nervous about. They don't get that you feel like they're holding your future happiness in their bellies! I told Diane how nervous I was, and let me tell you that opened the conversation up faster than anything else I said. She was stunned and confessed to me how nervous she was. We bonded over being scared to talk!

— Celebrities. First of all, who doesn't love the movies or television? She may not have been able to afford to go to the movies recently, but I bet you she knows who Brad Pitt is (and he's an adoptive dad) or Angelina Jolie. You may have been discussing single parenting and why she feels she wouldn't or couldn't do that (regardless of your marital status). You could then use this as a launchpad to ask her what she thinks of single adoptive parents like Calista Flockhart, Sharon Stone, or Meg Ryan (keep in mind that these women may be perceived as living somewhat racy lifestyles if your birth mother is from a conservative upbringing). Or you could talk about celebrity adoptive couples like Hugh Jackman (he played Wolverine in the movie *X-Men*) or Steven Spielberg and their wives. Either way, talking and laughing about movies, television and celebrities could lighten things up for a moment and keep you on the phone longer.

— Your profile. Ask her which is her favorite picture or what about your profile attracted her to you.

Be prepared for her to say things that are offensive to you and hard to hear. I often heard comments such as: "You must be so sad you can't have your own baby" or "You must hate me because I'm pregnant and I don't even want it." Let it roll off your back. Respond simply with something about how grateful you are to women who are considering making adoption plans. Because, let's face it, we *are* grateful!

The first conversation doesn't have to be very long. It could last fifteen minutes or three hours. After a good conversation you have a sense of whether she will move forward toward a more serious commitment to you. At the end of the conversation you need to tell her how much you enjoyed speaking with her and that you would love to speak to her some more, but at this point you would like her to speak with your adoption professional to learn what steps need to be taken to make an adoption plan together. If you weren't too crazy about this birth mother, alarms are going off in your head, or you are otherwise nonplussed, don't worry. You do not have to make a decision today about whether to adopt this woman's baby. You will—hopefully—have more chances to talk to determine if your first instinct was right. Oftentimes your first impression is not right; both of you were so nervous that neither of you came across the way you really are. Many an adoptive mom has realized that the first conversation did not accurately reflect her birth mother's personality, and she's wound up doing a complete about-face and loving the birth mother she was initially ambivalent about. By all means set up another time to talk, but emphasize that she must contact your adoption professional (or that your agency or attorney will be calling her) for you to be able to pursue this relationship seriously.

If you're pursuing an independent adoption and/or this first phone call wasn't arranged by a third party like your agency or attorney, another tactic to help establish the legitimacy of the particular situation or birth mother with whom you've just spoken is to get her phone number during your first call and then, after you've hung up, immediately call back with a follow-up question ("Umm, I'm so sorry to bother you but I forgot to ask . . ."). This is a well-known tactic, however, and if your birth mother has spoken with other adoptive parents and they've done this, you may alienate her. I personally feel it is safer to ask her to contact your adoption professional or for permission for the professional to contact her. By putting the onus on her to contact your attorney or agency, however, you really ask her to go the extra mile and prove her commitment. For the nervous or scared birth mother (who may be very committed to making an adoption plan), this may be too much to ask. Use your judgment and decide whether asking for a phone number, asking whether your attorney or agency can call her, or asking her to call your attorney or agency is the most appropriate for each individual birth mother.

The bottom line is that you need her to make a commitment to you by speaking with an adoption professional and taking steps toward formalizing your relationship in order for you to safely expend precious emotional energy on something that may not pan out. Too many of my friends (and I did it too) have spent hours and hours on the phone talking with pregnant women who either chose other families to parent their children, were scamming us (which I will discuss in a moment), or chose to parent. Keep in mind that you don't want to give up too much of your time and energy to someone who may not decide to place her baby with you or isn't necessarily serious about making an adoption plan.

I have spent hours on the phone with needy pregnant women who chose to keep their children. I didn't need to spend so much time talking with them and being their shrink. It would have been sufficient to speak with them for a half hour or three-quarters of an hour, let them get to know me, get to know them, and then let my adoption professional take over to determine whether these women were good matches. A birth mother who likes you—even a little bit—will agree to talk with your attorney or agency. A birth mother who is on the fence, not serious, or scamming you will balk, stall and otherwise do everything humanly possible to avoid talking seriously about making an adoption plan. Do not, I repeat, do not waste hours and hours of your time and energy talking with a birth mother who won't take the steps to make a commitment to you, gives you excuse after excuse as to why she hasn't called your adoption professional, or who consistently and repeatedly blows off your phone calls. A birth mother who is sincere and legitimate will follow through, I promise!

Whether it is your first or thirty-third conversation with a birth mother, be prepared to hear very personal and sometimes alarming details of her life. I have spoken before about the fact that all birth mothers are in crisis, and the vast majority of them are not leading easy lives. I have spoken with thirtysomething birth mothers who have their act together, have gone to college, have a professional life, have gotten pregnant, don't believe in abortion, and are thus making an adoption plan. This does happen, but is very rare. More likely, you are going to hear at least one very sad story, and you need to be prepared to suspend all judgment. Get rid of every judgmental bone in your body and try to be supportive, no matter how startled or alarmed you may be by what you're hearing. Birth fathers or birth mothers who are in jail aren't uncommon, nor is a family history of abuse or drug addiction, abandonment and poverty. You name it, you may hear it. As I said, not every story will be sad or ugly, but many of them will be. You may not be able to relate to it, but you need to accept it.

If you don't think you can handle hearing this stuff, talk with your adoption professional about how calls can be prescreened by the professional or conversations limited to particular subjects. It is not always possible or advisable to set limits on how, when, or why you will take calls, but if you really think you might blow it if you hear the birth mother is calling you from the state penitentiary, talk to your professional before you've got to handle this type of call. (And for the record, I've spoken with a lot of birth mothers, and this never came up for me. It did come up for a few friends, though!)

Try to always keep your calls light and upbeat or to end them on an upbeat note. You want to be supportive but not sickly sweet, realistic but not intrusive. And remember, she's as scared as you are!

Dealing with Birth Mothers Who Choose to Parent or Who Aren't Really Serious About Making an Adoption Plan: Scoping Out the Scammers and Identifying the Risky Situations

One of every adoptive parent's biggest fears is that a birth mother will choose to parent, either before or after the baby is born. Having been there twice, I can tell you that no matter when it happens, it *sucks*. It is pretty ghastly, however, when it happens after birth and why I recommend not taking a baby home while a birth family may still exercise its right to parent the baby. But let's talk first about the warning signs that a birth mother might choose to parent.

Assessing Placement Risk

Identifying one of the following risk factors in your prospective situation doesn't mean that your birth mother will keep the baby, and even presenting several factors doesn't mean she will. *The birth mother least committed to an adoption plan can place a baby, while the most committed to her adoption plan may choose to parent.* The following list (in no particular order) is really composed of a series of life facts that present red flags that you're walking into a higher-risk situation and need to proceed cautiously:

- The birth grandmother (most specifically the birth mother's mother) is not supportive of the adoption plan. In my opinion this is the biggest factor in an adoption plan going awry.

- Too much discussion of money. Be wary of the birth mother or birth father who is overly concerned with how much you will pay for things and how soon you will be sending that money.

- Inconsistent stories. A birth mother should tell you the same story she tells your professional. While she may later elaborate on certain elements of her history, the story should not substantively change each time you speak with her.

- An ongoing or on-again, off-again relationship with the birth father. There are birth parents who are married and place their child for adoption (even when they have other children) due to poverty or other extenuating circumstances. However, a birth mother who is single and is still involved (even tenuously) with the birth father and secretly (or not so secretly) hopes that he will ultimately step up to the plate and help her parent is not a good thing and is someone to watch carefully. You don't need to be a pawn in her plan to coerce, trap or otherwise convince the baby's birth father that he should parent.

- Sounds too good to be true. Any birth mother who sounds too confident, too secure, or too scripted is probably not for real.

- Not having a postplacement plan. Birth mothers who are serious about placing their babies for adoption likely will have made or will be making a plan for their life postadoption. Usually the adoption is a catalyst for a birth mother to get her life together. Although she may not succeed in following through on her postadoption life plan, having such a plan is a good sign. A birth mother who has not thought about her life after the adoption may not be serious about placing the baby and thus will not be making plans for life without the baby.

- She lives in a big city. Birth mothers who live in a big city may feel more protected by the anonymity the city offers and the common acceptance of single mothers.

- She was single parented, is single parenting another child, or has friends who are single parenting. A birth mother who was raised by a single parent, is parenting by herself, or has friends who are single parenting may feel more comfortable being a single parent than someone who is unfamiliar or unaccepting of single-parent homes.

- She is on welfare. A birth mother who is already on public assistance may not be overly concerned with the financial difficulties of parenting a child and may feel protected by the state welfare system.

- She plans a home birth. Most women who give birth at home are more committed to the child they carried and are unwilling or unable to place the baby for adoption after bonding at birth.

- She has a difficult delivery. A birth mother who has a difficult delivery may feel more connected with her child and reluctant— after perhaps almost losing the baby during birth—to let someone else care for the baby forever.

- She (and the birth father) are very young. A very young birth mother may not be aware of the reality of the challenges of parenting a baby or child or may be more likely to be persuaded by friends or family to raise the baby herself with their help.

- She is not religious. A birth mother who is not religious may not feel any social stigma about being a single parent.

- She is a high school dropout or no one in her family has achieved a secondary education. Statistically speaking, the more educated your birth mother or her family, the more likely she is to want to pursue other dreams and feel confident in her decision to place a baby for adoption in a loving home.

- The baby is due at or near Christmas and the holidays. Adoption professionals have warned me about it, and I have witnessed it with several couples who were attempting to adopt a baby born at or near the Christmas holidays: there is an extremely high rate of failed placements for babies born between Thanksgiving and New Year's. It is a very emotionally charged time of year, and many well-intentioned birth families find they cannot proceed with adoption plans during this time.

Now that I've listed all these red flags, you're probably freaking out at the fact that one or more birth-family situations meet one or more of these risk criteria. Relax! As I said before, the least-committed birth mother may very well choose to place her child with you; you can never tell. Certainly, a birth mother whose situation presents more than one of these flags is worth being concerned about. My recommendation when you have a high-risk situation is to speak frankly with your adoption professional.

Depending on whether you are doing an agency or independent adoption and the state law(s) that govern your adoption, there may be a rather long window after birth during which the birth mother could choose to parent after you've taken the baby home (see the Appendix for various state laws as they apply to relinquishment situations). It may be wiser to ask your attorney or agency to find a transitional care facility or foster family to care for the baby until all legal paperwork has been completed and the birth mother cannot choose to parent. I wish I had had the courage to do this with one of the birth mothers we worked with (we'll call her Heather) who decided to parent after we took the baby home. I now look back (hindsight is 20/20, after all) and realize that Heather subtly and not-so-subtly told me she was going to parent (her mother showing up a frantic wreck within hours of the baby's birth really should have had us running in the other direction). While Heather had already signed her relinquishment papers, she still had a thirty-day window under the applicable state law to choose to parent, so she was well within her right to ask for the baby back only three days after placement. Diane (David's birth mother), in contrast, chose to parent before she had to sign her relinquishment paperwork, but she was giving off clear signs to our adoption agency's caseworker that she was having serious second thoughts (the presumed birth father showing up in the hospital room and not knowing anything about us was not such a favorable event). At least in this instance we had an adoption professional present who knew Diane well and was able to recognize problems and tell us things were going bad fast. Fortunately, things turned around in the end, and Diane did decide to place David for adoption.

Like Diane and Heather, the vast majority of birth mothers who choose to parent do so within the forty-eight hours of the baby being born (Heather was really closer to seventy-two hours, but who's counting?). Many birth mothers also choose to parent within the first few months after finding out they're pregnant. Your best bet is to work with a birth mother who is well into her third trimester and who has had counseling or is willing to get counseling (even if you have to pay for it). And you should have a plan for who will take the baby home from the hospital if the birth mother is undecided or expressing any concerns. You can usually arrange for the baby to stay in the hospital for an extra day or so, but after that you may need the baby to be discharged to a licensed foster-care family or adoption agency. I don't care how strong you think you may be—no one should have to live through the experience of giving a baby back to its birth mother!

Avoiding the Scammers

Another scenario you want to watch out for is that of the scammer. If you're lucky, you won't come across this. Unfortunately, I did, and too many of my friends have. Indeed, there is a woman wandering the United States of America as I write this (we will call her Delila), who, according to the best guesses of several adoption professionals, has scammed upwards of fifteen adoptive families, has a warrant out for her arrest in the state of California, has had her name posted on almost every adoption bulletin board, and is known to many agencies and attorneys, and is still out there scamming!

Due to some psychotic need on Delila's part, she pretends to be pregnant and contacts prospective adoptive parents off the Internet with a very real-sounding story (although the story she told to each family was a little different). She even has pictures of "her" pregnant belly (there was no glimpse of her face in the picture, however, so no one has been able to prove it was her abdomen) and an ultrasound tape of a baby (someone's baby—I don't believe it's hers) that she can send you. It is only after prospective parents start working with her seriously that things start getting weird. She disappears for days or weeks and then is suddenly living in another state for bizarre reasons (as adoptive parents who've been scammed by Delila have shared with me, it's usually because she is working with another adoptive couple in that area). She will meet with attorneys and agencies but not be able to provide details or medical records that verify her pregnancy. For example, she will provide the name of a clinic or doctor, but when that doctor is contacted, he or she reveals that Delila has cancelled multiple appointments or refused to be examined. By the latest accounts over the last four years, Delila has delivered at least three babies, one of whom she is parenting but doesn't always have custody of. The easiest and most reliable way to spot a scammer: her story is initially convincing but not verifiable or differs from what she told someone else (different facts conveyed to different adoption professionals on your team), and when pushed to provide specific details or documentation, she flakes out.

* * *

Take it slowly with prospective situations. As hard as it is not to fall in love with a birth family, a baby and the prospect of becoming a parent in the very near future, the reality of our lives as domestic adoptive parents is the initial uncertainty of it. As my beloved caseworker told me in the beginning, go forward in good faith, be open-minded, and *guard your heart.* It is very much like living through the uncertainty of the first trimester of pregnancy. For most pregnant people there are no issues or concerns, and they go on to have a healthy baby. For others, there are setbacks and scares and sometimes miscarriages. Compared to pregnancy, however, adoption is guaranteed! You will take home a baby, and if you're careful and lucky, it will be with little heartbreak and lots of joy!

∾ 6 ∾

WAITING FOR PLACEMENT

To Shower or Not to Shower

(A Baby Shower, That Is)

One of the best ways to manage your wait is to find fun things to do to prepare for when baby actually arrives. Unlike during a pregnancy, there are no rules or cultural guidelines for what you should or should not do right now. And you have a lot of fun decisions to make, like what kind of nursery you're going to decorate, whether you want to try to breast-feed and whether you're going to have a baby shower! Come on, you're expecting to adopt. How cool is that?!

To Shower or Not to Shower

I know many of you are absolutely terrified that something will go wrong and your baby won't come home, so you don't want to have a baby shower before placement. This is, of course, your choice, but let me tell you something as the adoptive mother of two children who either didn't come home as initially planned or went back to a birth mother after placement (and as I write this book, I'm in the process of adopting again)—you're going to be a parent at some point in the not-too-distant future, so if you want to have a real girly-girl baby shower or a Jack-n-Jill (where boys are invited) type of shower, *go for it!* Having a baby shower is part of the ritual process of becoming a parent, and there's absolutely no reason you should be denied this experience. Unless you've got religious reasons for waiting or are extremely superstitious, I enthusiastically recommend having a baby shower. Even my friends who waited long periods of time—much longer than the national average—relished having their baby showers and were so grateful when they finally did get their babies that they had all the goods from the shower and had less shopping to do. By all means throw a welcome-home party if you're more comfortable with something like that, but I am planning my first-ever baby shower, and I am *blissed out!* I know this baby may not come home, but I am going to have another (probably my last) child through adoption, and I refuse to be denied any longer. I regret not having that baby shower for David, and I am going to have one for his sibling.

There are many great adoption-themed shower games you can play to make the party more appropriate for your situation. Let's face it, measuring the size of your belly and having people guess how big it is is really not for us. (I sure as hell don't want someone measuring my waist right about now!) But playing a guess-what-state-the-baby-will-be-born-in game (unless you've disclosed this information already) might be fun. Adoption Web sites have great ideas on themes, games and general invitation language that may be more appropriate for our unique perspective on becoming parents. One recommendation I have is that if you do have a baby shower ahead of time, ask people to give you—in addition to baby goods—gift cards to Blockbuster, Netflix, takeout chains, Starbucks and things like that. These gift cards can reduce your costs when you travel to get baby and also provide an activity or outing (going to rent a movie instead of paying the hotel rental fees). You can always use the gift cards at home too! But don't let the uncertainty of our situation as domestic adoptive parents deter you from having a baby shower if you want one.

Deciding Whether to Decorate a Nursery and Other Steps in Preparation for the Baby's Arrival

Nursery planning is another thing people hold off dealing with ahead of time. I have to tell you: it is a *bad* idea to wait to do the nursery. First of all, it usually takes about twelve weeks for a crib and changing table to come in after being ordered. So if you wait until après bébé to be ordering that stuff, you've got to have some other sleeping and changing arrangements for your little one. Babies outgrow bassinets very quickly, so don't think you can get by with one for very long. Second, and way more important, you're not going to have the time to shop for this stuff after placement!

If you think that after your little Adam or Eve arrives that you're going to have time for a regular shower (forget the baby shower, let's talk soap, shampoo and nice warm water cascading down your back) let alone time to shop, paint or pick out wallpaper borders, you've got another think coming! I cannot tell you how many times newly adoptive parents have expressed their shock at how much time and attention such a small person can suck from their lives and how exhausted they are. Like you're really going to want to schlep to buybuyBABY to brave the crowds and lack of adequate service while you are holding a screaming, hungry newborn to try to shop for a crib, changing table, glider and all the accoutrements. Get a grip *now* and go shopping *now!*

Pick a theme and start decorating! You don't have to have it perfect or complete, but you really need to plan ahead on this one. Charlie and I went shopping and planned the nursery ahead of time. I was completely up front with the store we bought our nursery furniture from and told them we were adoptive parents. The store was totally experienced—way more than I was—and told us they would hold our stuff as a layaway if the furniture was delivered to the store before the baby. All I had to do was give them a week's notice to arrange delivery when I knew I needed the furniture. And let me tell you something, we didn't get a lot of notice when Diane picked us to parent David. I had less than three weeks before he was born to get everything organized. Since I was doing it all myself, that wasn't a lot of time.

Most of the adoptive moms I've worked with have expressed their gratitude that I encouraged them to complete the nursery. Even when David didn't come home right away, I sat in his nursery and was able to envision—for the first time in my life—actually being a mom. Knowing that there was a beautiful room all ready and waiting comforted me.

I sat in David's nursery night after night, pumping breast milk after Diane decided to parent him. That nursery gave me hope; it didn't add to my grief. Really, most adoptive moms will tell you that it doesn't make you sad to have that room ready even when you have a failed match or placement. It is reassuring. It is a reminder of the *inevitability* of your parenthood.

While I may've been sad at points, sitting there in the middle of the night pumping and looking at the moon and stars painted on his wall, the crib and changing table, his mobile—those are some of the most treasured moments of my life.

Which leads me to my next question: have you considered breast-feeding?

Deciding Whether to Breast-Feed: Yes, It Can Be Done

Are you over the shock yet?

I know, most of you didn't know that nonbiological moms *could* breast-feed and make real breast milk. And guess what? It isn't even that complicated or hard. It just takes dedication and commitment—the same kind of dedication and commitment that biological moms have to give to the experience, because breast-feeding can be hard for any woman, regardless of her status as a biological or adoptive mom.

Breast-feeding for the vast majority of biological moms *is* hard. It takes time to learn how to do it right, and it takes time to get over the discomfort. There is no doubt that pumping isn't a lot of fun, and this is a critical component of adoptive breast-feeding, but biological moms will tell you that the first few weeks of their breast-feeding experience wasn't fun either. It takes hard work to be a successful breast-feeder. When it is right for you—and the only way you'll know it's right for you is to try it—it is the most amazing thing in the world.

I found the process of inducing lactation to be the most normalizing experience. I feel so defective as a woman because my body cannot make or hold a baby within it. But I can breast-feed. This makes me feel more "normal" and more "whole." A part of me that was stolen by my infertility was restored when I started making milk for my child. The fact that it worked blew me away; the fact that I had 1,200 frozen and stored ounces of breast milk for David when he came home and that we actually managed to figure out the whole latching thing (he was six months old when he came home) was just awesome.

I didn't enjoy the pumping so much, but I've since learned my pump wasn't emptying my breasts effectively (some of my bio-mom friends have said the same thing; you have to try different pumps to find the one that works best for you) and I wound up with a nasty case of double mastitis (a rather painful infection of the breast tissue). Still, I pumped and pumped and pumped. And every four-ounce bag of breast milk that went into the deep freezer (that I bought solely to store my breast milk) was a trophy and a reminder that my body could do something right.

When David came home, I didn't care as much as I had in the beginning of the process about being able to be his sole supply of nutrition. First of all, this wasn't a realistic expectation, as he was 20 pounds and eating solids, but I had also realized by this time that I was breast-feeding for bonding. I think this is a really critical component to being successful with the process if you choose to induce lactation. Do not expect to be able to meet your baby's exclusive nutritional needs. Many biological moms have to supplement with formula or donated breast milk (what, you think they invented the Lact-Aid nursing supplement device for adoptive moms?), and many give up entirely, finding the experience too tiring and difficult. Building up an adequate milk supply is hard work.

If you decide to try breast-feeding, take the pressure off yourself, and assume that at some point you'll need to supplement with formula. And frankly, at 2 A.M., it isn't the worst thing in the world to hand your baby off to your partner with a nice warm bottle of formula or breast milk and get some sleep. And no, I don't buy into that whole nipple-confusion thing. I know my husband especially enjoyed being able to bond with David by giving him bottles.

So hopefully, I've piqued your curiosity, and you want to know how to do this breast-feeding thing. There are several different approaches and, while I discuss them all briefly here, I urge you to do your research and figure out what type of induction is right for your boobs. With David I followed the Newman-Goldfarb Protocol (see the Resources section for information on this protocol). I took birth control pills continuously for three months to mimic the changes in my breasts that would occur with a pregnancy and assist me in making milk. Toward the end of this time period I added a medication called domperidone (also known as Motilium), which is a medication used to reduce nausea and has the side effect of increasing your prolactin level. Prolactin is the hormone that causes you to produce breast milk (regardless of your gender). A few weeks before David's birth, I abruptly stopped the birth control pills, increased my dosage of domperidone, and started double pumping (both boobs at the same time) six to eight times a day. And yes, I woke up at least once each night to pump.

The first time I pumped, I actually produced dark yellow droplets, enough to fill a teaspoon. I even took pictures of the teaspoon filled with the milk and put it in my scrapbook. While initially I was told that adoptive moms cannot make colostrum (the premilk that biological moms make that contain antibodies and other pro-immunity components), the color of my early milk so resembled colostrum that I did some more research to find out what was causing the color to be so yellow. Surprise, surprise—adoptive moms' first breast milk is very similar to biological moms' colostrum! So if you produce it, save every bit of those first drops.

From then on it was just a ritual of double pumping (both sides simultaneously), drinking a ton of water, and trying to build up my milk supply. The double pumping tricks your body into thinking you're nursing twins, which further raises your prolactin level and helps bring in more milk. I took some herbs to help with my supply and drank plenty of water, and it really worked.

You do not have to take birth control pills to induce lactation. You can use estrogen patches or bring in milk by pumping alone without any medicinal/hormone support, or in combination with the domperidone. You can also try putting a baby to your breast and doing nothing else (you will *have* to supplement with formula or donated breast milk with this method). The birth control pills increase your likelihood of producing larger quantities of breast milk, but nothing can guarantee that you will be successful with them. Many adoptive moms are just as successful without using birth control pills.

You can tailor any of the following basic options to suit your lifestyle better, but seek advice from someone with experience before adapting the methods (see the Resource section):

- Put baby to breast and allow nature to bring in your milk supply.

- Use hormonal support prebaby (birth control pills or estrogen supplementation) and domperidone and/or herbs in combination with a ritual of double pumping prebaby to bring in your milk supply.

- Use domperidone and/or herbs (without hormonal support) and a ritual of double pumping prebaby to bring in your milk supply.

Adoptive breast-feeding is much more common than it used to be, and there are several Web sites (see the Resources section) on which you can get very experienced help to find the right way for *you* to induce lactation. The important thing to remember if you try to breast-feed your baby is that breast-feeding is hard for biological and adoptive moms alike, and no one is guaranteed to have a good supply of milk—regardless of whether they gestated a baby for nine months or followed the Newman-Goldfarb Protocol. (Check the Resources section for some of my favorite places to learn and get support for adoptive breast-feeding.)

Deciding Whether to Attend the Birth, Sit in the Waiting Room, or Stay Home and Wait for a Phone Call

Most of the time you don't get a choice with this. If you're using an agency, it may have policies about adoptive parents not attending the birth. In fact, some hospitals have policies like this. However, my friend Mary—who used an agency for her adoption—was her birth mother's labor coach and cut Carrie's cord. If this is something that is of interest to you, make sure your adoption professional knows it, and then try talking about it with your birth mother. Every hospital and agency/attorney has its own policies for adoptive parents attending births.

Putting aside your agency's or attorney's recommendation (and that is all it is, a recommendation), hospital policies are sometimes hard to contend with. An antiquated understanding of the relationship between adoptive and birth families often means that a hospital won't let adoptive parents attend the birth or even see the baby until the relinquishment papers are signed (this infuriates me). Other hospitals will let just about anyone attend a birth provided the person doesn't get in the doctor's way while he or she is delivering the baby. Some hospitals don't let you record the birth (legal liability, I presume), and others will let TV network cameras in. Go figure. If you have to, you can become the designated labor coach. The hospital has very few rights to refuse you entry as the birth mother's labor coach regardless of your role as an adoptive parent. And feel free to argue with the hospital administrators if they give you a hard time. Remember, you're going to have to start dealing with misconceptions and misunderstandings about adoption at some point. What better reason to become a warrior than to be present at your child's birth?

In addition to determining whether the birth mother's hospital will permit you to be there, you should take some time to consider whether it's a good idea for you to be there. Sometimes you're involved in a higher-risk situation, in which case not being present at the birth might save you some grief. And some people are just plain grateful to have a nice clean, dressed, sleeping baby handed to them. Not everyone handles the bloody part of a baby's delivery well. How many stories have you heard of a dad fainting during delivery? Are you going to faint? If so, don't go!

If you choose not to attend the delivery, however, I don't know that staying home and waiting for your attorney or agency to tell you to come and get your baby is such a good idea, either. While many agencies and attorneys will counsel you to "wait for the phone call" before getting on a plane to pick up your baby, the scramble to get packed and get yourself to your birth mother quickly is not fun. Just try getting a flight out of JFK in New York to LAX in Los Angeles during a holiday weekend. It isn't going to happen! Many an adoptive birth parent has sat in an airport waiting lounge on the verge of tears waiting for a seat (or two) to open up on the next flight to his or her baby's birth city. And I don't know that it's so safe to drive at ungodly speeds across countless states in the scrambled, disoriented state you may find yourself in (I was so strung out going to get David that I was physically ill; if we had been in a car, I would've been asking my husband to pull over every five minutes to accommodate my severe gastrointestinal distress).

You may very well minimize your risk of flying or driving home with an empty car seat by waiting at home for that phone call (and it probably is a lot less disheartening to be waiting for a seat on a plane than to fly home empty-handed), but is it worth missing out on a single minute of your baby's life and stressing yourself trying to get on a plane or in the car to drive hours in a blinding rain with half a mind? Be sure to read the next chapter for information on planning for your trip.

I still wonder if things would have gone differently if we were at the hospital when Diane delivered our adopted son, David. Having us there to support her may have meant he came home at birth instead of six months later. I will never know. It was certainly easier to be at home waiting for her to decide whether she was going to parent and to cope with my grief when she did take David home from the hospital. But next time, I'm going to be sitting in that waiting room, and if I can, I want to be there to cut the cord.

When in doubt, my recommendation is to travel (if you can afford it).

~ 7 ~

BRINGING BABY HOME

The Joyous Part of Your Life and the Sleep-Deprivation
(and No Showers) Finally Begin

You waited and waited, got a phone call, dropped everything, zoomed off perhaps thousands of miles across the continental United States, and now someone has handed you a baby. Oh my God! Are you completely overwhelmed and scared to death yet?

Don't worry, we all are! Even biological parents are more than a little freaked out that someone sends them home from the hospital with a newborn and thinks they know how to take care of him or her. You don't know how to take care of this baby even if you took infant CPR and baby-care classes, and that's okay. Babies are resilient little things, for the most part, and they're remarkably tolerant of all the mistakes you're about to make. The good news is they won't remember this part of your parenting and won't be able to hold it against you sixteen years from now. (Just wait a few years—they discover really early how to make you feel guilty!) I was so freaked out on the flight to get David that I spent most of it in the bathroom puking; not too far off from many other adoptive-parent last-minute-jitters stories I've heard.

Traveling to Get Baby: Buying Plane Tickets and Making Travel Arrangements Ahead of Time

There are some basic dos and don'ts for traveling. If you do decide to purchase plane tickets or make hotel arrangements in anticipation of a baby's arrival (after you've matched with a birth mother but prior to placement), please check with your air carrier and hotel about restrictions and penalties for last-minute cancellations or rescheduling. Most airlines—especially if you tell them you're adopting when you book the flight—will help you purchase a class of ticket that enables you to reschedule your flight for a nominal fee or even to use your ticket at a moment's notice for up to a year (provided there are seats available on the flight you want; you can often check seat availability online before going to the airport). Be very careful if you're using frequent-flier miles to pay for your ticket, as these often come with tremendous restrictions on them unless you're buying first class (which many adoptive parents recommend doing because of the larger seats and better service during a stressful time—flying with a baby for the first time can be a nerve-racking experience).

Try to book a bulkhead seat (more room for all your newly acquired baby paraphernalia), and put the baby's car seat (if you buy a plane ticket for the baby, which I recommend you do, since you're going to have a car seat with you anyway) near the window so you don't have to climb over it to go to the bathroom. If you don't purchase a seat for the baby, make sure you've got a front carrier (like a Babybjörn, Snugli or a sling; see the Resources section) for the baby to hold him or her safely against you during the flight. This also will help restrain the baby during turbulence. (Please note that most front carriers have weight requirements, and if your baby is too small to use a Babybjörn, you may need to use a sling instead.)

Keep in mind that most airlines have a policy that if there is an empty seat available and you're traveling with an infant, they have to relocate you and the passenger near that empty seat to provide you with a seat for your baby and an infant car seat. So never, ever forget to check with the gate attendant about locating an empty seat if you don't purchase one for your baby. (Again, I recommend taking the extra expense and buying the baby a seat.) You also are more likely to have access to an empty seat if you fly during off hours. But remember, if you've been waiting for interstate clearance (see the Glossary) and have been in a hotel for a few days and are sleep-deprived, traveling home at 11 P.M. may not be ideal!

When making your hotel accommodations, try to get a suite (so one of you can sleep while the other watches the baby) with a kitchenette and microwave (for cooking and/or sterilizing bottles). Most hotel chains have residential or longer-term hotels for business travelers that are perfect for adoptive parents. You get a mini-apartment with all the amenities of home!

Don't forget to make arrangements with someone at home to care for your pets, plants and home.

The Essential Domestic Expecting-to-Adopt Travel Checklist

☐ Cameras and video equipment.

☐ Airline tickets, passports for identification and all rental car information in one easy-to-access envelope. (You will be amazed at how disoriented and fussed you are when you're traveling to get your baby.)

☐ Car seat (can't leave the hospital or agency without one). You can check this at the airport gate on the way down if you are flying to pick up your baby or arrange to ship it ahead of time to the hotel or your adoption professional.

☐ Car seat stroller. A universal car seat stroller or other stroller that accommodates your car seat will be handy to have while you're away, waiting for interstate approval to travel. If you're brave enough to venture outside your hotel with the baby (and you've got a pediatrician's okay to do so), it will make life easier than carrying a car seat for the adventure (they get surprisingly heavy very quickly). It also will be much easier in the airport to have a stroller, because you will have way more carry-on luggage going home with the baby, and you can transport some of this through the airport in the storage rack at the bottom of the stroller. You can gate-check both the stroller and the car seat on the way to get your baby and the stroller on the way home; airline personnel will retrieve them for you prior to deplaneing. *Do not purchase bags to carry the car seat or stroller in, as this will ensure that the items go into the cargo hold instead of ready-access storage and will mean you have to pick them up at a special location in your airline terminal, even if they are marked for gate-checking purposes.* Alternatively, you can purchase your car seat stroller when you arrive at your destination. I don't normally recommend this, as you don't know how much time you'll have while you're there. If you're going to pick up a baby that already has interstate clearance to come home, you conceivably (pardon the pun) could be flying there and back within a twenty-four-hour period. I believe that having the car seat and stroller ahead of time will make things easier in the long run.

- [ ] An extra empty suitcase to bring home all the extra stuff you bought while you were waiting to come home. (You can pack this inside one of your larger suitcases for the trip to get your baby.)

- [ ] Parenting books. At least two of them: one that covers the basics of newborn care and another that covers behavior issues (like one of the books by William Sears, MD, or T. Berry Brazelton, MD, respectively; see the Resources section for suggested titles).

- [ ] Pediatrician's phone number at home and one in the area you will be staying in, in case of emergency.

- [ ] One case of premade, prebottled formula, the brand recommended by your pediatrician. (Enfamil and Similac both make small premade bottles that you just attach a nipple to. You can buy them online at their Web sites, at a baby store or even at the supermarket, although you may have to special-purchase the nipples to fit the bottles from the manufacturer.) Despite what others may tell you, you *cannot* count on your hospital or agency to provide you with enough formula to get you through the first forty-eight hours. I have heard too many complaints of having to run out and buy formula (we did) after picking up baby. Having a supply with you will save you an emergency trip to the store.

☐ One package of newborn-size diapers (again, you cannot count on the hospital or agency to provide you with these, and you want to save yourself as many trips to the store as possible).

☐ Two clothing outfits per day (babies soil clothes easily!) for the baby in a variety of sizes (you may have a super-teeny-weeny, normal or large baby, so make sure you've got at least one preemie outfit, just in case), *prewashed in Dreft or Ivory Snow detergent,* for approximately five days (ten outfits). You don't want to have to be washing clothes at the laundromat unless absolutely necessary.

☐ One roll of quarters in case you have to do laundry while you're waiting for interstate clearance to travel.

☐ At least two comfortable outfits (as in sweatpants) for parent(s) per day for approximately five days.

☐ Five (or more) prewashed infant washcloths (you likely will be told not to use store-bought moist wipes for the first few weeks and will instead rely on wet, warm washcloths to clean dirty tushies).

☐ Front-holding baby carrier or sling. (Please note that there are size and weight requirements on these, and not all newborns are big enough to fit in them. It is still handy to have one, especially if your baby is big enough.)

☐ Diaper bag.

☐ Presterilized pacifiers in a Ziploc bag (at least six, they get lost easily!).

☐ List of local restaurants with takeout service (ask the concierge in the hotel or go online before you travel). You don't want to rely on expensive room service every day of your stay, and in all likelihood the hotel staff isn't going to know about all the inexpensive takeout joints around it (they will, of course, know about all the pricey places).

☐ A list of local baby stores and a map to help you find them. (The hotel will not be able to help you on this, *trust me*, and you will be shopping for things like microwave sterilizers while you're down there.)

☐ Any breast-feeding equipment and books on breast-feeding, if you're attempting to breast-feed.

☐ The names and numbers of any friends or family members in the area in case you need a helping hand, or the number of the local doula service. (See the Resources section for more information on doulas. You may want to call ahead on this to prearrange some assistance for the first few days you are staying in the hotel or as an emergency backup.)

☐ A laptop computer to e-mail pictures and check flight times. (If you don't have one, borrow one.)

☐ A bottle of very expensive champagne (if you drink).

Now, first things first. Go get that video camera out and film *every minute* of the trip to pick up your baby and take him or her back to your hotel (or to your home, if you're lucky enough to have the baby born near where you live). Then take a deep breath and plunge into your new life!

Living in a Hotel with a Newborn:
Let's Give the Term "Honeymoon" New Meaning

Hopefully you arrived ahead of the baby's delivery and had time to check in at your hotel before collecting your bundle of joy, or perhaps you went straight to the hospital or adoption agency and collected your bouncing baby. Either way, you're heading back "home" a little freaked out, with a new member of your family to care for. Relax, you can so totally do this! You have been through so much already—you're stronger and more equipped than you think (remember boot camp?)!

Let's get the new parenting priorities in order: First, you need to eat! You cannot care for baby properly when you're hungry. (You can, as you will soon discover, properly care for baby on less than two hours' sleep. Combine sleep and food deprivation, however, and you're doomed to failure.) So, pick up that phone and order some room service, or one of you go get something from a local takeout joint. Recommendation: Go easy on the rich and greasy food, as your stomach is likely to be a wee bit upset. You don't want to be dealing with gastrointestinal problems tonight!

The next step in parenting priorities: You need to celebrate! Get that bottle of champagne and sit and stare at that tiny little baby, and toast to the good things in life—*your child!* Recommendation: Go easy on the champagne, as it's going to be a long night. You'll also have all night to drink it. (What, you thought you'd actually sleep tonight? *Puh-lease!*) No need to tie one on here; you're heading into the walking-zombie-zone now (known only to parents of young children), so pace yourself and use the champagne to properly celebrate this historic event—*you're finally a parent!*—and if need be to take the edge off the stress a little bit. (If you're breast-feeding, now would be a good time to learn about "pumping and dumping" . . . disposing of any breast milk containing alcohol and using formula either in a bottle or in a nursing supplement device.)

Priority number three: After you've eaten, had a glass of champagne, and sent e-mails to everyone (attaching the pictures you've

Plan Ahead for Your Hotel Stay

My good friends Jake and Lisa had a fairly easy adoption experience, as far as domestic adoption goes. They had a good perspective and sense of humor, so the waiting process wasn't difficult for them. When Jake and Lisa matched with their birth mother and arranged for their trip to Florida to pick their baby up after birth, Jake and Lisa decided to make a vacation out of it. They booked themselves into the honeymoon suite at the local Ritz Carlton Hotel. (Nice way to do it if you can afford it, yes?)

What they didn't realize was that the Ritz Carlton Hotel chain doesn't ordinarily provide fridges (larger than the mini-bar variety), microwaves or other things that adoptive parents need when staying in a hotel with a newborn, waiting days and sometimes weeks for approval to travel across state lines! Being the relaxed, easygoing couple that they are, however, the lack of in-room amenities was hardly a difficult aspect to overcome. In fact, their favorite story of living in a hotel with their new baby is about Jake going down to the kitchen in this five-star hotel at one o'clock in the morning to sterilize baby bottles with the chef!

been taking all day) letting them know all is well, turn off the phone and start your family honeymoon.

One of the nicer things about being adoptive parents who go out of state to adopt their baby (and the vast majority of us do) is that we get this nice little honeymoon phase in a hotel where we cannot be bothered by well-meaning but horribly annoying friends and family members. The front desk can take messages, and you can just sit and stare at your baby all day without the doorbell ringing and your mother-in-law pestering you to let her change the baby (for the tenth time this hour) or telling you that you aren't burping the baby properly. The bad news is that you're stuck in a hotel without friends and family for support.

I personally think the honeymoon aspect of domestic interstate adoption is undervalued, and that if you plan carefully and can take advantage of it, it's a time to look back on as pure bliss with your new baby. Because face it, in about three weeks, you're going to be just like everyone else at home with a new baby who is dealing with friends and family wanting to come over and walking into furniture at 2 A.M., looking for a binky to stop the plaintive squawking from the bassinet. When else in your parenting experience are you going to have daily maid service, room service, and no relatives calling?

So important are these few days of privacy that I recommend that even if you aren't doing interstate adoption, think about checking into a hotel for a few days with the baby—or creating a similar experience at home—to have a private honeymoon with your brand-new family.

To make living in a hotel really work to your advantage and not be too stressful, here are some tips from friends and colleagues:

The Essential Domestic Adoption Living-in-a-Hotel Checklist

☐ If you can afford to do room service and stay in a hotel with daily maid service, *do it!*

☐ Try to get a mini-suite with a living room so you have plenty of room to spread out; at the very least, get a king-size bed and a handicapped-accessible bathroom (they're bigger so you'll have more room for all your stuff and all the baby stuff).

☐ Make sure you've got a room with a kitchenette or at least a microwave and mini-fridge so you can sterilize bottles using a microwave sterilizer that you can buy in a baby store. Otherwise, make sure to use preprepared, disposable bottles from your formula company.

☐ Try to stay in a hotel with a complimentary breakfast and/or happy hour with some kind of free food every morning and afternoon (one of you can get out of the room for a break and bring back food for the other).

☐ Ask for a room away from the elevator but close to the laundry room (if your hotel has self-service laundry), or ask for a *quiet* room.

☐ Make sure your hotel has high-speed Internet access so you can send pictures to friends.

☐ Make sure your hotel offers movies on demand or rents VCRs or has DVD players (or use your laptop to play DVDs). Make a list of movies you want to rent/watch, and take some time to lie in that big king-size bed, staring dreamily at your baby and catching up on some good movies.

☐ Take turns with the baby at night. One of you take the early shift while the other sleeps, and one of you take the late shift while the other sleeps. Otherwise, both of you sleep when the baby sleeps. (Single parents should *not* travel alone to pick their baby up. Take someone with you!)

☐ Have an emergency plan, a list of places you can go to escape and get fresh air. (You probably need to pick something up for the baby, like diapers or pacifiers, right?)

☐ Stay on top of your adoption professional to make sure you know when paperwork is being filed and have an idea when you're going to fly home. As badly as you want to go home, *do not rush* to the airport with a newborn the minute you find out you've got interstate clearance to travel home. Airports and airplanes are dirty, crowded, loud places. *Check with your air carrier first* to make sure there are seats available, and if need be, stay another night in the hotel so you can travel home relaxed and not rushed. (It's worth the extra credit card payment not to be stressed out when traveling home.)

☐ Try to fly home direct, without a layover. Most babies are not terribly appreciative of air-pressure changes during takeoff and landing and will complain vociferously about them. (*Make sure to feed the baby during takeoff and landing, as sucking and swallowing will help clear the baby's ears.*)

Postbirth Checkup

One of the outings you might take with that beautiful new baby is to the pediatrician. Check with your pediatrician at home before you leave to get your new little person, but know that most newborns need to see a pediatrician within forty-eight hours of birth. If you know you're going to be waiting more than forty-eight hours to fly home (let's say the baby was born on Friday morning; interstate paperwork won't even get filed in the applicable state capital until the following Monday morning), you're going to need to go to a local pediatrician for the first checkup. It is preferable to get the name of someone in the area from your pediatrician at home, but if need be, you can follow up with the pediatrician who saw your baby in the hospital (in his or her office, not the germy hospital, if possible), or get the name of someone from your adoption professional. You are definitely going to have questions, and your pediatrician at home is not going to be able to answer them over the phone, as he or she is going to need to see your baby to tell you, "Yes, it's perfectly normal for the baby to be screaming all the time," or "No, it's *not* perfectly normal that she's so yellow, she looks like she has self-tanner on. We call this jaundice, and she needs to go to the hospital." Catch my drift here, newbie parent? You need a *local* pediatrician to call with questions, and you will in all likelihood have to venture out for a routine examination regardless of your parenting competence.

Other than a trip to the pediatrician, take walks with your little one to break up the monotony. Bundle baby up according to the weather (remember, newborns cannot regulate their own body temperature, so they need more clothing or less clothing, depending on weather conditions; there is a list of recommended parenting and advice books in the Resources section), and put her in that front carrier or the car seat, attach it to the stroller, and take a walk outside if it's a nice day, or go to the mall if the weather is bad. But please remember to follow your pediatrician's advice regarding contact with people during the first few days of life. Some pediatricians are very mellow about this, while others are not. The bottom line, however, is that if you're flying home, your little one will be exposed to a good number of germs whether any of you like it or not, and a trip outside to save your sanity before that long, germy flight home is not going to hurt anyone. Staying inside and going stir-crazy, on the other hand, is going to hurt all of you. You need to use this time to save your strength, because before you know it, you're going to be walking through the front door of your home, and then the onslaught will begin!

Coming Home: Managing Friends and Family, Sleepless Nights, Piles of Laundry and the Postadoption Blues

One of the few things I remember about our experience traveling to get David was walking through our front door carrying him in my arms, and of Charlie looking over his shoulder at us with an expression of such pure and utter bliss that it took my breath away and made me start crying with joy. And I didn't stop crying for quite some time. At first I thought I was just so emotional and tired from new motherhood that I was prone to tears (and besides, I already cry at every Disney movie ever made). But after a few days I realized I was crying for a whole host of reasons I could only begin to understand. I didn't have time to deal with it, however, because everyone in the world wanted to come over and meet the little guy.

Parenting priority number four: set limits. One hour, two hours, one day a week, whatever it is that works for you—set clear and specific limits on how often and for how long people can visit. And by all means, assign your visitors tasks. They want to hold the baby, you need them to bring you a meal! They want to change the baby, you need them to help you fold laundry while he or she sleeps. Do not hesitate to put people to work! They will ask you before they come over, "Is there anything I can bring you or do for you?" Say *yes!* Don't be a fool here; take whatever help is offered, and then ask for *more*. It someone asks if he can run to the grocery store, say yes, and tell him what you need (and pay for it, of course). If someone asks if she can stop at the deli for you, have her get you a tuna sandwich, potato chips and a soda (and pay for it, of course). All this good-natured, willing-to-help assistance is very short-lived. Please take advantage of it while it lasts. This too is a honeymoon—a honeymoon during which people help you!

Let them help you now, because before you know it, you're going to be alone with this kid and five baskets of dirty laundry, no diapers, a dishwasher overflowing with dirty dishes, no clean dishes, no sleep under your belt, and hair so greasy you'll look like a contestant on *Survivor* (actually, you are a contestant on the parent edition of *Survivor*). Grab that gift card you got to Starbucks at your baby shower and head out for some caffeine reinforcement and fresh air. Then tackle one item of housework, and only one item.

Once everyone has left you alone with the baby and the honeymoon is over, don't try to do everything all at once by yourself (or even with help). Everything is going to be overwhelming at first. Every new adoptive parent I've spoken with has expressed complete and utter shock at how much time a little tiny baby can take from the day and how much laundry accumulates in the blink of an eye. We all struggle with learning to balance the household chores and the baby-care responsibilities. (Why do you think your social worker asked you about it during your home study?) Learn to live out of the dishwasher and to wash essential items only (clean bed sheets, unless the dirty ones have been peed on by an angry pet, are not essential anymore), like baby clothes and your pajamas. And when in doubt about food, order takeout!

The sleep-deprivation really catches up with you about three weeks after you've brought baby home. That is also about the time that the dishwasher isn't the only thing overflowing; you're crying a lot and coping with what has now been recognized as postadoption depression. I am not talking about the shock of how hard parenting is or how many dirty dishes you have. I am talking about serious hormonal changes, which have absolutely nothing to do with gestating a child, that come with your new role as a parent. It is a rough change; life is upside down and inside out, you're sleep-deprived and completely stressed out and overwhelmed, and I truly think that can cause chemical changes in the brain. I could talk at length about the role of neurotransmitters and cortisol and their effect on mood, but you don't really care. All you need to know is that this is normal for adoptive parents.

It is real—not some figment of your imagination—and if you need to get some help from a physician, get a prescription for an antidepressant. I have spoken to far too many newly adoptive parents (domestic and international) who describe exactly what mothers with postpartum depression describe, and I've read too many articles by professionals and parents to dismiss this. I went through it myself! If you think you're struggling more than you should be, if you're having trouble getting out of bed in the morning, if you don't feel like yourself, if you're crying all the time, get some professional help. It is my experienced, compassionate and (donning my faux doctor's jacket) "professional" opinion that postadoption and postpartum depression should really be called new-parent depression.

Another common reaction that is less severe but often goes hand-in-hand with new-parent depression is the discovery that you feel nothing for your new baby. You look at this beautiful thing, and you feel blank. Not everyone falls in love with their child at first sight— not even biological parents. You are not a bad person if you feel this way. Let me share the experience of my good friend Caroline.[1]

Caroline is a good friend and member of one of my adoptive-parent support groups. She is a single Hispanic mom who adopted an

---

1. At Caroline's request certain details surrounding her adoption and experience with bonding and postadoption depression have been modified to protect her privacy. The essential theme and feelings conveyed through Caroline's story are an accurate depiction of her experience.

African American newborn boy. She knew she was biting off a lot when she chose to adopt outside her own ethnicity, but she felt very connected to her child's birth mother. Caroline lined up a ton of support for when she and Nathan came home; she had meals in the freezer for months, a cleaning service paid for by her parents, and friends offering to babysit one night a week so she could catch six hours of uninterrupted sleep. Caroline had planned well and done everything she could've done to ease her transition into single parenthood. The problem was that she and Nathan didn't exactly bond from day one.

Nathan was a colicky baby who seemed only to be soothed by strangers. Caroline felt he was rejecting her every time he stopped crying when someone else held him. He also had his days and nights reversed (not uncommon for newborns), so Caroline's schedule was completely upside down. But what she worried about more—and what was exacerbated by Nathan's schedule and his colic—was that she didn't feel anything for Nathan when she looked at him. She later confided in me that there were times when she wanted to give him back to the adoption agency, fearing she had made some horrible mistake.

That is, until the day Caroline took Nathan to one of his regular pediatrician appointments. The pediatrician reassured Caroline that all was well with Nathan. He was a beautiful, thriving, healthy baby (albeit with a nasty case of colic), but that things would get easier. Caroline just needed to be patient with him and with herself. She was too embarrassed to tell her pediatrician that she hated being a mother and wasn't exactly interested in Nathan. She was too ashamed.

This pediatrician visit happened to be one of those during which the little one gets stuck with needles. Nathan had been calm and reasonably content thus far at the pediatrician's office. However, the minute one of those needles went into his chubby thigh, Caroline said she heard a primal scream the likes of which she had never heard from his (or anyone else's) lungs. Startled at first by the noise he made, Caroline only got more upset when the next needle went into his other thigh, and Nathan wailed louder and harder.

Suddenly, every ounce of "mother-ness" that Caroline had been denying existed inside her reverberated from Nathan's protestation at being immunized. Caroline turned on her pediatrician like a mother bear protecting her cub and demanded that the pediatrician put down the next needle, or *else!* She scooped up her baby and put him to her chest and soothed and shushed as only an experienced, bonded, and confident parent would. And she cried as loud as Nathan did at the unjust pain inflicted on his little tiny legs and that it had taken so long for her to feel him in her heart.

What surprised Caroline even more, however, was that despite the fact that she finally fell in love with her baby, she continued to struggle. She dragged for months, no matter how much caffeine she drank. Eventually she emerged from what she calls the dark days of new motherhood and became an extremely confident and content parent. But Caroline—like other adoptive moms, including me— felt she made her transition to parenthood much harder by not recognizing the signs of depression and not asking for help. Caroline wishes she had sought medical help for herself rather than "gutting it out." But even now she feels ashamed that she had such a hard time and has great difficulty discussing what it was like for her.

The postadoption blues are not unusual or abnormal, and I don't want you to judge yourself for not loving your baby instantly or for hating being a parent. If you need help, please get it! And even if you don't have full-blown depression, cut yourself some slack. It is so totally *okay* to say that parenthood is not what you expected! The bottom line is that eventually, we all have a magic moment in which we realize that we would do *anything* for our child, and that this experience is the best in the world!

PART THREE

GOING INTERNATIONAL

Around the World in 180 Days

~ 8 ~

MANAGING AN INTERNATIONAL ADOPTION

Agencies, Attorneys and Immigration Issues
Demystified for the Soon-to-Be Jet-lagged

I love international adoption. I think that having set timetables and adopting a child who is an orphan is wonderful. The racial and ethnic diversities are truly magnificent. If we have another child, you can bet I will be lobbying to do an international adoption. While it is a more straightforward and easier-to-navigate process, international adoption is more expensive and presents its own set of issues for you to contend with (like making sure your dossier is absolutely perfect).

One of the first steps in pursuing an international adoption is deciding the country from which you want to adopt. Making this decision first will help you choose your adoption professional and determine your costs and your time frame for becoming a parent. Some people know right off the bat when they decide to pursue an international adoption that they want to adopt a baby girl from China or a toddler from Russia. But not everyone knows this instinctively, and you may need to spend some time thinking about what type of family you envision for yourself. Then, consider whether there are any restrictions imposed by countries based on your age, marital status or sexual orientation.

If you haven't already picked a country from which you will adopt, take another run through the questions in chapter 1. Then consider your family (will your relatives open their arms to a baby from Ethiopia?), your age (some countries place limitations on adoptions for older and even younger parents), marital status and sexual orientation (some countries permit gay families to adopt, others don't; some countries permit singles to adopt, others impose quotas or only permit it if you adopt an older child). Also consider whether you're willing and able to travel to get your baby; some countries require multiple trips or long (like four to six weeks) stays in the country. Other countries will provide an escort, someone who brings the baby to you in the United States. How do these requirements or restrictions impact your decision?

Then close your eyes and fantasize. Do you see a baby in your mind's eye? What does he or she look like? Do you have an affinity for or a familiarity with a particular culture? I know one couple that adopted from China because the wife's roommate and best friend in college was Chinese, and she had spent many vacations and holidays with her college buddy. She felt comfortable adopting from China because she felt she knew and understood the culture better than she did Russian or Greek culture.

Choosing a Country

Let's take a look at some of the requirements and restrictions of some of the most common countries from which people adopt. Please note that I am breaking down these criteria only for the more popular countries; this list is by no means exhaustive, and if you're interested in adopting from a different country, check the Resources section for links to the U.S. State Department's Web site (which provides an outline of adoption requirements for all countries from which Americans may adopt) and for a list of Web sites keeping up-to-date lists of countries that are actively accepting applications from American families.

China

Parent's Age(s)	Parents must be between the ages of 30 and 55. Parents over age 45 may only adopt toddlers, and those over age 50 may only adopt school-age children.
Parent's Marital/ Familial Status	Singles and married partners; there are quotas on the number of adoptions allowed by single parents. No adoptions are permitted by gay parents.
Timeline from Completion of Paperwork	From completion of dossier to referral, 6 to 8 months. Shorter waiting times for special-needs adoptions and adoptive parents of Chinese descent.
Estimated Fees and Expenses[1]	$15,000–$30,000, with 50% of adoptive parents spending $20,000–$25,000.
Travel Information	One parent must travel to China for an average period of 10 to 14 days.
Information about Available Children	50% are under 1 year of age; and 50% 1–4 years of age. 95% of the children adopted from China are female due to population control policies. Special-needs children are available for adoption.

1. Unless otherwise stated, all fee and expense information is from *Adoptive Families Magazine,* "Affording Adoption," February 2006, vol. 39, no. 1, p. 33.

Guatemala

Parent's Age(s)	No restrictions.
Parent's Marital/ Familial Status	Singles and couples may adopt.
Timeline from Completion of Paperwork	From completion of dossier to final adoption, 6–9 months.
Estimated Fees and Expenses	$25,000–$35,000. 67% of adoptive parents spent $25,000–$30,000, according to statistics from 2005.
Travel Information	Escorts are available to bring the baby to you in the United States; otherwise, one brief 2- to 3-day trip required.
Information about Available Children	Both genders adopted in approximately equal numbers. 76% under 1 year old.

Kazakhstan

Parent's Age(s)	No age restrictions imposed on married applicants. Singles must be at least 16 years older than the child being adopted.
Parent's Marital/ Familial Status	No marital status requirements. According to the U.S. State Department prior to 2005, single applicants had found it difficult to adopt, but that situation is apparently improving. Check with your agency or attorney about any restrictions if you're single and seeking to adopt from this country.

Timeline from Completion of Paperwork	You will receive an invitation to travel and stay in-country to finalize the adoption 2–4 months after completing your dossier.
Estimated Fees and Expenses	$25,000–$35,000. 61% of adoptive parents spent over $30,000, according to statistics from 2005. The U.S. State Department reports average adoption costs at $18,000–$25,000 per child.
Travel Information	4–8 weeks in-country; may be broken into two trips. Kazakhstan requires one 14-day period in-country for bonding that cannot be waived, and another 15-day waiting period to finalize the adoption (can be waived, but usually is not).
Information about Available Children	Both genders adopted in approximately equal numbers. Majority of children placed for adoption are over 1 year old. (Average age range 6 months–3 years), although it is possible to adopt a baby under 1 year.

Russia

Parent's Age(s)	Married couples have no age restrictions. Singles must be at least 16 years older than the child they are adopting.
Parent's Marital/ Familial Status	Singles and married couples are permitted to adopt.
Timeline from Completion of Paperwork	The average wait time from USCIS approval of the I-600A Petition to final approval to travel is 5 months.

Russia, continued

Estimated Fees and Expenses	$25,000–$35,000. Over 66% of adoptive parents spent more than $30,000, according to statistics from 2005. The U.S. State Department reports the average cost to be $20,000.
Travel Information	Usually two trips are required. The first trip may be by one parent to accept the referral; the second trip to complete the adoption must be made by both parents if a married couple is adopting.
Information about Available Children	Both genders adopted in approximately equal numbers. 50% are 1–4 years of age. Sibling groups and special-needs children are available for adoption.

South Korea

Parent's Age(s)	Adoptive parents must be between the ages of 25 and 44 (subject to certain exceptions; check with your agency).
Parent's Marital/ Familial Status	No singles. Must be eligible to adopt under the laws of your U.S. state of residency and/or laws of the United States.[2] Must be married for a minimum of 3 years.

---

2. According to the U.S. State Department, South Korean administrative guidelines provide that in order to adopt from South Korea, a couple must be eligible to adopt pursuant to the laws of their state of legal residence. Accordingly, a married gay couple residing in a state that recognizes gay marriage (Massachusetts) *may* be eligible to adopt from South Korea (please check with your adoption agency for specifics). However, a gay couple residing in Florida would not, under these guidelines, be eligible to adopt, because the state of Florida does not permit gay individuals to adopt children.

Timeline from Completion of Paperwork	From application to placement of the child in adoptive home, 10–16 months.
Estimated Fees and Expenses	$15,000–$25,000. 56% of adoptive parents spent $20,000–$25,000, according to statistics from 2005.
Travel Information	Escorts are available, or one or both parents may travel to South Korea.
Information about Available Children	Predominantly male, 94% under 1 year. Special-needs and older children are available for adoption (age restrictions are usually waived for special-needs adoptions).

Choosing Your Adoption Professional

You may not have a choice on this one. The country you have decided to adopt from may require that you use an agency to process your application, although many countries will permit you to work with a local attorney or facilitator. Whatever route you choose, agency or attorney, *please* make sure your agency and/or attorney is accredited and well experienced at completing adoptions in your chosen country. You do not want to be the first family placing a baby in a particular country through your agency. The amount of red tape you'll experience because it's your agency's first time will be overwhelming to both you and it. An agency and/or attorney with a well-established and respected reputation in the country from which you are adopting will mean that the process will go much more smoothly, and if there are problems, there are names and faces at your agency recognized in the foreign country to work out the issues on your behalf.

Choose Your Adoption Professional Carefully to Ensure a Smooth Process

James and Brianna were experienced adoptive parents who were going back for baby number two. They had chosen a country to adopt from and were in process with their agency (accredited and experienced in that country) when their program abruptly closed. Hey it *sucks,* but it happens! When it became apparent that they would no longer be able to adopt from this country, they chose to continue working with their agency but in a country in which the agency had yet to complete an adoption.

While ultimately James and Brianna (and big sister Lucy) brought home a beautiful baby girl, the process took about three times as long as it normally does for other adoption agencies operating in that country. The delays were due solely to the fact that their adoption agency did not have contacts, attorneys, connections, resources or accreditation in or from the country they were working with. James and Brianna were the agency's guinea pigs. In order to facilitate the process of bringing home baby Ava, Brianna moved to Ava's country of birth to change their visa status and to be there to answer questions, shepherd paperwork, and appear before judges and members of the consulate. They don't regret a moment of their adoption experience, but not everyone is as strong-willed and determined as Brianna.

Choose your adoption professional carefully, or be prepared to go the extra mile to make your adoption happen!

Hiring an Agency

The most important thing you need to check when hiring an agency—and the vast majority of international adoptions are handled by private, U.S.-based agencies—is that it's accredited with the countries you're interested in adopting from and has a lot of experience working with these countries. After that, it comes down to facts and figures and references from other adoptive parents. Go online and to adoptive-parent support groups to seek out recommendations for agencies that people have had positive experiences with when adopting from the country(ies) you're considering. Check with your Better Business Bureau, the U.S. State Department's Web site, and, if you can, the U.S. embassy in the capital city of the country you're looking into to see what the agency's reputation is like. Some questions you might want to ask the agency include:

- What is the total cost, including travel, of adopting through the program(s) I am interested in?

- Do you provide a breakdown of fees and expenses, and when they are due and to whom?

- What costs aren't covered by the agency fee?

- Do you provide a contract that establishes our respective rights and obligations?

- Do you have a professional service that you recommend for preparing my dossier?

- If I am not approved, will I be able to find out why?

- How many children have you placed from the program(s) I am interested in?

- How long have you been working in the country(ies) I am interested in?

- How often do representatives from the agency travel to the country(ies) I am interested in to check on the orphanages and/or foster-care families?

- What other assistance—besides placing children in adoptive homes—do you provide to the country(ies) I am interested in?

- What materials do you provide to demonstrate that the child I am adopting is a documented orphan?

- What happens to my application if my program closes? Can I get a refund of my fees, or will you apply them to another program?

- Do you help make travel arrangements? Do adoptive parents travel alone or as a group? Does a representative from the agency travel with me or the group? Do you provide any guidance for preparation to travel?

- Do you have translators available when I am in my child's country of birth?

- Do you have medical professionals in the country(ies) I am considering for taking care of medical emergencies when I am traveling?

- Do you offer escorts (if they are available from the program you're interested in)?

- What is the process like for meeting my baby in his or her country of birth?

Hiring a well-known, well-established agency to assist you with your international adoption is a smart choice. It is not hard to do the research to find adoptive parents who sing the praises of a particular agency or others who uniformly complain about an agency.

Hiring an Attorney

Most countries do not permit independent adoptions (those that take place using an attorney in the United States and/or an attorney or facilitator abroad). Therefore, the likelihood that you will be hiring an attorney to assist you in connection with an international adoption is small. That said, there are countries (like Guatemala) that permit attorneys in the United States to help you—instead of using a U.S.-based agency. The questions you'll want to ask the attorney are much the same as those listed above for hiring an agency and those outlined in chapter 4 for hiring an attorney. If you're hiring an attorney, please review that section. Here are some additional questions you might want to ask regarding international adoptions:

- Do you help make travel arrangements? Do adoptive parents travel alone or as a group? Does a representative from your office travel with me or the group, or is there a representative from your office available when we are in country?

- Do you provide any guidance for preparation to travel?

- Do you have translators available when I am in my child's country of birth?

- Do you have medical professionals in the country(ies) I am considering for taking care of medical emergencies when I am traveling?

- Do you offer escorts (if they are available for the program you're interested in)?

- What is the process like for meeting my baby in his or her country of birth?

What I do want you to be aware of and conscientious about is the rather substantial risks presented by using an attorney and doing an independent international adoption. You do not want to overlook the possibility that the attorney you're hiring is (inadvertently or not) presenting you with a black-market adoption situation, inadequate medical information, and/or a lack of proper documentation regarding the baby's status as an orphan (necessary for all international adoptions). While I fortunately have never met anyone who went through something like this, I have read far too many articles written by adoption agencies about couples coming to them after experiencing tremendous difficulties working toward an international adoption with an attorney.

You will also likely have many more responsibilities than you will if you go through an agency. Although some of the more reputable attorneys will be able to help you with a lot of this stuff, you need to be aware that working with an attorney may very well put more of the work in your lap. While you'll be required to obtain a home study like every other adoptive parent, you may have to locate the professional to conduct your home study yourself (perhaps an adoptive-parent friend can recommend someone). You'll need to check with your social worker whether he or she can provide the home study report directly to you (in addition to your state of residence) or whether it must be forwarded to the country from which you're adopting. (Some states do not permit social workers to share the home study report with the adoptive parents before it has been filed with the appropriate authorities.) If the home study must be filed with the authorities, you need to make sure you know exactly who it needs to be sent to and in what form. Indeed, it will be incumbent upon *you* to ensure that you know and understand the adoption procedures in your chosen country and how to coordinate your adoption with the requisite foreign agencies and Uncle Sam. You also will have less guidance filling out your dossier and USCIS paperwork. You will need to know exactly what documents your country requires, in what form (original, certified, notarized, apostilled, or photocopies of same) and how many.

Many people have had successful adoptions using domestic and/or foreign attorneys and facilitators. Independent international adoption is definitely more complicated and more risky. If you're considering working with an attorney toward an international adoption, please work only with someone who has been referred to you by more than one other adoptive parent and who is a member of the American Academy of Adoption Attorneys. Then be the savvy consumer I know you are and make sure every *t* is crossed and every *i* is dotted on all your paperwork and filed by your attorney. Be careful, choosy and (as always) proactive, and this can work!

Completing Your Dossier and USCIS Forms (Without Losing Your Mind and Eyesight)

The paperwork you need to complete for an international adoption can be staggering. I thought I had a lot of paperwork to complete for a domestic adoption until I saw the stack on my girlfriend's desk one day as she was pursuing an adoption from Guatemala. Fortunately, you can get help preparing the paperwork, and since many adoptive parents are working full time or otherwise aren't terribly organized, it may be worth a few extra dollars (see below) to hire someone to assist you in preparing your dossier. (The Resources section has a list of companies that help prepare dossiers for international adoptions.) Regardless of whether you do it yourself or have someone help you, you need to understand what goes into your application and in what form. Some documents must be original and certified for one form, but then original, certified, notarized and apostilled (I'll explain in a moment; all terms are also listed in the Glossary) for some other part of the adoption process.

Getting Started with the Paperwork

The first pieces of paperwork to cross your desk will come from your agency or attorney and will have to do with basic information about you in preparation for your home study or just to get approved by the agency (or both). After that you may need to compile a bunch of documents for your home study (see chapter 3 for detailed information about home studies).

Hold onto everything you get copies of and file them somewhere that is easy to access and by an easy-to-reference name. It is more than likely that another copy of this document will be needed again

in your adoption process, and the last thing you want to be doing at
3 A.M. is scratching your head, swearing and digging through a stack
of papers looking for that copy of your partner's original certified
birth certificate. I also recommend keeping copies of correspon-
dence related to that document or any notes you took in connection
with obtaining it for later reference. For example, if you're married,
you will undoubtedly need at least one original certified copy of your
marriage license (order a few if you can when you order them; it may
save you time down the road if someone loses one or you need to
order another original for another part of the process). File it under
"marriage license," and keep all documents relating to your marriage
license in this folder. Simple, yes? Seriously, file it separately and
keep a box or filing cabinet dedicated solely to your adoption appli-
cation/dossier. You'll be coming back again and again to this box.

I-600A and USCIS Documentation

Next on your paperwork list will be completing your I-600A, "Application for Advancing Processing of Orphan Petition." This is your
first contact with USCIS (formerly the Immigration and Naturalization Service). Your adoption professional will tell you when and how
to file your I-600A. (Depending on where you're adopting from, it
may go to USCIS or to the U.S. consulate in your child's country of
birth.) Here are some tips on completing the I-600A:

- The person with the greater income should be the primary
  petitioner (regardless of gender).

- On all future documents filed with USCIS, make sure you list
  the same primary petitioner.

- The form is filed either by you or your agency along with your
  approved home study and two sets of your fingerprints (on
  USCIS Form FD-258).[1]

---

1. As of the date of this writing, the USCIS was using form FD-258. Please check with your agency or
other professional regarding the current forms required in connection with filing your I-600A Petition.

- The form requires proof that at least one (or both) applicants is a U.S. citizen (use a valid U.S. passport, birth certificate or certificate of naturalization).

- The form requires proof of age.

- The form requires proof of marriage (if applicable); photocopies may be accepted of your marriage certificate, but when possible, send an original just to be safe.

- The form requires documentation of termination through divorce or death of any prior marriage(s); photocopies may be accepted of a death or divorce certificate, but when possible, send an original just to be safe.

- *Originals will never be returned.* You don't have to provide originals of your birth certificate, etc. Whenever possible, submit an original, provided you know and understand that you won't get it back (as I said above, request multiple original copies whenever possible). If you need the original and cannot obtain another or otherwise need to submit a photocopy (for example, you want to submit a photocopy of your passport, *not* the original), your regional office of the USCIS has a form that you can sign and include with your I-600A stating that the photocopies are true and unaltered.

- The form requires a certified check for the processing fee *plus* fingerprinting fee for each adult over eighteen for whom fingerprints are being submitted, made payable to the "U.S. Citizenship and Immigration Services."

- Never assume you have the most up-to-date information on USCIS policies regarding this form. Check with your agency or regional office about any recent changes.

- *Send your application by some means that is traceable,* either by Federal Express or other overnight carrier, or by United States Postal Service Certified Mail or Return Receipt Requested.

Since time is of the essence when getting this form filed, shell out the extra dollars and send it by overnight mail. Make sure to request a signature verifying delivery receipt.

• It takes two to three months for this form to be processed.

Once your I-600A has been approved, you will be sent form I-171H, "Notice of Favorable Determination Concerning Application for Advance Processing of Orphan Petition." Make sure to request that this notice also be sent to the U.S. embassy or consulate in the country from which you're adopting. Approval of your I-600A remains valid for eighteen months from the date the I-171H is created. If it expires before you've completed your adoption, you may file an application for an expedited refiling of the I-600A (you'll have to update your fingerprints). Check with your regional USCIS office for what documents it requires to expedite the reprocessing of your I-600A petition.

International Paperwork—Your Dossier

Next up on your paperwork agenda (need glasses yet?) is preparing your dossier. This is the most complicated part of the paperwork. If you have any questions or hesitation about your ability to complete your dossier or making sure each and every document is submitted in *exactly the right form and manner required* by the country you're adopting from, hire a professional to do it for you. This usually costs about $750 to $1,000 (see the Resources section).

Getting a dossier together means compiling a lot of documents evidencing things about you and your lifestyle and having them notarized, certified, apostilled and otherwise authenticated. You can have a document that is an original copy and notarized, but because it is not apostilled (has a seal from your secretary of state validating the notary's seal—is this overkill or what?), it will get rejected. Keeping track of what needs which type of authentication can be tedious except for those who are truly detail oriented (and I really mean anal-retentive).

Here is an example of what goes into a typical dossier. (Remember, the contents of your dossier will vary according to the requirements of the country from which you're adopting. *Make sure you are complying with your adoptive country's requirements,* not necessarily what's on my list).

- Adoption petition provided by your agency

- Postplacement agreement provided by your agency

- Form I-171H from the USCIS (a copy of this document usually is acceptable)

- For married adoptive parents, certified copies of birth and marriage certificates for each applicant

- For a single adoptive parent, certified copy of your birth certificate

- A statement attesting to your physical health (on your physician's letterhead providing a date of a recent physical examination)

- Financial information (this can be country-specific; sometimes it is simply your most recent tax return. Other times it is letters from your bank stating your current bank balances, and sometimes it is both)

- Certified copy of divorce decree or death certificate for any prior marriage(s)

- Copies of your passport photo and identification pages

- Copy of a criminal background check (you can obtain one from your local police department, or check with your agency to see if it conducts one as part of your agency acceptance and try to use that)

- Verification of employment (even if you're self-employed; check with your agency about what documentation to provide if you're self-employed)

- Photographs of you, your partner, your home, your pets (if any)

- A power of attorney (usually provided to your adoption agency)

- A certified copy of your home study report

- Letters of reference

- A copy of your agency's license (it must be current and valid)

One last note about the documents you send to USCIS and compile as part of your dossier: make copies of each of them and any documents authenticating them, and take them with you (*on the plane*) when you travel to get your baby. If there is a question or problem, you will be able to pull out the photocopy and show it to the appropriate official. *Never* provide these original, authenticated documents to anyone outside your adoption agency, an authorized representative thereof, or a licensed social worker; nor should you provide monies to anyone (especially anyone who is unlicensed) outside your agency. Trust your instincts—if something doesn't feel or sound right, check with your adoption professional before acting. Your dossier is too important to jeopardize!

Your adoption professional should be the person or entity responsible for getting your dossier into the appropriate foreign representative's hands for evaluation.

And now the waiting for the referral of your baby begins!

~ 9 ~

PREPARING FOR PARENTHOOD

Packing, Shopping,
Planning and Sleeping

O ne of the most exciting and overwhelming parts of becoming an international adoptive parent is planning for and traveling to get baby. Whether you're flying from Boston to Birmingham, Alabama, or Beijing, China, there are things to plan and prepare for. There are more things to plan for, however, when you're traveling to Beijing. First of all, it's not like you're going to have a CVS around the corner (although there are forty-nine Starbucks in Beijing!). Then there are the not-so-insignificant questions like "Can I get formula through customs?" "Do I need to pack medicine for the baby?" "What size clothes should I take?" "What food is safe to eat?" These and other questions are probably going to be waking you in the middle of the night. First among your big concerns is making your travel arrangements, as this comes with a big price tag, and the longer you wait to make those reservations, the more costly it becomes!

Traveling to Get Baby: Buying Plane Tickets and Making Travel Arrangements Ahead of Time

You may be traveling in a group or solo. If your agency is sending a group of adoptive parents to collect offspring all at one time, the agency likely will be booking your travel accommodations for you or will be able to give you some helpful hints.

If you participate in any frequent-flier programs, check to see which international carriers will accept your mileage plan (probably none), and then find out if you have enough miles to purchase ticket(s) or (more likely) upgrade the class of service. Buying first-class or business-class tickets from Boston to Beijing is phenomenally expensive (and worth every penny in comfort, if you can swing it), but if you have enough frequent-flier miles for an upgrade, now would be a good time to make that investment. You usually have a year from the date you request the mileage certificate to use the miles, so make sure when you're redeeming frequent-flier miles that your travel plans will take place within that year. Then hold onto the award certificate and contact a travel agent. Be very careful, however, if you're using frequent-flier miles to pay for your ticket, as these often come with tremendous restrictions on them unless you're buying first class.

If trying to negotiate how and when you use your frequent-flier miles is posing an issue for you, I recommend using a travel agent. In fact, using a travel agent will save you time, money and years of sanity. There are dozens of phone calls to be made to secure your reservation, and your travel date may change a few times. Having a professional deal with this is *ideal*. Let your travel agent know if you've got frequent-flier miles and/or what, if anything, you require for the flight, and then let the agent do his or her thing. The agent will know how to deal with frequent-flier restrictions, upgrades, and late-in-the-game changes to your travel date.

There are several agencies that specialize in booking travel arrangements for adoptive parents, and many of them are great (check the Resources section), but by all means use someone with whom you've worked in the past, especially if he or she knows your travel preferences. Most airlines—especially if you tell them you're adopting when you book the flight—will help you purchase a class of ticket that enables you to reschedule your flight for a nominal fee or even to use your ticket at a moment's notice for up to a year (provided there are seats available on the flight you want). And some of them even offer discounts to adoptive parents! Again, a travel agency— especially one that specializes in adoption—will know the best carriers and options for you.

The next major issue is how many tickets you purchase for the trip home. As international travel is such a large part of the cost of your adoption, you may be tempted not to buy a ticket for your little one. Adoptive parents argue this topic every day, and those arguments can get heated. My recommendation is that if you adopt a younger baby or child (under two) who weighs less than 25 pounds, do not buy a plane ticket. Instead, purchase an air travel security vest (see the Resources section) or use a front carrier to restrain him or her during the trip (especially during turbulence) and to keep your hands free if the baby falls asleep. If you're adopting an older or larger baby or child, get the extra seat. You are not going to want a sleeping 30-pound mound of child on you for eighteen hours, stuck in coach, jet-lagged, weary and experiencing whatever gastrointestinal bug you may have acquired (or gotten because of stress). This will also mean you have to schlep a car seat halfway around the world, but we address this issue in the checklist that follows.

If you don't buy a seat for the baby, keep in mind that most domestic U.S. airlines have a policy that if there is an empty seat available and you're traveling with an infant, they have to relocate you and the passenger near that empty seat to provide you with a seat for your baby and his or her car seat. The same often holds true for international carriers. So never, ever forget to check with the gate attendant about locating an empty seat if you don't purchase one for your baby (again, I recommend taking the extra expense and buying baby his or her own seat if he or she is over two). You also are more likely to have access to an empty seat if you fly during off hours.

Here are some general travel tips from experienced adoptive parents I've worked with:

The Essential International Expecting-to-Adopt Travel Checklist

☐ Try to book a bulkhead seat (more room for all your newly acquired baby paraphernalia) for the extra room and privacy. If you don't purchase a seat for the baby, make sure you've got a front carrier or travel vest for the baby to hold him or her safely against you during the flight. This also will help restrain him or her during turbulence and free your arms up to read a book if you're lucky enough to get him or her to fall asleep.

☐ Try to fly business or first class. Either purchase the tickets and suck up the expense, or upgrade using frequent-flier miles. You have no idea how uncomfortable flying coach with a baby on your lap for eighteen hours can be!

☐ I recommend you only buy baby a seat if he or she is over two years of age and you're traveling coach.

☐ If the baby is under two and you buy a ticket for him or her, you'll need a car seat, which many adoptive parents will tell you is extraordinarily difficult to lug around on a long journey. Although, if you want to do it (and some of us are admittedly safety freaks), I recommend purchasing a special bag to carry the car seat in (see the Resources section) and checking it with your luggage on the way there. Make sure you understand how to use the car seat in non–LATCH-equipped cars. (Most car seats are now made for U.S. cars with standard LATCH kits for installation. LATCH stands for "lower anchors and tethers for children.") Most European cars are not LATCH-equipped.

☐ When making your hotel accommodations, try to get a suite (so one of you can sleep while the other watches the baby) with a mini-kitchen and microwave (for cooking and/or

sterilizing bottles). Most hotel chains have residential or
longer-term hotels for business travelers that are perfect for
adoptive parents; if you're in a rural area you may not have
this option, but it never hurts to ask.

☐ If you're adopting from China, check into EVA Airways, a
well-known Asian air carrier (see the Resources section for a
URL). It has a class of service called Evergreen Deluxe
Coach, which has business-class-size seats for the price of a
coach ticket, lots of floor space and good food. It flies
through the Seattle-Tacoma International Airport (SETAC,
its main U.S. hub), which is where you will go through
customs. SETAC is rumored to have an extremely adoption-
friendly airport! EVA Airways also permits you to make
reservations well in advance of your travel date, which many
other international carriers don't permit.

☐ Consider getting prescriptions for antianxiety medication
and/or sleeping pills for the trip abroad and for while you're
in country (provided you're traveling with someone who can
alternate sleeping shifts with you so while one of you is
knocked out from an Ambien, the other is with baby). It is
imperative that you get a good night's sleep on the way over,
and sometimes people need a little help, not to mention the
anxiety factor about your imminent status as mom or dad! I am
not alone when I say that I spent the entire flight to Dallas to get
my son in the airplane bathroom experiencing gastrointestinal
problems. I didn't know about Valium back then! Think about
it, and discuss it with your physician. Also keep in mind that
you might want to try a test run of the medication when you're
at home to make sure you don't have an adverse reaction.

☐ Make arrangements with someone at home to care for your
pets, plants and home.

☐ Take cash for any remaining adoption fees and travelers
checks for miscellaneous expenses, such as laundry.

☐ Make sure to pack cameras and video equipment in your carry-on bag.

☐ Pack all airline tickets, passports for identification and copies of all your dossier documents in one easy-to-access envelope in your carry-on bag (you will amazed at how disoriented and fussed you will be when you're traveling to get your baby).

☐ Pack an extra empty suitcase to bring home all the extra stuff you bought while you were waiting to come home, such as souvenirs. (You can pack this inside one of your larger suitcases for the trip to get your baby.)

☐ Parenting books—at least two of them, one that covers the basics of infant care and another that covers behavior issues (like one of the books by William Sears, MD, or T. Berry Brazelton, MD. (See the Resources section for suggested titles.)

☐ Laptop or portable DVD player (a laptop will enable you to send pictures home via e-mail, but you also are encouraged to take something to play DVDs on for you and the little one).

☐ You will need to take formula with you, as the formula that is available overseas is not approved for use by most pediatricians and usually isn't iron-fortified. You can take powdered formula (the brand recommended by your pediatrician) either in the original sealed can or in Ziploc bags. (Enfamil makes individual serving packages that you could purchase and carry with you, thus saving the Ziploc bag and premeasurement issues.) Either way, please remember that people have tried to smuggle cocaine by disguising it as baby formula. Make sure you know how to say and write "baby formula" and "adopting baby" in the language of the country you're traveling to in case your bags are inspected by customs and anyone questions what is in the containers. If you take powdered formula, make sure you can obtain bottled water at your destination. You can also take premade, prebottled formula. (Enfamil and Similac both make small premade bottles that you just attach a nipple to. You can buy them online at their Web sites, at a baby store, or even the supermarket, although you may have to special-order the nipples to fit the bottles from the manufacturer.) These are much heavier to transport but eliminate concerns about bottled water and measuring quantities.

☐ Bottles and nipples (you will need about four per day, depending on how easy it will be for you to wash them; you can get by with fewer if you'll have a good place with hot water to clean them) and a nipple brush.

☐ One large package of diapers in the size that your orphanage has indicated will be appropriate and one package in a size larger (you cannot always depend on your orphanage to accurately represent your child's size). You can always donate the diapers that don't fit. When packing the diapers, take them out of their package and empty them into your suitcase in a flat layer. They'll take up much less space this way.

☐ One large package of diaper wipes, one package of Clorox wipes (removed from packaging and placed in a Ziploc bag with the label from the container), Purell instant hand sanitizer, dish soap wipes and extra Ziploc bags in a variety of sizes.

☐ Two clothing outfits per day (babies soil clothes easily!) in a size estimated to fit your child (err on the larger size, as you can always cuff pants and roll up sleeves), *pre-washed in Dreft or Ivory Snow detergent,* for approximately five days (ten outfits).

☐ At least two comfortable outfits (as in sweatpants) for parent(s) per day for approximately five days.

☐ Front-holding baby carrier, sling and/or hip carrier (a front carrier is better for bonding and for safety on the plane) and/or stroller (you can gate-check the stroller on both flights) depending on the size, age and weight of your child.

☐ Diaper bag.

☐ Pacifiers in a Ziploc bag (at least six, as they get lost easily!).

☐ An inflatable baby tub.

☐ An inflatable mattress topper. (Check into some of the smaller ones designed for travel. Depending on the country you're traveling to, the mattresses may be really bad, and you're going to need every minute of sleep.)

☐ Baby spoons, plastic disposable bowls and sippy cups. (You will throw all but the sippy cups away when you leave. You may want the sippy cups for your trip home.)

☐ Infant Tylenol, infant Motrin (if your child is over six months of age and your pediatrician says it's okay), diaper cream in a tube, teething gel (we liked Hyland's teething gel, but Orajel works well too), Q-tips, Band-Aids, saline spray for infants (like Little Noses brand; you can buy a prepackaged kit of travel remedies, such as Little Remedies), infant thermometer, Aquaphor lotion, powdered electrolyte formula in case of dehydration (try Kaolectrolyte).

☐ A few baby toys that are age-appropriate and soft books to play with, DVDs (*Sesame Street*, *Baby Einstein*, *Teletubbies* or *The Wiggles*) to watch in the hotel and on the plane trip home.

☐ Infant sunblock and insect repellent (approved by your pediatrician).

☐ Any prescriptions your pediatrician recommends you take in the event that your child is suffering from an ear infection or something like that when you arrive. (U.S. medications will be more effective than what is available from the orphanage; your pediatrician should be able to advise you on a broad-spectrum antibiotic that you can take with you, such as amoxicillin, or a scabies medicine, such as Elimite.)

☐ Adult-strength acetaminophen, ibuprofen, antibacterial cream, charcoal and antidiarrhea medicine, glycerin suppositories (for constipation), alcohol wipes, more Band-Aids, hydrocortisone cream, daily prescription or short-term prescription medications, vitamins (yes, a daily adult vitamin!), cold medicine (don't forget saline spray and decongestants) and any other remedies you might need and not be able to locate in a foreign country. If you're traveling to a country with mosquitoes, bring insect repellent with DEET (for mom and dad only!). Remember to leave all medications in their original packaging and to take them in your carry-on bag.

☐ Travel alarm clock.

☐ Umbrella.

International Adoption and Medicine: Talking to a Specialist and Getting Your Immunizations

Not only will you need to discuss your child's health with a medical professional prior to travel, but mommy and daddy need to get a checkup before they travel too! This exam will serve as a baseline in case you arrive home with some non-sleep-deprivation-related malady, and it will be an opportunity to get your immunizations. Depending on where you're traveling, it can take up to six months for your immunizations to be fully effective (the current hepatitis series takes a while to kick in and is perhaps most important). Depending on where you're traveling, you will need different vaccines, and your internist may not be up to speed on the current vaccine recommendations for travel to the Hunan province of China. You can check with the Centers for Disease Control and Prevention (see the Resources section for a URL to the CDC Web site with travel/immunization recommendations) for a list of recommended immunizations, or visit the International Society of Travel Medicine's directory to find a travel-medicine specialist (see the Resources section for a URL that will help you locate a physician) in your area. Some travel-medicine specialists may also recommend that you take prophylactic medicines to prevent diseases such as malaria (commonly prescribed for adoptive parents traveling to Guatemala). Most adoptive parents get the hepatitis series, polio, typhoid, and tetanus. *Make your appointment for immunizations as soon as possible after completing your dossier.* If it takes six or more months for all your vaccines to be effective and you travel seven months after your dossier has been submitted—well you can do the math!

You may also want to discuss with your physician the possibility of taking a prescription antibiotic to be used in case of food contamination or other infection, and/or sleep and antianxiety medication for traveling. When packing medicines for travel, remember to keep them in their original containers, and take more than you think you'll need. Also take a doctor's note naming the medications, what they're used for, and why you're traveling with them. Go over recommendations for what to eat and what not to eat. The rule of thumb is that you never eat anything raw. Make sure your food is boiled, pasteurized, peeled, washed, and/or sealed before it crosses your lips. Don't drink anything with ice in it, and don't purchase food from street vendors. Wash your hands frequently, and try to carry something like Purell *and* disposable antibacterial wipes in your pocket[book].

Lining Up a Pediatrician

You also will need to meet with a pediatrician prior to traveling. First and foremost, you need to establish a relationship with your regular pediatrician and introduce yourself, as you will need an appointment with him or her within the first forty-eight to seventy-two hours of returning home. Whether you also elect to speak with a pediatrician who specializes in international adoptive medicine (see the Resources section for a list) is completely up to you before you travel and is often dependent on where you're adopting from. Many countries now have established and reliable medical care. Others, such as Ethiopia and Russia, may cause you to want to review a child's medical history with a medical professional before you accept your referral or before you travel. Regardless of whether you actually see this physician before you travel, you need his or her name before you travel, and it's probably prudent to go meet in person just so you've got the introductions out of the way. In all likelihood, you'll be calling for an appointment or a phone consult shortly after returning home (I recommend within forty-eight hours), and having previously met with this physician (in addition to your regular physician, if they are different) will help facilitate making that appointment.

I strongly encourage you to establish a relationship with a pediatrician specializing in international adoptive medicine prior to traveling. If you're also seeing this pediatrician before you travel or accept your referral, there are specific things you'll want to go over. First, you want the doctor to explain the things your child may be at risk for, having been born in a particular country or been living in an orphanage setting. Then you will both want to pay close attention to the information provided by the adoption agency, such as the baby's size and growth pattern. A small head can be indicative of exposure to alcohol in utero or a birth-related defect. Children who have lived in an institutional setting are at risk for growth delay, so please consider the child's residential setting when evaluating information. Your pediatrician can help you assess growth in relationship to U.S. standards. I have seen statistics that indicate that every month a child lives in an orphanage equates to one month of growth retardation (not necessarily mental retardation; I'm talking *height* and *weight* here!). Only your pediatrician can assess whether this seems to be true for your child, and he or she also will consider malnutrition, residential concerns, and size when assessing whether there might be mild to severe developmental delays, if any. *Do not assume anything on your own!* Language and hearing issues can be assessed based on videos, as can gross and fine motor coordination. A general standard applied to institutionalized children is that a one-year-old child the size of an eight-month-old should demonstrate developmental characteristics consistent with an eight-month-old, not a one-year-old (see the Resources section for a link to a developmental chart prepared by *Adoptive Families Magazine*).

Don't Forget, This Is Supposed to Be a Special Time Too!

My friend Julia gave me permission to excerpt from her adoption diary. (By the way, you should totally keep a diary during this time, because *you're never going to remember your adoption journey otherwise.* I don't remember anything about my wedding, and I didn't want to risk not remembering our adoption experience! That journal is now something special I'm saving for David when he's older.)

I was especially moved by this entry in Julia's diary:

We took Hannah's paperwork to her new pediatrician, and she's a very healthy little baby! She needs a bit more iron, but everything else looks great. We are relieved and excited! We picked up some "just in case" prescriptions for amoxicillin and Elimite [a scabies medicine] to bring with us. When I got home with them, Peter and I realized they were the first things that had [her name] printed on them. Of course we got all teary and sappy. And then [we] spent the rest of the night staring sentimentally at a box of anti-scabies medication. Ah, parenthood!

Do not freak out if your pediatrician is concerned about size or developmental issues. Most of these issues can be overcome with early intervention, which is paid for by your state. If your pediatrician is concerned about potential delays, arrange to have an early intervention assessment performed a few weeks after returning home. (Your pediatrician can give you the number to call in your area.) Statistics are clear that children who receive early intervention often ultimately do as well as, if not better than, children who have no developmental delays at all. A little love and attentiveness on your part can go a long way toward overcoming delays caused by institutional care settings!

To Shower or Not to Shower

One of the blessed parts of international adoption is the knowledge that you're going to be a mom (or a dad), and it's going to happen in a specific amount of time. Unlike domestic adoptive moms, who worry that the birth mother with whom they are working may choose to parent, you know that on March 10, you're climbing aboard an aircraft bound for San Francisco International Airport, then on to Hong Kong and from there to Beijing. You have no worries that this kid ain't coming home. Because having a baby shower is part of the ritual process of becoming a parent, and you know with a greater degree of certainty than a domestic adoptive parent that this is really happening, you don't have any excuses not to indulge in this rite of passage. Unless you've got religious reasons for waiting or are extremely superstitious, I highly recommend having a baby shower. By all means, throw a welcome-home party if you're more comfortable with something like that, but seriously consider having a good old-fashioned baby shower!

There are many great adoption-themed shower games you can use to make the party more appropriate for your situation. Adoption Web sites have great ideas on themes (some of them country-specific), games and general invitation language that may be more appropriate for your unique perspective on becoming a parent. One recommendation I have is that, if you do have a baby shower ahead of time, ask people to give you—in addition to baby booty—gift cards for Blockbuster, Netflix, takeout chains, Starbucks (remember the forty-nine Starbucks in Beijing?) and things like that. These gift cards can reduce your expenses when you get home and can provide you with an activity when you're adjusting to life at home. And make sure to get a ton of baby goods, because believe me, the last thing jet-lagged and sleep-deprived parents want to be doing is shopping for Exer-saucers and baby clothes!

Deciding Whether to Decorate a Nursery

In fact, it's downright stupid *not* to decorate the nursery when you've got a travel date looming. Again, unlike domestic adoptive parents who're afraid to decorate a nursery for fear of jinxing the process or because they don't want to stare at an empty nursery for two years, you've got a date by which you must have accommodations for your child. Did you know that it usually takes about twelve weeks for a crib and changing table to come in after being ordered? So if you wait until après bébé to be ordering that stuff, you've got to have some other sleeping and changing arrangements for your little one. Unless you're doing the family bed thing, don't expect little Adam or Eve to appreciate sleeping in a Pack 'n Play for three months (some welcome home!). Second, and way more important, you're not going to have the time to shop for this stuff after you get home!

If you think that after you return home from a couple weeks of overseas traveling, sleep-deprived on top of jet-lagged and over-whelmed by new parenting responsibilities, attachment and bond-ing issues, you're going to have time for a regular shower (forget the baby shower, let's talk soap and shampoo) let alone time to shop, paint, or pick out wallpaper borders, you've got another think com-ing! I cannot tell you how many times newly adoptive parents have expressed their shock at how much time and attention such a small person—especially a small person who doesn't share your language and feels displaced and disoriented—can suck from their lives, and how exhausted they are. Like you're really going to want to trek to Babies "R" Us to brave the crowds and lack of adequate service while holding a screaming, squirming toddler who sees all sorts of cool toys and colors to try to shop for a crib, dresser, glider, stroller and all the accoutrements. Get a grip *now* and go shopping *now!*

Have all the booty ready when you get home to save yourself the headache. Knowing you've got five different brands of bottles and nipples at home waiting for miss-fussy-I-don't-like-this-bottle to try will give you way more peace of mind than you know or could possibly understand now in your blissfully sleep-enriched state. And speaking of bottles, have you considered breast-feeding?

Deciding Whether to Breast-Feed: Yes, It Can Be Done

Are you over the shock yet? Go back and read in chapter 6 a little bit about the ways you can induce lactation, and then flip back to this page.

As I said in chapter 6, adoptive breast-feeding is much more common than it used to be, and there are several Web sites (see the Resources section) on which you can get very experienced help to find the right way for *you* to breast-feed. The important thing to remember if you try to breast-feed your baby is that with an older baby, you'll need more help and support from a trained lactation consultant, and that you shouldn't expect to be the sole or even a substantial source of nutrition for your child. The purpose of attempting to breast-feed an older baby is mostly bonding-related. If you're able to produce milk (you go girl!), that is really just an added benefit for both of you. Make sure to line up good support before you attempt to do this and to cut yourself a lot of slack. It will take numerous attempts before it works.

I did it with David, and he was almost six months old (and was cutting teeth). You can do it too. Have patience and be persistent (and don't be afraid to ask for help)!

~ 10 ~

BRINGING BABY HOME

From Boston to Beijing and Back

Finally, the day has arrived! You have filled out endless reams of paperwork, passed home studies and criminal background checks, gotten your vaccinations, stared longingly at e-mailed pictures of your baby, packed and repacked your bags, visited pediatricians, and traveled three-quarters of the way around the world for this day (not necessarily to Beijing or to adopt a little girl, either): the day you meet your child for the first time! If you didn't already figure it out, you've been a parent or at least have been immersing yourself in the parent mind-set for a while, but now you move on to the scary stuff—actually caring for this little person!

Don't worry, we all freak out at the notion that someone is handing us another human being with the expectation that we know how to take care of him or her. Most of us don't really know what we're doing, but we learn fast! All babies and toddlers, and even little people, are surprisingly resilient and forgiving—at least initially—of our incompetence at changing their diapers or soothing their diaper rashes. You'll get the hang of it in no time!

Living in a Hotel in a Foreign Country with a Baby: Mattresses, Sightseeing and Sleep-Deprivation with Subtitles

What is harder to get the hang of is the sleep-deprivation combined with the jet lag and strange foods and smells while you're in-country getting used to parenting, all the while living in a hotel (or reasonable facsimile thereof).

Whether you're there for three days or three weeks, it can be overwhelming. My recommendation—and that of all of my adoptive-parent friends—is that when staying in a hotel with new offspring, try to make your stay a honeymoon. You have the advantage with an older infant of being able to go out and about and sightsee some. (Parents adopting newborns may receive warnings from their pediatrician to stay inside as much as possible.) You are going to want to take photographs of everything about the place in which your child was born to help him understand his history as he's growing up anyway, so plan a few sightseeing excursions around your video and digital (or 35mm, if you're a purist) cameras. You might even need to go to an Internet café for broadband Internet access to e-mail pictures and send messages home. These forays into the real world also will help reassure your little one, as he will be with you (still a relative stranger, pardon the pun!) but also seeing, hearing and smelling all things familiar.

Once you've taken all of the home videos and digital pictures, I strongly encourage you to hole up in your hotel room and bond with your baby. Your mattress may not be terribly comfortable (as if you could sleep anyway!) and your intestines may be complaining rather intensely at the strange foods you've been eating, so staying inside for a few days may not be such a bad idea. Hopefully, you're in a hotel with some kind of room service. If not, make sure one of you can get out once a day (alone) to grab some food (no street vendors, *please!*). You may have found a restaurant you like during one of your sightseeing adventures; go back and get take out as often as possible! If necessary, eat McDonald's a few times. Try to keep the food source consistent (if your stomach is upset), and follow the guidelines in chapter 9 about what foods to avoid eating.

The Essential International Adoption Living-in-a-Hotel Checklist

☐ If you can afford to order room service and stay in a hotel with daily maid service, *do it!*

☐ Try to get a mini-suite with a living room so you have plenty of room to spread out; at the very least get a king-size bed and a handicapped-accessible bathroom (they're bigger, so you'll have more room for all your stuff and all the baby stuff). This may not be something available to you in the country you've traveled to, but if it is, *do it.*

☐ Try to stay in a hotel with a complimentary breakfast and/or happy hour with some kind of free food every morning and afternoon (one of you can get out of the room for a break and bring back food for the other).

☐ Ask for a room away from the elevator but close to the laundry room (if your hotel has self-service laundry), or ask for a *quiet* room.

☐ Try to stay in a hotel that has high-speed Internet access to send pictures to friends.

☐ Make sure you have some way to play lullabies (download them to your laptop or make a CD before you leave).

☐ Make sure your hotel offers movies on demand or rents VCRs or has DVD players (or use your laptop to play DVDs). Take along some DVDs for mom and/or dad, and also take some for the baby (introduce him to *Sesame Street*, *Baby Einstein*, *Teletubbies* or *The Wiggles*).

☐ Take turns with the baby if he's not sleeping through the night. One of you take the early shift while the other sleeps, and one of you take the late shift while the other sleeps.

Otherwise, both of you sleep when the baby sleeps. (Single parents should *not* travel alone to pick up their babies. Take someone with you!)

☐ Take extra clothing for everyone so you don't have to do laundry unless absolutely necessary.

But seriously, stay inside with the baby as much as possible and get to know each other. This is the only time you're going to be truly free to be alone as a family unit.

Before you know it, you're going to be home with friends and family members literally beating down your door to meet your child. Now is the time for your family to just bond. And don't hesitate to impose a quarantine when you arrive home too. When we got home with David, our pediatrician told us to stay at home with him one-on-one for two to three weeks with few (if any) visitors and to "wear" him to facilitate bonding. The self-imposed hotel or home quarantine is amazingly helpful (even if you go a little stir-crazy) to give you all time to get to know each other.

Traveling with Baby: From Beijing to Boston— Hold On, You're in for a Bumpy Ride

At last you've entered the final leg of your journey. You are getting settled for your long journey home. As you're packing to go home, you're going to be shocked at the vast array of stuff you have to take back. Fortunately, you packed an extra suitcase for all the souvenirs and baby-related paraphernalia you bought. You will still need to divest yourself of some of the stuff unless you want to be paying extra weight charges to whatever air carrier is shepherding you home. Now is the time to give away diapers, wipes, medicines and any clothing you don't absolutely need. You will have a CVS around the corner at home and can replace these items. You don't need to take them home and schlep heavy bags filled with the extra stuff you packed "just in case." Your orphanage or other adoptive parents will be grateful for your hand-me-downs. Orphanges *always* like donations; the medicines you brought (if unopened) are extremely valuable, as are formula, diapers and wipes. Every little bit counts for every little baby left behind to wait for his or her forever parent(s) to arrive. And many adoptive parents have been grateful for the extras left behind by other adoptive parents, especially at 9 P.M., when the local pharmacy is closed and they call their in-country contact desperately seeking infant Tylenol.

Pack only the essentials for your trip home in your carry-on bag (packing the same stuff in your carry-on as you did flying from the United States), and dispose of the rest. You might want to keep some clothing for the baby as a keepsake (like whatever he was wearing when you brought him "home" to your hotel), and of course any souvenir clothing you bought. But other than that, take all the baby stuff and give it to your orphanage or to personnel from your agency to distribute to orphanages, foster families or other adoptive parents who find themselves without that infant Tylenol. If you followed my advice, most of what you packed for you (mom and/or dad) was sweatpant-type clothing that should be easily replaceable at your local Gap or Target. Keep enough diapers and wipes and medicine for one extra day (assuming you get stranded—heaven help you—in an airport somewhere) but give or throw away everything else!

Make sure everything on the following list is packed in your carry-on bag and is easily accessible:

The Essential Traveling Home on an Airplane for Eighteen Hours Checklist

- ☐ The sippy cup or bottles are ready to be used (as in contain drinkable liquid), and you have plenty of snacks (which you may have had to purchase at the airport).

- ☐ Movies for your laptop or DVD player.

- [ ] Toys and books.

- [ ] Front or hip carrier.

- [ ] Camera and/or DVD player (to record the tantrum he will undoubtedly throw nine hours into your journey).

- [ ] Blankets, pillows and sweatshirts for warmth and back/neck support.

- [ ] Eye shade for mom and/or dad.

- [ ] Any prescription antianxiety medications you've discovered actually work, Tylenol or other over-the-counter (don't forget saline spray to combat dry airplane air) and/or prescription medicines you might need to combat a headache.

- [ ] Antibacterial wipes and lotion.

- [ ] Benadryl in case of baby overload. (Check with your pediatrician beforehand, but many adoptive parents have discovered it is sometimes helpful to "assist" baby to sleep on the plane. One word of warning: sometimes Benadryl has the opposite effect and makes babies hyper. If your pediatrician says it's okay to use Benadryl to help with the plane trip, test it out in the hotel first—that is, unless you want to be murdered by your fellow plane passengers.)

- [ ] Two changes of clothing for baby and one for mom and/or dad (or your traveling companion) in case of spills or spit-up.

Consider walking up and down the aisles of the plane with the baby. You will both be grateful for the opportunity to stretch your legs, and he'll no doubt delight other passengers and give you all something to talk about (like how cute he is!). Check with your flight attendant *first,* as some airlines require everyone to stay seated the entire flight, but it's well worth a little friendly persuasion to let the little one explore rather than have a screaming child cooped up for an ungodly length of time sitting on your lap and playing patty-cake.

Coming Home: Managing Friends and Family, Sleepless Nights, Piles of Laundry and the Postadoption Blues

From the bottom of my heart, I offer you this one piece of advice: do not, I repeat, do not allow anyone to meet you at the airport! I know you're in shock that I am telling you this; you've seen so many videos of giant groups of family members welcoming the baby to his or her new country. *Bad idea,* in my not-so-humble and educated opinion. Too many adoptive parents have told me that they seriously regretted the welcoming committee at the airport. The baby did not appreciate being passed around and meeting a dozen strangers and being kissed and pinched and thrown in the air. Everyone is going to be tired and cranky; it is going to be overwhelming and disorienting to have people in your face and asking questions. More important, however, you're in the middle of serious bonding and attachment time. Introducing a ton of strangers all at once is going to disrupt that process and scare the living daylights out of your child. Whatever is involved in getting from the airport to your residence without the assistance of friends and family, suck it up and endure the hassle. Your baby will benefit from it (and therefore so will you)!

Adjusting to the time difference when you get home is going to be really hard (that is somewhat of an understatement). Make sure someone stopped by and left several meals in your fridge for you and stocked you up on diapers, wipes, clean laundry, milk, juice, eggs—you get the idea. Get *one* person to come help you for the first few days you're home. This person should be someone that the baby will be close to over the long term so that he or she has an introduction to bonding with someone who will be an important part of life.

If you don't have any relatives who can help, you might want to arrange for a doula to come stay for a few days (see the Resources section). These are like paid family members who will come take care of the baby and do the dishes. Whomever you enlist, make sure this person understands that she is there to *help you.* She should be prepared to stay up late at night, wash dishes, cook meals, take care of the baby, and hold you when you cry from exhaustion. This is not a guest coming to meet the baby. This person is coming to *work* so you can get some rest or downtime after a very long and stressful few weeks. All of you are going to be jet-lagged, sleep-deprived and overwhelmed. You want someone you can order around without feeling guilty!

Expect the first few weeks at home to be challenging. The first week will be awful as you all get on a schedule relative to the current time zone. Try not to wash too many of the baby's blankets or burp cloths (especially if you had them in-country). You want as many things to smell as familiar as possible while she adjusts to her new environment. Show her the same videos she watched when you were in the hotel and on the airplane, and introduce as little as possible for the first few days. Then gradually start exposing her to more of her new world. If possible, wear or carry her (your weight, her weight, and your physical well-being should be considered before wearing a child as Charlie and I wore David—going from regular life to being attached to a 20-pound monster may not be such a great idea for your back; I wound up having back surgery a year later!), and sleep with her. If you're anti–family bed (many people are), make sure you have a baby monitor near her crib, and the minute she cries, get to her and pick her up. This is not the time to sleep train! Organizing her sleep schedule around the time zone is important, but leaving her alone in a crib in a strange new world to cry it out is cruel. If you have any concerns or questions about how to assist her in transitioning, bonding and attaching, check out the Resources section for books on attachment issues and parenting techniques.

You will need some longer-term assistance as well. Once that initial adjustment to reality has taken place and life starts into a daily schedule, it's going to hit you: you are a parent and this is tough work! I am not just talking about taking care of the baby, but taking care of her and the rest of your life at the same time without losing your mind. The dishes and laundry are going to reproduce at an alarming rate, and it'll be hard to keep up with them. One morning you're going to wake up and stand in your kitchen crying at 7 A.M. because the bathroom needs to be cleaned, the carpets need vacuuming, the fridge is empty, and you're out of diapers and—by far the worst on this list—coffee. We all have to learn to juggle household chores on three hours of sleep. You're going to have to learn to do them on three hours of sleep while recovering from being in a completely different time zone with a child who is still learning your language! That is not an easy combination, even for a super-mom. And you're trying to do this while still encouraging and fostering bonding. You may still be in the quarantine zone when the reality of parenting life at home hits you. I promise, it's going to be *okay*!

Here are some survival tips for helping you cope and getting some "people" time in without breaking the quarantine/bonding period:

- Live out of the dishwasher, and wash only the essential items of laundry. Clean bed sheets, unless the dirty ones have been soiled by a leaking or overflowing diaper, aren't essential anymore. Neither are clean towels or clothing. Clean underwear, sweatpants, pajamas and baby's cute clothes are essential!

- When the fridge is bare, order out or go online for groceries. Better yet, arrange with people before you leave to bring you a meal or some groceries every few days, starting about ten days after you get home (hopefully, you've had live-in help for those ten days). People will ask you how they can help; take them up on it and ask for a food run. They get to see the baby briefly when they drop the food off; you get a brief bit of human companionship and one less meal or grocery-store trip to worry about.

- Make sure to visit the pediatrician shortly after coming home. Make sure to have the doctor evaluate any potential illnesses that could have (even in the absence of symptoms) been contracted by your child in her country of birth and any attachment or adjustment concerns.

- Arrange with someone (the same person, if possible) to come over every few days to give you a break to shower, sleep, or take a walk. Making sure it is the same person every time for brief periods of time won't overwhelm your new charge and will give you a much-needed break. Even if you're married or have a great life partner, you're going to need breaks.

- Remember that this is overwhelming for every new parent (biological or adoptive) and that it takes time—sometimes months—to adjust. Don't expect perfection or even an uninterrupted night's sleep for quite some time. If things are going swimmingly and you're getting a ton of sleep and baby seems to be adjusting well, count yourself among the lucky, but do not expect it to be easy.

- Make sure to use all those gift cards you got at your baby shower to rent movies or grab a cup of coffee to give you some downtime. It is perfectly okay to watch an adult movie while baby plays quietly on the floor (no violence, please). You need your sanity, and pretty soon baby's going to control the television programming (*The Wiggles* rapidly becomes a child's obsession). You'll never get to watch what you want. (Scarier still is when *you* start singing a Wiggles tune while on line— alone, without child—for the checkout counter at the supermarket. Very embarrassing, unless the person behind you happens to join in!)

- Take baby out for walks (weather permitting). Wear her if possible; if not, zoom around with that fancy new stroller Great-Aunt Agatha bought you.

The sleep-deprivation really catches up with you about three weeks after you've brought baby home. That is also about the time that the dishwasher isn't the only thing overflowing; you're crying a lot and coping with what has now been recognized as postadoption depression (see the Resources section for more information). I am not talking about the shock of how hard parenting is or how many dirty dishes you have. I am talking about serious hormonal changes, which have absolutely nothing to do with gestating a child, that come with your new role as a parent. It is a rough change; life is upside down and inside out, you're sleep-deprived, and you're completely stressed out and overwhelmed. I truly think that causes chemical changes in the brain. I could talk at length about the role of neurotransmitters and cortisol and their effect on mood, but you don't really care. All you need to know is that this is *normal* for adoptive parents too. If you want to see where you are on the scale of normal adjustment versus depression, flip back to chapter 7 and read about my friend Caroline's experience with the postadoption blues.

As Caroline's story makes clear, this is real, not some figment of your imagination, and if you need to get some help from a physician, get a prescription for an antidepressant. I have spoken to far too many newly adoptive parents (domestic and international) who describe exactly what mothers with postpartum depression describe, and I've read too many articles written by professionals and parents to dismiss this. I went through it myself! If you think you're struggling more than you should be, if you're having trouble getting out of bed in the morning, if you don't feel like "you," if you're crying all the time, get some professional help. It is my experienced, compassionate and (donning my faux doctor's jacket) "professional" opinion that postadoption and postpartum depression should really be called "new-parent depression."

You will get over it, through it, and past it and will move on to the next hurdle in being a parent—something along the lines of toddler tantrums, food refusal and potty training. Oh, joy!

Welcome to the club, my friend! It is a nice place to be after all this time, isn't it?

AFTERWORD

Becoming and being an adoptive parent is an amazing and challenging experience. As I've been writing this book, I've been preparing and planning to adopt baby number two. I am again overwhelmed by the process, the reams of paperwork and the apprehension. I am an experienced and confident parent, but I know what I'm in for now, and part of me is terrified of the change in our fragile daily routine (what routine?). And yet I've never been happier in my life, and that's being said by someone who is profoundly sleep-deprived. Being a parent is the best job I've ever had, and it was worth every notarized, certified piece of paper and every hiccup in our adoption process. I can't wait for you to hold your child for the first time or for it to hit you that you're a mom or dad!

Watching our children grow fills us all with awe, but adoptive parents have a more unique perspective. We worked hard to get here and do not take a single moment for granted. It is more than awe-inspiring for most of us; it is a blissful, magnificent life.

My final words of advice: Make your adoption experience focused on your baby, not on the steps in the process or what you're feeling today. A baby-centered adoption, one that focuses on the best interests of your soon-to-be child, is one that will be successful for all of you. While birth parents may choose to parent their child and countries and programs may close and change, if you focus on the needs of the child, you'll recognize that the stress you feel today is insignificant. Somewhere out there is a baby or child who needs you, and you will do everything to get to him or her. It is an essential component of shifting from the child-free lifestyle to the paradigm of parenting: learning to put baby first.

I remember trying to describe to someone the experience of coming home from the grocery store with an overtired and angry baby. Screw the groceries, the eggs, the milk and the ice cream (not to mention my bladder); everything was unimportant until he was peacefully asleep in his crib. If you can start thinking that way as you plan your adoption ("This is not about me!" and "What is really important in this moment?"), you've gone a long way toward becoming a centered and focused parent. When the paperwork gets overwhelming or the cell phone isn't ringing, remember that this is your time to learn to roll with the punches and to shift perspective to putting someone else before almost everything else in your life.

Speaking of perspective: Please, try to keep your sense of humor! It is way too easy to take this too seriously.

I also encourage you to make your transition to parenthood easier by joining adoptive-parent support groups, making friends with other new parents (whether biological or adoptive) and finding playgroups and classes to attend with your little one. Read up on raising adopted children (see the Resources section), attachment and other styles of parenting, attachment and bonding issues, baby-care basics, lifebooks and video diaries (creating a record of your child's life that will help make sense of the adoption experience; this will help you remember your trip to get baby as well as embrace some of the issues you may one day face), and spend time *enjoying* the time you have now to sleep, go to the movies (without paying a babysitter) and prepare for your new life.

This is your time to be expectant, "pregnant" and full of life and possibilities. Enjoy it! And by the way, ***congratulations!***

PART FOUR

~ ~ ~

APPENDICES

RESOURCES

Chapter 1
Domestic Versus International Adoption

National Adoption Organizations and Resources

A more comprehensive list can be found in the *Adoptive Families Magazine* Adoption Guide available online at: www.adoptivefamilies.com/adoptionguide.php

Adoptive Families Magazine
42 West 38th St., Suite 901
New York, NY 10018
toll-free number: (800) 372-3300
phone: (646) 366-0835
fax: (646) 366-0842
www.adoptivefamilies.com

American Academy of Adoption Attorneys (AAAA)
Box 33053
Washington, DC 20033-0053
phone: (202) 832-2222
www.adoptionattorneys.org

American Academy of Pediatrics Section on Adoption and Foster Care
141 Northwest Point Blvd.
Elk Grove, IL 60007-1098
phone: (847) 434-4000
www.aap.org/sections/adoption

American Adoption Congress
1025 Connecticut Ave. NW, Suite 1012
Washington, DC 20036
phone: (202) 483-3399
www.americanadoptioncongress.org

The Dave Thomas Foundation for Adoption
4288 West Dublin-Granville Rd.
Dublin, OH 43017
toll-free number: (888)ASK-DTFA
www.davethomasfoundationforadoption.com

The Evan B. Donaldson Adoption Institute
120 Wall St., 20th Floor
New York, NY 10005
phone: (212) 269-5080
fax: (212) 269-1962
www.adoptioninstitute.org

Institute for Adoption Information
PO Box 4405
Bennington, VT 05201
phone: (802) 442-7135
www.adoptioninformationinstitute.org

Child Welfare Information Gateway
Children's Bureau/ACYF
1250 Maryland Ave., SW, 8th floor
Washington, DC 20024

phone: (703) 385-7565
fax: (703) 385-3206
www.childwelfare.gov

National Resource Center for Special-Needs Adoption
Spaulding for Children
16250 Northland Dr., Suite 120
Southfield, MI 48075
phone: (248) 443-0306
fax: (248) 443-7099
www.nrcadoption.org

RESOLVE
7910 Woodmont Ave., Suite 1350
Bethesda, MD 20814
phone: (301) 652-8585
toll-free help line: (888) 623-0744
fax: (301) 652-9375
e-mail: info@resolve.org
www.resolve.org
RESOLVE has chapters nationwide.

Stars of David International, Inc.
3175 Commercial Ave., Suite 100
Northbrook, IL 60062-1915
phone: (847) 509-9929
fax: (847) 509-9545
www.starsofdavid.org

USCIS
U.S. Citizenship and Immigration Services
www.uscis.gov
To locate your regional or field office:
www.uscis.gov/graphics/fieldoffices/index.htm

Adoptive-Parent Support Groups

A Bond of Love, Inc.
6732 Pasadena Dr.
Tallahassee, FL 32317
phone: (850) 671-5793
e-mail: abondoflove@hotmail.com
www.abondofloveinc.com

Adoption Knowledge Affiliates
PO Box 4082
Austin, TX 78765
phone: (512) 442-8252
e-mail: aka@adoptionknowledge.org
www.adoptionknowledge.org

Adoption Mosaic
PO Box 18102
Portland, OR 97218
phone: (503) 318-8273
e-mail: mina@adoptionmosaic.org
www.adoptionmosaic.org

Adoption Network
1667 East 40th St., Suite B-1
Cleveland, OH 44103
phone: (216) 881-7511
e-mail: betsie@adoptionnetwork.org
www.adoptionnetwork.org

Adoption Paths
PO Box 2746
Santa Cruz, CA 95062
phone: (831) 476-7252
e-mail: sara@adoptionpaths.com
www.adoptionpaths.com

Alabama Post Adoption Connections
181 West Valley Ave., Suite 300
Birmingham, AL 35209
phone: (205) 949-2722
e-mail: csegars@casapac.org
www.casapac.org

Adoptive Parents Committee, Inc.
PO Box 3525, Church St. Station
New York, NY 10008-3525
phone: (718) 380-6175
www.adoptiveparents.org
APC has regional chapters throughout the tri-state area.

Adoption Resource Network
PO Box 178
Pittsford, NY 14534
phone: (585) 586-9586
e-mail: info@arni.org
www.hillside.com/services/adoption.htm

Chicago Area Families for Adoption
PMB 108, 1212 Naper Blvd., Suite 119
Naperville, IL 60540-8360
phone: (630) 585-4680
e-mail: caffamember@aol.com
www.caffa.org

Families for International Children
3124 Midland Dr. SE
Grand Rapids, MI 49506
phone: (616) 949-6758
www.fficgr.org

Families with Children from China
FCC has chapters nationwide and worldwide. A comprehensive list
can be found at www.fwcc.org
If your state or region does not have a chapter of FCC, the
organization encourages the formation of local chapters.

FCC of Greater NY
PO Box 237065, Ansonia Station
New York, NY 10023
phone: (212) 579-0115
www.fccny.org

FCC of New England
8 Berkeley St.
Cambridge, MA 02138-3464
phone: (617) 876-3042
fax: (617) 441-5449
www.fccne.org

Friends in Adoption
PO Box 659
Auburn, WA 98071
phone: (206) 264-5136
e-mail: friendsinadoption@yahoo.com
www.friends-in-adoption.org

ODS Adoption Community of New England
1750 Washington St.
Holliston, MA 01746-2234
phone: (508) 429-4260
toll-free number: (800) 932-3678
e-mail: info@odsacone.org
www.odsacone.org

For more information on locating an adoption support group,
go to: www.adoptivefamilies.com/support_group.php.

Heritage Trips

www.adoptivefamilytravel.com
www.concordialanguagevillages.org
www.heritagecamps.org

Chapter 2
Affording Adoption

Cost of Adopting

Adoptive Families Magazine poll, 2002
www.adoptivefamilies.com/articles.php?aid=317

Adoptive Families Magazine poll, February 2006, vol. 39, no. 1, p. 33
www.adoptivefamilies.com/adoption-cost.php

Budgeting Spreadsheet

www.adoptivefamilies.com/planner

Employer Adoption Benefits

Lists of Adoption-Friendly Workplaces:
Best Employer Benefits
www.adopting.org/adoptions/adoption-benefits-from-
    employers.html

Employers with Adoption Benefits
www.adoptionfriendlyworkplace.org/employers.asp

Creating an Adoption-Friendly Workplace
www.adoptionfriendlyworkplace.org
"How to Lobby Your Employer for Adoption Benefits" by Elizabeth
    Mair
www.adoptivefamilies.com/articles.php?aid=168

Benefits Guides
www.benefitsguides.com

Military Adoption Benefits
military.adoption.com/army/military-adoption-benefits.html

Adoption Loans

Adoption Network Law Center
www.adoptionnetwork.com/adoptiveparents/credit-based-adoption-
    loans.shtml
toll-free number: (800) FOR-ADOPT
e-mail: info@adoptionpro.com

National Adoption Foundation
100 Mill Plain Rd.
Danbury, CT 06811
www.nafadopt.org

Adoption Grants

Lifetime Adoption Foundation
Adoption Grants
PO Box 1116
Nevada City, CA 95959
phone: (530) 432-7383
www.lifetimefoundation.org

WACAP Financial Assistance Programs
PO Box 88948
Seattle, WA 98138
phone: (206) 575-4550
toll-free number: (800) 732-1887
fax: (206) 575-4148
www.wacap.org/FinancialAssistance.asp

The Dave Thomas Foundation for Adoption
4150 Tuller Rd., Suite 204
Dublin, OH 43017

toll-free number: (800) ASK-DTFA or (800) 275-3832
e-mail: adoption@wendys.com
www.davethomasfoundation.com/index.asp

Fore Adoption Foundation
For pending adoptions
www.foreadoption.com/grant/

Gift of Adoption Fund
101 East Pier St., 1st Floor
Port Washington, WI 53074
phone: (262) 268-1386
toll-free number: (877) 905-ADOP (2367)
fax: (262) 268-1387
e-mail: info@giftofadoption.org
www.giftofadoption.org/grant.asp

National Adoption Foundation
NAF Grant Program
100 Mill Plain Rd.
Danbury, CT 06811
www.nafadopt.org

A Child Waits
For Eastern European adoptions
1136 Barker Rd.
Pittsfield, MA 01201
phone: (866) 999-CHILD (2445)
fax: (518) 794-6243
e-mail: cnelson@achildwaits.org
www.achildwaits.org

Federal Adoption Tax Credit

Information on the Adoption Tax Credit from the IRS:
www.irs.gov/taxtopics/tc607.html

Form 8839—Tax Benefits for Adoption:
www.irs.gov/instructions/i8839

Adoption Taxpayer Identification Number:
www.irs.gov/individuals/article/0,,id=96452,00.html

"The Adoption Tax Credit Explained," by Mark McDermott
www.adoptivefamilies.com/articles.php?aid=377

Adoption Insurance

Adoption Assurance
www.adoptionassurance.com/home.aspx

Foster-Adoption Waiting Children

Freddie Mac Foundation Wednesday's Child
www.adopt.org/wednesdayschild
Has links to local Wednesday's Child programs nationwide.

New York's Wednesday's Child Program
www.nyc.gov/html/acs/html/become_parent/wednesdays_child.shtml

Adoption Assistance for Children Adopted from Foster Care
A Fact Sheet for Families:
Child Welfare Information Gateway
www.childwelfare.gov/pubs/f_subsid.cfm

Special-Needs Adoption

North American Council on Adoptable Children
Subsidies to help parents pay for ongoing treatments:
www.nacac.org/adoptionsubsidy.html

Adoption Subsidy
www.adopting.org/adoptions/adoption-subsidy-negotiating-and-
renegotiating-your-childs-contract.html

Other Resources for Financing

Adoption Subsidies by State
Nonrecurring Adoption Expense Reimbursement
Families who adopt from the public system may be eligible for
reimbursement for some adoption-related expenses
www.nacac.org/subsidy_stateprofiles.html

Military Subsidies
www.childwelfare.gov/pubs/f_milita.cfm

National Endowment for Financial Education
"How to Make Adoption an Affordable Option"
phone: (888) 878-3256 (item #508-F)
www.nefe.org/adoption

Burke Family's Web Site
List of adoption funding sources
www.angelfire.com/journal/adoptionhelp/adopthelp.html

Chapter 3
The Infamous and Anxiety-Provoking Home Study

Online Discussion Boards for Home-Study Process
Thinking About the Home Study—Adoption Journals
journals.adoption.com

home-study.adoption.com

Chapter 4
Beginning a Domestic Adoption

Agencies

Below is a sampling of national adoption agencies. A more comprehensive list can be found in the *Adoptive Families* Adoption Guide, www.adoptivefamilies.com/adoptionguide.php, or at www.adoption.com.

A.A.C. Adoption
735 E. Hwy 56
PO Box W
Berthold, CO 80513
phone: (917) 532-3576
(303) 444-5001
e-mail: aacadopt@frii.com
www.aacadoption.com
Also has offices in Utah.
Specializing in Korean and Chinese adoption.

Adoption Alliance
7303 Blanco Rd.
San Antonio, TX 78216
phone: (210) 349-3991
toll-free number: (800) 626-4324
www.adoption-alliance.com
Specializing in domestic adoption.

Adoptions from the Heart—Main Office
30-31 Hampstead Circle
Wynnewood, PA 19096
phone: (610) 642-7200
toll-free number: (800) 355-5500
www.adoptionsfromtheheart.org

Specializing in domestic adoption and international adoption from
China, Guatemala, India, Kazakhstan, Lithuania, Russia,
Ukraine and Vietnam.

Bethany Christian Services
901 Eastern Ave. NE
PO Box 294
Grand Rapids, MI 49501-0294
phone: (616) 224-7610
e-mail: info@bethany.org
Specializing in domestic adoption and international adoption from
Albania, China, Colombia, Guatemala, Haiti, Hong Kong, India,
Lithuania, Philippines, Russia, South Korea and Ukraine.

The Gladney Center for Adoption
6300 John Ryan Dr.
Fort Worth, TX 76132-4122
phone: (817) 922-6000
toll-free number: (800) GLADNEY
www.adoptionsbygladney.com
Also has offices in New York.
Specializing in domestic adoptions and international adoptions
from China, Colombia, Ethiopia, Guatemala, Kazakhstan,
Russia and Ukraine.

Spence-Chapin
6 East 94th St.
New York, NY 10128
phone: (212) 369-0300
e-mail: info@spence-chapin.org
Specializing in adoptions from Asia, Eastern Europe, Latin
America, and the United States.

Wide Horizons for Children
38 Edge Hill Rd.
Waltham, MA 02451
phone: (781) 894-5330
e-mail: contact@whfc.org
www.rainbowkids.com/widehorizonsagency.htm
Specializing in domestic adoption and international adoptions from
    China, Colombia, Ethiopia, Guatemala, India, Korea, Moldova,
    Philippines, Russia and Ukraine.

World Association for Children and Parents (WACAP)
    (pronounced Way-cap)
PO Box 88948
Seattle, WA 98138
toll-free number: (800) 732-1887
www.wacap.org
Specializing in domestic adoption and international adoptions from
    China, India, Korea, Romania, Russia and Thailand.

Adoption.com's online database of agencies may be found at
directory.adoption.com/services/Adoption_Agencies.html

Attorneys

American Academy of Adoption Attorneys
PO Box 33053
Washington, DC 20033
phone: (202) 832-2222
e-mail: info@adoptionattorneys.org
www.adoptionattorneys.org
A directory of all member attorneys can be found on the AAAA
    Web site.

Chapter 5
Managing a Domestic Adoption

Letters to Birth Mothers

For more information on drafting your birth mother letter, please see the following Web sites and book:

www.openadopt.org/families/index.html
www.parentprofiles.com/
www.adoptionhelp.org/families/index.html
www.linkadoption.com/adprof.htm

Dear Birthmother, Thank You for Our Baby
Kathleen Silber & Phylis Speedlin (Corona Publishing, 1998)

Adoptive-Parent Profile Professionals

For more information on preparing your adoptive-parent profile using professional support, see the following:

Adoption Profiles, L.L.C.
459 N. Gilbert Rd., Suite C-121
Gilbert, AZ 85234
phone: (480) 633-3006
toll-free number: (800) FAMILY-NOW
fax: 480-894-2338
www.parentprofiles.com

Adoption Network Law Center
toll-free number: (800) FOR-ADOPT
adoptionnetwork.com/adoptiveparents/parentsintake.shtml

Adoption Profile Assistance
toll-free number: (866) 741-8989
www.adoptionprofileassistance.com/contact.html

Daisy Profiles
www.daisyprofiles.com

Lisa O'Hair
750 2nd St. NW
Hickory, NC 28601
phone: (828) 322-2192
cell: (828) 244-2790
e-mail: lohair@charter.net

Chapter 6
Waiting for Placement

Adoptive Breast-feeding

Newman-Goldfarb Protocols for Induced Lactation
www.asklenore.com/breastfeeding/abindex.html

The Adoptive Breastfeeding Resource Website
www.fourfriends.com/abrw

LaLeche League International
1400 N. Meacham Rd.
Schaumburg, IL 60173-4808
phone: (847) 519-7730
www.lalecheleague.org/NB/NBadoptive.html

Suggested Reading

Breastfeeding the Adopted Baby
Debra Stewart Peterson (Corona, rev. ed., 1994)

*Breastfeeding Book: Everything You Need to Know about Nursing Your
    Child from Birth through Weaning*
Martha Sears (Little, Brown & Co., 2000)

The Nursing Mother's Companion
Kathleen Huggins (Harvard Common Press, 2005)

The Nursing Mother's Problem Solver
Claire Martin (Simon & Schuster, 2000)

Ultimate Breastfeeding Book of Answers: The Most Comprehensive Problem-Solution Guide to Breastfeeding from the Foremost Expert in North America
Jack Newman, MD, and Teresa Pitman (Crown Publishing Group, 2000)

Chapter 7
Bringing Baby Home

Travel Agencies

Access Travel
Sue Sorrels
4020 North MacArthur, #118
Irving, TX 75038
toll-free number: (800) 345-8894
fax: (972) 717-1751
e-mail: accessirving@worldnet.att.net

All Ways International Travel Agency
225 West 34th St., Suite 2001
New York, NY 10122
phone: (212) 947-0505
fax: (212) 947-7197
www.awintl.com

Federal Travel's Adoption Travel Services
www.federaltravel.com/index2

Lotus Travel, Inc.
lotustours.net

Baby Travel Paraphernalia

Air Travel Security Vest
Baby B'Air Infant Products Flight Vest Travel Harness
www.babyuniverse.com
www.onestepahead.com

Hands-Free Car Seat Bag
Car Seat Carrier by Dex Products
www.babyabby.com

See also:

Babybjörn front carrier, available online and at almost every baby store (they even make one out of a mesh material for hot climates!)

Baby sling like the New Native Baby Carrier available online at www.newnativebaby.com

A good selection of hip carriers and slings available at www.mammasmilk.com

One Step Ahead catalog, available online at www.onestepahead.com

Ride On Carry On convertible car seat/stroller

The Pac Back car seat back pack carrier

Eddie Bauer car seat travel bag available online at www.amazon.com

Stroller travel bags at www.stroller.com (available for many different models and in many different sizes). Please note that if you gate-check a stroller in a bag, it will be placed in the aircraft's hold and not separately checked; you will have to retrieve it with other oversize items at your airline's package desk. It is not recommended that you gate-check a stroller if you will need it when deplaning.

Doulas

A doula is a trained professional who can provide support during
labor or during your first few days home. She will take care
of the baby, cook meals, do laundry, even go shopping
for you! Please make sure to locate a postpartum
doula (different than a labor doula).
Some even have training in breast-feeding.

DONA International
PO Box 626
Jasper, IN 47547
phone: (888) 788-DONA (3662)
fax: (812) 634-1491
www.dona.org

See also:
www.childbirth.org/doula123.html

Postadoption Depression Suggested Reading

Post-Adoption Blues: Overcoming the Unforseen Challenges of Adoption
Karen J. Foli and John R. Thompson (Rodale Press, Inc., 2004)

Down Came the Rain: My Journey Through Postpartum Depression
Brooke Shields (Hyperion, 2005)

"You're Not Alone: Addressing the Common Problem of Post
    Adoption Depression" by Kelly Burgess
iparentingadoption.com/resources/articles/postadoption.htm

Post Adoption Depression—The Silence and the Secrecy
First printed in *Adoptions from the Heart* newsletter, Summer 2003
www.rainbowkids.com/2004/07/attachment/post_adoption_
    depression.chtml

Parenting Books

The following is a list of suggested titles on parenting and caring for a newborn or infant. By all means locate other books; this is merely a suggested reading list.

The Baby Book: Everything You Need to Know about Your Baby from Birth to Age Two (Revised and Updated)
William M. Sears, Martha Sears, Robert Sears and James Sears (Little, Brown & Company, 2003)

Dr. Spock's Baby and Child Care
Benjamin Spock, concept by Robert Needlman (Simon & Schuster Adult Publishing Group, 2004)

Healthy Sleep Habits, Happy Child
Marc Weissbluth (Ballantine Publishing Group, 1999)

The No-Cry Sleep Solution: Gentle Ways to Help Your Baby Sleep Through the Night
Elizabeth Pantley (McGraw-Hill Companies, 2002)

Secrets of the Baby Whisperer: How to Calm, Connect, and Communicate With Your Baby
Traci Hogg with Melinda Blau (Random House, Inc., 2002)

The Sleep Book for Tired Parents
Becky Huntley (Parenting Press, Inc., 1991)

Touchpoints Essential Reference: Your Child's Emotional and Behavioral Development: Birth to Three
T. Berry Brazelton (Perseus Publishing, 1994)

What to Expect the First Year
Heidi E. Murkoff, Arlene Eisenberg and Sandee Hathaway (Workman Publishing Co., Inc., 2003)

What to Expect the Toddler Years
Heidi E. Murkoff, Arlene Eisenberg and Sandee Hathaway
(Workman Publishing Co., Inc., 1996)

Your Baby and Child: From Birth to Age Five
Penelope Leach (Knopf Publishing Group, 1997)

Chapter 8
Managing an International Adoption

Agencies

Below is a sampling of national adoption agencies. A more comprehensive list can be found in the *Adoptive Families* Adoption Guide (www.adoptivefamilies.com/adoptionguide.php) or on www.adoption.com.

A.A.C. Adoption
735 E. Hwy 56
PO Box W
Berthold, CO 80513
phone: (917) 532-3576
fax: (303) 444-5001
e-mail: aacadopt@frii.com
www.aacadoption.com
Also has offices in Utah.
Specializing in Korean and Chinese adoption.

Adoption Alliance
7303 Blanco Rd.
San Antonio, TX 78216
phone: (210) 349-3991
toll-free number: (800) 626-4324
www.adoption-alliance.com
Specializing in domestic adoption.

Adoptions from the Heart—Main Office
30-31 Hampstead Circle
Wynnewood, PA 19096
phone: (610) 642-7200
toll-free number: (800) 355-5500
www.adoptionsfromtheheart.org
Specializing in domestic adoption and international adoption from
China, Guatemala, India, Kazakhstan, Lithuania, Russia,
Ukraine and Vietnam.

Bethany Christian Services
901 Eastern Ave NE
PO Box 294
Grand Rapids, MI 49501-0294
phone: (616) 224-7610
e-mail: info@bethany.org
www.bethany.org
Specializing in domestic adoption and international adoption from
Albania, China, Colombia, Guatemala, Haiti, Hong Kong, India,
Lithuania, Philippines, Russia, South Korea and Ukraine.

The Gladney Center for Adoption
6300 John Ryan Dr.
Fort Worth, TX 76132-4122
phone: (817) 922-6000
toll-free number: (800) GLADNEY
www.adoptionsbygladney.com
Also has offices in New York.
Specializing in domestic adoptions and international adoptions
from China, Colombia, Ethiopia, Guatemala, Kazakhstan,
Russia and Ukraine.

Spence-Chapin
6 East 94th St.
New York, NY 10128
phone: (212) 369-0300

e-mail: info@spence-chapin.org
www.spence-chapin.org
Specializing in adoptions from Asia, Eastern Europe, Latin America
and the United States.

Wide Horizons for Children
38 Edge Hill Rd.
Waltham, MA 02451
phone: (781) 894-5330
e-mail: contact@whfc.org
www.rainbowkids.com/widehorizonsagency.htm
Specializing in domestic adoption and international adoptions from
China, Colombia, Ethiopia, Guatemala, India, Korea, Moldov,
Philippines, Russia and Ukraine.

World Association for Children and Parents (WACAP)
(pronounced Way-cap)
PO Box 88948
Seattle, WA 98138
toll-free number: (800) 732-1887
www.wacap.org
Specializing in domestic adoption and international adoptions from
China, India, Korea, Romania, Russia and Thailand.

Adoption.com's online database of agencies can be found at
directory.adoption.com/services/Adoption_Agencies.html

Attorneys

American Academy of Adoption Attorneys
PO Box 33053
Washington, DC 20033
phone: (202) 832-2222
e-mail: info@adoptionattorneys.org
www.adoptionattorneys.org
A directory of all member attorneys can be found on the AAAA
Web site.

Country-Specific Information Sites

United States Department of State International Adoption Country-Specific Information
travel.state.gov/family/adoption/country/country_369.html

International Adoption
international.adoption.com

RainbowKids.com: The International Adoption Publication
www.rainbowkids.com/countries

Joint Council on International Children's Services
www.jcics.org/country_information.htm

Dossier Services

The following provides a sample of the services available to assist you in preparing your dossier.

Legal-Eaze
Legal-Eaze CT Headquarters
290 Willow Rd.
Guilford, CT 06437
phone: (203) 458-6007
fax: (203) 458-6008
e-mail: ctoffice@legal-eaze.com

Legal-Eaze NYC Office
366 Amsterdam Ave., Suite 275
New York, NY 10024
phone: (845) 642-2990
e-mail: nyoffice@legal-eaze.com

The Paper Midwife
Jill S. Touloukian
International Adoption Dossier Services
3790 El Camino Real #114
Palo Alto, CA 94306

phone: (650) 465-0137
(fax) 650 329-9907
www.papermidwife.com

World Partners Adoption, Inc.
Cindy Harding, Executive Director
2205 Summit Oaks Ct.
Lawrenceville, GA 30043
phone: (770) 962-7860
toll-free number: (800) 350-7338
Fax: (770) 513-7767
(Office hours 9:00 A.M.–5:00 P.M. Eastern Standard Time)
e-mail: wpadopt@aol.com

Over the Rainbow Dossier
Sherry Majewski, Dossier Preparer
Lambertville, MI
phone: (734) 856-8584
e-mail: overtherainbowdossier@yahoo.com

Journey of Love Dossier Service
Teresa Baldinucci
phone: (516) 662-2831
e-mail: dosdoula@optonline.net

ABC International Dossier Services, Inc.
Pam Eidson
13614 Las Brisas Way
Jacksonville, FL 32224
phone: (904) 221-6068
e-mail: eidson91@comcast.net

Adoption CoordiNations
Sonia Baxter
612 Center Ave.
Pittsburgh, PA 15215

phone: (412) 781-7343
fax: (412) 781-6718
e-mail: soniabee@aol.com
hometown.aol.com/soniabee

Adoption Ark
phone: (510) 235-3818
toll-free number: (877) 889-3192
e-mail: adopt@adoptionark.com or kids@adoptionark.com
www.adoptionark.com

European Children Adoption Services
6050 Cheshire Lane North
Plymouth, MN 55446
phone: (763) 694-6131
fax: (763) 694-6104
e-mail: info@ecasus.org

Genesis Adoptions
Main Office
phone: (678) 518-3911
fax: (678) 518-3919
Central South Georgia Office
Tammy Freilich, Director
phone: (678) 432-9118
fax: (770) 957-3549

West Coast Branch Office
Jennifer Greenfield, Attorney at Law
706 Aquarius Way
La Grande, OR 97850
phone: (541) 963-9639
fax: (541) 963-9219

Chapter 9
Preparing for Parenthood

Travel Agencies

Access Travel
Sue Sorrels
4020 North MacArthur, #118
Irving, TX 75038
toll-free number: (800) 345-8894
fax: (972) 717-1751
e-mail: accessirving@worldnet.att.net

All Ways International Travel Agency
225 West 34th St., Suite 2001
New York, NY 10122
phone: (212) 947-0505
fax: (212) 947-7197
www.awintl.com/home.html

Federal Travel Adoption Travel Services
travelagency.net

Lotus Travel, Inc.
lotustours.net

Airlines

EVA Airways Corp.
www.evaair.com/html/b2c/english

Northwest Airlines Special Delivery
www.nwa.com/features/adopt.shtml

Baby Travel Paraphernalia

Air Travel Security Vest
Baby B'Air Infant Products Flight Vest Travel Harness
www.babyuniverse.com
www.onestepahead.com

Hands-Free Car Seat Bag
Car Seat Carrier by Dex Products
www.babyabby.com

See also:

Babybjörn front carrier, available online and at almost every baby store (they even make one out of a mesh material for hot climates!)

Baby sling like the New Native Baby Carrier available online at www.newnativebaby.com

A good selection of hip carriers and slings available at www.mammasmilk.com

One Step Ahead catalog, available online at www.onestepahead.com

Ride On Carry On convertible car seat/stroller

The Pac Back car seat back pack carrier

Eddie Bauer car seat travel bag available online at www.amazon.com

Stroller travel bags at www.stroller.com (available for many different models and in many different sizes). Please note that if you gate-check a stroller in a bag, it will be placed in the aircraft's hold and not separately checked; you will have to retrieve it with other oversize items at your airline's package desk. It is not recommended that you gate-check a stroller if you will need it when deplaning.

Parenting Books

The following is a list of suggested titles on parenting and caring for a newborn. By all means locate other books; this is merely a suggested reading list.

The Baby Book: Everything You Need to Know About Your Baby From Birth to Age Two (Revised and Updated)
William M. Sears, Martha Sears, Robert Sears and James Sears (Little, Brown & Company, 2003)

Dr. Spock's Baby and Child Care
Benjamin Spock, Concept by Robert Needlman (Simon & Schuster Adult Publishing Group, 2004)

Healthy Sleep Habits, Happy Child
Marc Weissbluth (Ballantine Publishing Group, 1999)

The No-Cry Sleep Solution: Gentle Ways to Help Your Baby Sleep Through the Night
Elizabeth Pantley (McGraw-Hill Companies, 2002)

Secrets of the Baby Whisperer: How to Calm, Connect, and Communicate With Your Baby
Traci Hogg with Melinda Blau (Random House, Inc., 2002)

The Sleep Book for Tired Parents
Becky Huntley (Parenting Press, Inc., 1991)

Touchpoints Essential Reference: Your Child's Emotional and Behavioral Development: Birth to Three
T. Berry Brazelton (Perseus Publishing, 1994)

What to Expect the First Year
Heidi E. Murkoff, Arlene Eisenberg and Sandee Hathaway (Workman Publishing Co., Inc., 2003)

What to Expect the Toddler Years
Heidi E. Murkoff, Arlene Eisenberg and Sandee Hathaway (Workman Publishing Co., Inc., 1996)

Your Baby and Child: From Birth to Age Five
Penelope Leach (Knopf Publishing Group, 1997)

Travel Immunization Recommendations

Centers for Disease Control and Prevention
www.cdc.gov/travel/vaccinat.htm

International Travel Medicine
www.travelmedicine.com/index.htm

International Adoptive Medicine Pediatricians

American Academy of Pediatrics
Contact: Mary Crane
e-mail: adoption@aap.org
www.aap.org/sections/adoption

Jane Aronson, MD
151 East 62nd St., Suite A
New York, NY 10021
phone: (212) 207-6666
www.orphandoctor.com

International Adoption Clinics
www.chinaconnectiononline.com/clinics.htm

International Adoption Medical Clinics
www.comeunity.com/adoption/health/clinics.html

Patrick Mason, MD, PhD
International Adoption Center
8505 Arlington Blvd., Suite 100
Fairfax, VA 22031
phone: (703) 970-2651

Schneider Children's Hospital Evaluation Center for Adoption
269-01 76th Ave.
New Hyde Park, NY 11040
phone: (718) or (516) 470-3000
www.schneiderchildrenshospital.org

Tufts New England Medical Center International Adoption Clinic
750 Washington St.
Boston, MA 02111
phone: (617) 636-5000
www.nemc.org/adoption

Yale Adoption Clinic
333 Cedars St.
PO Box 208064
New Haven, CT 06520-8064
phone: (203) 737-1623
www.yalemedicalgroup.org

Breast-feeding

Newman-Goldfarb Protocols for Induced Lactation
www.asklenore.com/breastfeeding/abindex.html

The Adoptive Breastfeeding Resource Website
www.fourfriends.com/abrw

LaLeche League International
1400 N. Meacham Rd.
Schaumburg, IL 60173-4808
phone: (847) 519-7730
www.lalecheleague.org/NB/NBadoptive.html

Suggested Reading

Breastfeeding the Adopted Baby
Debra Stewart Peterson (Corona, rev. ed., 1994)

*Breastfeeding Book: Everything You Need to Know about Nursing Your
    Child from Birth through Weaning*
Martha Sears (Little, Brown & Co., 2000)

The Nursing Mother's Companion
Kathleen Huggins (Harvard Common Press, 2005)

The Nursing Mother's Problem Solver
Claire Martin (Simon & Schuster, 2000)

*Ultimate Breastfeeding Book of Answers: The Most Comprehensive
Problem-Solution Guide to Breastfeeding from the Foremost Expert
in North America*
Jack Newman, MD, and Teresa Pitman (Crown Publishing Group,
2000)

Chapter 10
Bringing Baby Home

Doulas

A doula is a trained professional who can provide support during
labor or during your first few days home. She will take care
of the baby, cook meals, do laundry, even go shopping
for you! Please make sure to locate a postpartum
doula (different than a labor doula).
Some even have training in breast-feeding.

DONA International
PO Box 626
Jasper, IN 47547
toll-free number: (888) 788-DONA (3662)
fax: (812) 634-1491
www.dona.org

See also:
www.childbirth.org/doula123.html

Books on Attachment Issues and Attachment Parenting

Attaching in Adoption: Practical Tools for Today's Parents
Deborah D. Gray (Perspectives Press, 2002)

*The Attachment Parenting Book: A Commonsense Guide to
Understanding and Nurturing Your Baby*
Martha Sears, Deborah Baker (ed.) (Little, Brown & Co., 2001)

Launching a Baby's Adoption
Patricia Irwin Johnston (Perspectives Press, 1998)

Raising Adopted Children: Practical, Reassuring Advice for Every
  Adoptive Parent
Lois Ruskin Melina (Harper Perennial, 1998)

Postadoption Depression

Post-Adoption Blues: Overcoming the Unforseen Challenges of Adoption
Karen J. Foli and John R. Thompson (Rodale Press, Inc., 2004)

Down Came the Rain: My Journey Through Postpartum Depression
Brooke Shields (Hyperion, 2005)

"You're Not Alone: Addressing the Common Problem of Post
  Adoption Depression" by Kelly Burgess
iparentingadoption.com/resources/articles/postadoption.htm

Post Adoption Depression—The Silence and the Secrecy
First printed in *Adoptions from the Heart* newsletter, Summer 2003
www.rainbowkids.com/2004/07/attachment/post_adoption_
  depression.chtml

Afterword
Please see the chapter 1 resource list for adoptive-parent support
groups and national organizations that may be of assistance to you.

Suggested Reading
Do not let me limit you; there are a myriad
of wonderful titles on adoption!

Adoption Is a Family Affair! What Relatives and Friends Must Know
Patricia Irwin Johnston (Perspectives Press, 2001)

Adoption Nation: How the Adoption Revolution is Transforming America
Adam Pertman (Basic Books, 2000)

Adopting After Infertility
Patricia Irwin Johnston (Perspectives Press, 1992)

Attaching in Adoption: Practical Tools for Today's Parents
Deborah D. Gray (Perspectives Press, 2002)

Creating Ceremonies: Innovative Ways to Meet Adoption Challenges
Cheryl A. Lieberman, PhD Rhea K. Bufford, LICSW (Zeig, Tucker
   & Co., 1999)

Family Bound: One Couple's Journey Through Infertility and Adoption
Carrie Ostrea (iUniverse, 2003)

Family Nobody Wanted
Helen Grigsby Doss (Northeastern Univ. Press, 2001)

Launching a Baby's Adoption
Patricia Irwin Johnston (Perspectives Press, 1998)

Lifebooks: Creating a Treasure for the Adopted Child
Beth O'Malley, MEd (Adoption-Works, 2004)

The Open Adoption Experience
Lois Ruskin Melina, Sharon Kaplan Roszia (Harper Perennial, 2003)

*Raising Adopted Children: Practical, Reassuring Advice for Every
   Adoptive Parent*
Lois Ruskin Melina (Harper Perennial, 1998)

Secret Thoughts of an Adoptive Mother
Jana Wolf (Vista Communications, 2000)

STATE ADOPTION LAWS

The Search

The following is an analysis of state adoption laws as they may pertain to your search for a birth family.

Please check with a member of the American Academy of Adoption Attorneys who is practicing in your state before relying on any of the information set forth herein. A local practitioner will know the specific laws relevant to your particular situation.

The following summaries also include citations to the pertinent sections of the states' laws, to help direct and define your conversation (if any) with your adoption professional. Should you and your adoption professional need to discuss one of the issues addressed in the following table in greater detail, you will be able to direct your adoption professional to the statutory basis for your thoughts or concerns.

Please note, however, that the following table presents a summary of the law and is not intended to be exhaustive.

Does this state require that an adoption agency be involved in my adoption?[1]	May I advertise in this state to locate a birth mother?	Does this state permit me to use a facilitator to help me locate a birth mother?

Alabama

No Ala. Code § 26-10A-34 (2006).	No. It is unlawful for any person, organization, hospital or agency to advertise verbally, through print, electronic media or otherwise that they will adopt children or assist in the adoption of children. Ala. Code § 26-10A-36 (2006).	No. It is a felony for any person or agency to receive any money or other thing of value for placing, assisting or arranging a placement of a minor. Ala. Code § 26-10A-34 (2006).

Alaska

No Alaska Stat. Tit. 25, Ch. 23 §§ 5-240 (Mitchie 2006).	Alaska statutes do not address advertising. Please check with a local practitioner for advertising practices in this state. Alaska Stat. Tit. 25, Ch. 23 §§ 5-240 (Mitchie 2006).	Not clear; probably not. Alaska statutes do not address the use of facilitators. Alaska Stat. Tit. 25, Ch. 23 §§ 5-240 (Mitchie 2006).

1. Please note that while a state may require an agency to be involved in your adoption, you also may be permitted to work with a private attorney toward an adoption. You do not necessarily need to use an agency to locate the birth mother, but rather the agency may need to be involved for actual placement and finalization with the court. Please check with independent legal counsel located in your jurisdiction before relying on any statements or representations contained herein, as laws change frequently.

Does this state require that an adoption agency be involved in my adoption?	May I advertise in this state to locate a birth mother?	Does this state permit me to use a facilitator to help me locate a birth mother?

Arizona

No *See, e.g.,* Ariz. Rev. Stat. § 8-130 (C) (2006).	The Arizona statutes do not address advertising. Please check with a local practitioner for advertising practices in this state. Ariz. Rev. Stat. §§ 8-101–8-135 (2006).	No. It is illegal for any person not employed by an adoption agency licensed by the state of Arizona to solicit or accept employment for compensation by or on behalf of a parent or guardian for placement of a child for adoption or to locate a child for adoption. Ariz. Rev. Stat. § 8-130 (B) (1) & (2) (2006).

Arkansas

No *See, e.g.,* Ark. Code Ann. § 9-9-211 (5) (Mitchie 2006).	Arkansas statutes do not address advertising. Please check with a local practitioner for advertising practices in this state. Ark. Code Ann. §§ 9-9-101–9-9-224 (Mitchie 2006).	Not clear; probably not. Arkansas statutes do not address the use of facilitators. *See, e.g.,* Ark. Code Ann. § 9-9-211 (5) (Mitchie 2006).

Does this state require that an adoption agency be involved in my adoption?	May I advertise in this state to locate a birth mother?	Does this state permit me to use a facilitator to help me locate a birth mother?

California

| No | No. Only licensed persons or agencies may place advertisements. | Yes. The state also licenses and regulates the operation of facilitators. |
| *See, e.g.,* Cal. Code § 8610 (b) (West 2006). | Cal. Code § 8609(a) (West 2006). | Cal. Code §§ 8623– 8638 (West 2006). |

Colorado

| Yes | Colorado statutes do not address advertising. Please check with a local practitioner for advertising practices in this state. | No. Only agencies, physicians and attorneys may serve as paid intermediaries. |
| Col. Rev. Stat. § 19-5-205.5 (West 2005). | Col. Rev. Stat. §§ 19-5-200.2–19-5-403 (West 2005). | Col. Rev. Stat. § 19-5-213 (West 2005). |

Connecticut

| Yes | Connecticut statutes do not address advertising. Please check with a local practitioner for advertising practices in this state. | Not clear; probably not. Connecticut statutes do not address the use of facilitators. |
| Conn. Gen. Stat. Chap. 803 § 45a-724a (2005). | Conn. Gen. Stat. Chap. 803 § 45a-728d (2005). | *See* Conn. Gen. Stat. Chap. 803 §§ 45a-706–770 (2005). |

Does this state require that an adoption agency be involved in my adoption?	May I advertise in this state to locate a birth mother?	Does this state permit me to use a facilitator to help me locate a birth mother?

Delaware

Yes	No	No
Del. Code. Ann. tit. 13, chap. 9 § 904 (2006).	Del. Code. Ann. tit. 13, chap. 9 § 930 (2006).	Del. Code. Ann. tit. 13, chap. 9 §§ 904 & 906 (2006).

District of Columbia

Yes	D.C. statutes do not address advertising. Please check with a local practitioner for advertising practices in the District. D.C. Code Ann §§ 16-301-316, 4-1401–1410 (2006).	No
D.C. Code Ann. § 4-1405(a) (2006).		D.C. Code Ann. § 4-1410 (2006).

Florida

No	No. Only a licensed or registered adoption entity may place advertisements. *See* Fla. Stat. Ch. 63.212 (1)(g) (2005).	No
See Fla. Stat. Ch. 63.032 (3) (2005)		*See* Fla. Stat. Ch. 63-032, 63.039 & 63.085 (2005).

Does this state require that an adoption agency be involved in my adoption?	May I advertise in this state to locate a birth mother?	Does this state permit me to use a facilitator to help me locate a birth mother?

Georgia

No	No	No
See Ga. Code Ann. § 19-8-1(3) (2004).	Ga. Code Ann. § 19-8-24(a) (2004).	Ga. Code Ann. § 19-8-24(a)(2) (2004).

Hawaii

No Haw. Rev. Stat. § 578-2 (2006).	Hawaii statutes do not address advertising. Please check with a local practitioner for advertising practices in this state. *See* Haw. Rev. Stat. Ann. §§ 578-1–578-17 (Michie 2005).	Not clear; probably not. Hawaii statutes do not address the use of facilitators. *See* Haw. Rev. Stat. Ann. §§ 578-1–578-17 (Michie 2005).

Idaho

No Idaho Code § 16-1504 (2005); Idaho Code § 18-1512(A) (4) (2005).	Only an authorized agent or employee of Idaho's Department of Health and Human Services may advertise in furtherance of an adoption. Idaho Code § 18-1512(A) (2).	Not clear; probably not. Idaho statutes do not address the use of facilitators. *See* Idaho Code § 18-1511 (2005).

Does this state require that an adoption agency be involved in my adoption?	May I advertise in this state to locate a birth mother?	Does this state permit me to use a facilitator to help me locate a birth mother?

Illinois

No *See* 720 Ill. Comp. Stat. § 525/4.1 (g) (West 2005).	Illinois statutes do not address advertising. Please check with a local practitioner for advertising practices in this state. *See* 720 Ill. Comp. Stat § 525/4.1 (West 2005).	Not clear; probably not. Illinois statutes do not address the use of facilitators. *See* 720 Ill. Comp. Stat. § 525/4.1 (g) (West 2005).

Indiana

Yes Ind. Code § 31-19-7-1 (2005).	Indiana statutes do not address advertising. Please check with a local practitioner for advertising practices in this state. *See* Ind. Code §§ 31–35 (2005).	No Ind. Code § 35-46-1-9(a) (2005).

Does this state require that an adoption agency be involved in my adoption?	May I advertise in this state to locate a birth mother?	Does this state permit me to use a facilitator to help me locate a birth mother?

Iowa

No *See* Iowa Code § 600.1–600.25 (2004)	Iowa statutes do not address advertising. Please check with a local practitioner for advertising practices in this state. *See* Iowa Code § 600.1–600.25 (2004).	Yes Iowa Code § 600.9 ("Any person assisting in any way with the placement or adoption of a minor person shall not charge a fee which is more than usual, necessary, and commensurate with the services rendered") (2004).

Kansas

Yes Kan. Stat. Ann. § 59-2112 (c) (2005).	No. Only a licensed adoption agency may advertise. Kan. Stat. Ann. § 59-2123 (a)(1) & (b)-(c)(1) (2005).	No Kan. Stat. Ann. § 59-2123 (a)(2)-(a)(3) (2005).

Kentucky

No Ky. Rev. Stat. Ann. § 199.590 (3) (2005).	No Ky. Rev. Stat. Ann. § 199.590 (1) (2005).	No Ky. Rev. Stat. Ann. § 199.590 (3) (2005).

Does this state require that an adoption agency be involved in my adoption?	May I advertise in this state to locate a birth mother?	Does this state permit me to use a facilitator to help me locate a birth mother?

Louisiana

No	No	No
La. Children's Code § 1170 A (1)-(2) (2005).	La. Rev. Stat. Ann. § 46:1425 (A) (2005).	La. Rev. Stat. Ann. § 14:286 (B)-(C) (2005).

Maine

No	No. Only a licensed adoption agency may advertise.	Not clear; probably not. Maine statutes do not address the use of facilitators.
See Me. Rev. Stat. Ann. tit. 18A § 9-306 (West 2005).	Me. Rev. Stat. Ann. tit. 18A § 9-313 (West 2005).	*See* Me. Rev. Stat. Ann. tit. 18A § 9-306 (West 2005).

Maryland

No	Maryland statutes do not address advertising. Please check with a local practitioner for advertising practices in this state.	No
See, e.g., Md. Code Ann. Family Law § 5-3B02 (effective January 1, 2006).	*See* Md. Code Ann. Family Law §§ 5-3A-3B, 5-362 (effective January 1, 2006).	Md. Code Ann. Family Law §§ 5-362, 5-3B-32, 5-3A-45 (effective January 1, 2006).

Does this state require that an adoption agency be involved in my adoption?	May I advertise in this state to locate a birth mother?	Does this state permit me to use a facilitator to help me locate a birth mother?

Massachusetts

Yes Mass. Gen. Laws Ch. 28A § 11(c) (2005).	No. Only a licensed adoption agency may advertise. Mass. Gen. Laws Ch. 210 § 11A (2005); Mass Gen. Laws Ch. 28A § 14 (2005).	No Mass. Gen. Laws Ch. 210 § 11A (2005).

Michigan

No Mich. Comp. Laws §§ 710.23(a) (3), 710.55a (2005).	Michigan statutes do not address advertising. Please check with a local practitioner for advertising practices in this state. Mich. Comp. Laws §§ 710, 722 (2005).	Yes, but facilitators are defined as child-placing agencies or adoption attorneys. Mich. Comp. Laws §§ 710.55(1), 722.124b (c)-(d) (2005).

Minnesota

Yes Minn. Stat. §§ 259.22, 259.47 (2005).	Minnesota statutes do not address advertising. Please check with a local practitioner for advertising practices in this state. Minn. Stat. § 259 (2005).	No Minn. Stat. §§ 259.21, 259.47, 259.55 (2005).

Does this state require that an adoption agency be involved in my adoption?	May I advertise in this state to locate a birth mother?	Does this state permit me to use a facilitator to help me locate a birth mother?

Mississippi

Yes Miss. Code. Ann. §§ 93-17-5, 93-17-9 (2005).	Mississippi statutes do not address advertising. Please check with a local practitioner for advertising practices in this state. Miss. Code. Ann. § 93 (2005).	Not clear; probably not. Mississippi statutes do not address the use of facilitators. Miss. Code. Ann. § 93 (2005).

Missouri

No Mo. Rev. Stat. § 453.014 (2005).	Missouri statutes do not address advertising. Please check with a local practitioner for advertising practices in this state. Mo. Rev. Stat. §§ 453, 568 (2005).	No Mo. Rev. Stat. § 453.014 (2005); Mo. Rev. Stat. § 568.175 (2005). ("It is illegal to offer, give, receive or solicit money or any other form of consideration in exchange for delivery or offer of a child for adoption or consent to a future adoption.")

Does this state require that an adoption agency be involved in my adoption?	May I advertise in this state to locate a birth mother?	Does this state permit me to use a facilitator to help me locate a birth mother?

Montana

Yes Mont. Code Ann. § 42-2-301(4) (2005).	No. Only a licensed adoption agency may advertise. Mont. Code Ann. § 42-7-105 (1)(a) (2005).	No Mont. Code. Ann. § 42-7-105 (3) (2005).

Nebraska

Yes Neb. Rev. Stat. § 43-701 (2005).	No. Only a licensed adoption agency may advertise. Neb. Rev. Stat. § 43-701 (2005).	No Neb. Rev. Stat. § 43-701 (2005).

Nevada

Yes Nev. Rev. Stat. §§ 127.240, 127.285 (2005).	No Nev. Rev. Stat. § 127.310 (1)(b)-3 (2005).	No Nev. Rev. Stat. § 127.300 (2005).

Does this state require that an adoption agency be involved in my adoption?	May I advertise in this state to locate a birth mother?	Does this state permit me to use a facilitator to help me locate a birth mother?

New Hampshire

Yes N.H. Rev. Stat. Ann. § 170-B:5 (2005).	No. Only a licensed person or agency may advertise. N.H. Rev. Stat. Ann. §§ 170-B-E (2005).	Not clear; probably not. New Hampshire statutes do not address the use of facilitators. N.H. Rev. Stat. Ann. §§ 170-B-E (2005).

New Jersey

No. You may use an attorney, provided your home study was conducted through an approved agency. N.J. Stat. Ann. § 9:3-39.1 (2005).	New Jersey statutes do not address advertising. Please check with a local practitioner for advertising practices in this state. N.J. Stat. Ann. § 9:3-39.1 (2005).	No. N.J. Stat. Ann. § 9:3-39.1(d) (2005). ("A person, firm, partnership, corporation, association, intermediary or agency other than an approved agency which pays, seeks to pay, receives, or seeks to receive money or other valuable consideration in connection with the placement of a child for adoption shall be guilty of a crime. . . .")

Does this state require that an adoption agency be involved in my adoption?	May I advertise in this state to locate a birth mother?	Does this state permit me to use a facilitator to help me locate a birth mother?

New Mexico

Yes N.M. Stat. Ann. § 32A-5-12 (Michie 2005).	New Mexico statutes do not address advertising. Please check with a local practitioner for advertising practices in this state. N.M. Stat. Ann. § 32A (Michie 2005).	No, subject to certain exceptions. The exchange of information between persons regarding the existence of a potential adoptee or adoptive family is not prohibited. However, no one other than a licensed adoption agency may select or arrange for the selection of an adoptive family or adoptee. N.M. Stat. Ann. § 32A-5-42 (Michie 2005).

New York

No. You may use an attorney or agency for placement of a child for purposes of adoption. *See, e.g.,* N.Y. Dom. Rel. § 115 (1)(a) (McKinney 2005).	New York statutes do not address advertising. Please check with a local practitioner for advertising practices in this state. N.Y. Dom. Rel. § 115 (McKinney 2005).	Not clear; probably not. New York statutes do not address the use of facilitators. N.Y. Dom. Rel. § 115 (McKinney 2005).

Does this state require that an adoption agency be involved in my adoption?	May I advertise in this state to locate a birth mother?	Does this state permit me to use a facilitator to help me locate a birth mother?

North Carolina

Yes N.C. Gen. Stat. § 48-3-201 (2005).	No. Only a licensed agency may advertise. N.C. Gen Stat. § 48-10-101 (2005).	No. North Carolina prohibits a person or entity from giving or receiving compensation for placing or arranging for the placement of a child, except for those expenses authorized by other provisions in the statute (medical and legal services). N.C. Gen. Stat. §§ 48-3-202, 48-10-102, 48-10-103 (2005).

North Dakota

No. N.D. Cent. Code §§14-15-05, 50-06-01.4 (2005).	No. Only an agency licensed by the state may advertise in furtherance of the placement of a child through adoption. N.D. Cent. Code §§23-16-08, 50-11-06, 50-19-11, 50-12-17 (2005).	Yes, but only persons licensed by the department of human services may facilitate an adoption. N.D. Cent. Code §50-12-17 (2006).

Does this state require that an adoption agency be involved in my adoption?	May I advertise in this state to locate a birth mother?	Does this state permit me to use a facilitator to help me locate a birth mother?

Ohio

No. However, an attorney may not represent both the birth family and the adoptive parents. Ohio Rev. Code Ann. §3107.011 (West 2006).	No. Only an agency licensed by the State may advertise in furtherance of the placement of a child through adoption. Ohio Rev. Code Ann. §5103.17 (West 2006).	Any person may "informally aid or promote an adoption by making a person seeking to adopt . . . aware of a minor who will be or is available for adoption." Ohio Rev. Code Ann. §3107.011 (West 2006).

Oklahoma

Yes Okla. Stat. tit. 10 § 7503-2.1 (4) (2005).	No. Only a licensed agency may advertise. Okla. Stat. tit. 21 § 866 (A)(1)(e) (2005).	No Okla. Stat. tit. 21 § 866 (A)(1) (2005).

Oregon

Yes Or. Rev. Stat. §§ 109.309, 109.311 (3) (2003).	Yes. A licensed agency or person who has completed his or her home study and received a favorable recommendation may advertise. Or. Rev. Stat. § 109.311 (4) (2003).	No Or. Rev. Stat. § 109.311 (3) (2003).

Does this state require that an adoption agency be involved in my adoption?	May I advertise in this state to locate a birth mother?	Does this state permit me to use a facilitator to help me locate a birth mother?

Pennsylvania

| No. You may use an intermediary or facilitator, subject to certain limitations regarding payments. | Pennsylvania statutes do not address advertising. Please check with a local practitioner for advertising practices in this state. | Yes, subject to limitations regarding type and amount of payment to the facilitator. |
| *See* 23 Pa. Cons. Stat. §§ 2102, 2530, 2533 (2005). | 23 Pa. Cons. Stat. §§ 2102, 2530, 2533 (2005). | 23 Pa. Cons. Stat. § 2533 (d) (2005); 18 Pa. Cons. Stat. § 4305 (2005). |

Rhode Island

| Yes | Rhode Island statutes do not address advertising. Please check with a local practitioner for advertising practices in this state. | Not clear; probably not. Rhode Island statutes do not address the use of facilitators. |
| R.I. Gen. Laws § 15-7-4 (2005). | R.I. Gen. Laws § 15 (2005). | R.I. Gen. Laws § 15 (2005). |

South Carolina

| Yes | South Carolina statutes do not address advertising. Please check with a local practitioner for advertising practices in this state. | No |
| S.C. Code Ann. §§ 20-7-1650 (e), 20-7-1670 (2005). | S.C. Code Ann. §§ 20-7-1650–1690 (2005). | S.C. Code Ann. §§ 20-7-1690(F), 20-7-1650 (e) (2005). |

Does this state require that an adoption agency be involved in my adoption?	May I advertise in this state to locate a birth mother?	Does this state permit me to use a facilitator to help me locate a birth mother?

South Dakota

Yes S.D. Codified Laws § 25-6-8 (Michie 2005).	South Dakota statutes do not address advertising. Please check with a local practitioner for advertising practices in this state. S.D. Codified Laws § 25-6 (Michie 2005).	No. Offering, giving, or receiving unauthorized consideration for adoption is a felony under South Dakota laws. Any payment of any monies in connection with an adoption not otherwise approved by the court or fees charged by an agency are impermissible. S.D. Codified Laws §§ 25-6-4.2, 25-6-4.1 (Michie 2005).

Tennessee

Yes *See, e.g.,* Tenn. Code Ann. § 36-1-108 (2005).	Tennessee statutes do not address advertising. Please check with a local practitioner for advertising practices in this state. Tenn. Code Ann. § 36-1-108 (2005).	No. No person may receive payment for the placement or selection of a child for adoption, or arranging the bringing together of children and families. *See, e.g.,* Tenn. Code Ann. §§ 36-1-108(a), 36-1-109(a)(2) (2005).

Does this state require that an adoption agency be involved in my adoption?	May I advertise in this state to locate a birth mother?	Does this state permit me to use a facilitator to help me locate a birth mother?

Texas

Yes Texas Code Ann. § 162.05 (2005).	No. Only a licensed agency may advertise. Texas Code Ann. § 25.09 (2005).	No. Attorneys counseling parties to an adoption are exempt from the penalties for accepting payment for work in connection with an adoption. Texas Code Ann. §§ 25.08 (2), 162.025 (2005).

Does this state require that an adoption agency be involved in my adoption?	May I advertise in this state to locate a birth mother?	Does this state permit me to use a facilitator to help me locate a birth mother?

Utah

Yes.	No.	Yes, however, no money may be exchanged between the facilitator and prospective adoptive parents or any other party to the adoption.
Utah Code Ann. §62A-4a-602 (1) (2006).	Utah Code Ann. §62A-4a-602 (2) (b) (2006).	
However, "an attorney, physician, or other person may assist a parent in identifying or locating a person interested in adopting the parent's child, or in identifying or locating a child to be adopted. However, *no payment, charge, fee, reimbursement of expense, or exchange of value of any kind, or promise or agreement to make the same, may be made for that assistance.*"		Utah Code Ann. § 62A-4a-602 (2)(a) ("An attorney, physician, or other person may assist a parent in identifying or locating a person interested in adopting the parent's child, or in identifying or locating a child to be adopted. However, *no payment, charge, fee, reimbursement of expense, or exchange of value of any kind, or promise or agreement to make the same, may be made for that assistance.*" (emphasis added) (2006).
Utah Code Ann. § 62A-4a-602 (2)(a) (emphasis added) (2006).		

Does this state require that an adoption agency be involved in my adoption?	May I advertise in this state to locate a birth mother?	Does this state permit me to use a facilitator to help me locate a birth mother?

Vermont

Yes Vt. Stat. Ann. tit. 15A § 2-101 (a)-(d) (2005).	Vermont statutes do not address advertising. Please check with a local practitioner for advertising practices in this state. Vt. Stat. Ann. tit. 15A (2005).	No. "A person may not pay or give or offer to pay or give to any other person . . . or accept any money or anything of value, directly or indirectly for: (1) the placement of a minor for adoption; (2) the consent of a parent, a guardian, or an agency to the adoption of a minor; (3) the relinquishment of a minor to an agency for the purpose of adoption. . . ." Vt. Stat. Ann. tit. 15A § 7-105 (a) (2005).

Does this state require that an adoption agency be involved in my adoption?	May I advertise in this state to locate a birth mother?	Does this state permit me to use a facilitator to help me locate a birth mother?

Virginia

No. "The birth parent or legal guardian of a child may place his child for adoption directly with the adoptive parents of his choice. . . ." Va. Code Ann. § 63.2-1230 (2005).	No Va. Code Ann. § 63.2-1218 (2005).	No. "No person or child-placing agency shall charge, pay, give, or agree to give or accept any money, property, service or other thing of value in connection with a placement or adoption or any act undertaken pursuant to this chapter except (i) reasonable and customary services provided by a licensed or duly authorized child-placing agency and fees paid for such services. . . ." Va. Code Ann. § 63.2-1218 (2005).

Does this state require that an adoption agency be involved in my adoption?	May I advertise in this state to locate a birth mother?	Does this state permit me to use a facilitator to help me locate a birth mother?

Washington

No. You may utilize the services of an attorney or other intermediary or facilitator toward placement of a child or finalization of an adoption. *See, e.g.,* Wash. Rev. Code § 26.33.390 (2005).	Yes. Only a licensed agency or a person who has completed a home study with a favorable report may advertise. Wash. Rev. Code § 26.33.400 (2005).	Yes Wash. Rev. Code §§ 26.33.020(14)(o), 26.33.390(2)-(3) (2005).

West Virginia

Yes W. Va. Code § 49-3-1 (2005).	West Virginia statutes do not address advertising. Please check with a local practitioner for advertising practices in this state. W. VA. Code §§ 48–49 (2005).	No W. Va. Code § 48-22-803 (2005).

Does this state require that an adoption agency be involved in my adoption?	May I advertise in this state to locate a birth mother?	Does this state permit me to use a facilitator to help me locate a birth mother?

Wisconsin

No. You may be represented by an attorney. Wis. Stat. § 48.837 (1) ("A parent having custody of a child and the proposed adoptive parent or parents of the child may petition the court for placement of the child for adoption in the home of a person who is not a relative of the child if the home is licensed as a foster home or treatment foster home under *s. 48.62*"), and § 48.837 (8) ("The same attorney may not represent the adoptive parents and the birth mother or birth father") (2005).	Yes. Only a licensed agency or a person who has completed a home study with a favorable report may advertise. Wis. Stat. § 48.825 (2005).	Not clear; probably not. Wisconsin statutes do not address the use of facilitators. Wis. Stat. § 48 (2005).

Wyoming

No. "A petition may be filed by any single adult or jointly by a husband and wife who maintain their home together. . . ." Wyo. Stat. Ann. § 1-22-104 (2005).	Wyoming statutes do not address advertising. Please check with a local practitioner for advertising practices in this state. Wyo. Stat. Ann. § 1-22-101 et. seq. (2005).	Not clear; probably not. Wyoming statutes do not address the use of facilitators. Wyo. Stat. Ann. § 1-22-101 et. seq. (2005).

STATE ADOPTION LAWS

Consent and Expenses

The following is an analysis of state law as it applies to *consent, revocation of consent and the payment of birth parent expenses.* Please note that the following analysis does not address state laws as they pertain to adoptions of children and infants of Native American descent. Many states have laws in addition to the federal Indian Child Welfare Act. Please check with a member of the American Academy of Adoption Attorneys who is practicing in your state before relying on any of the information set forth herein. A local practitioner will know the specific laws relevant to your particular situation.

The following summaries also include citations to the pertinent sections of the states' laws, to help direct and define your conversation (if any) with your adoption professional. Should you and your adoption professional need to discuss one of the issues addressed in the following table in greater detail, you will be able to direct your adoption professional to the statutory basis for your thoughts or concerns.

Please note, however, that the following table presents a summary of the law and is not intended to be exhaustive.

Who may/must consent?	When can consent be obtained/ withdrawn?	What birth parent expenses are permissible?

Alabama

The birth parents, including the presumed father regardless of paternity; or the agency to whom the adoptee has been relinquished or which holds permanent custody; or the putative father, if he has responded to notice, must consent.	Consent can be obtained any time prior to or after the birth of the child.	Adoptive parents can pay a birth mother's maternity-connected medical or hospital expenses, necessary living expenses of the mother preceding and during pregnancy-related incapacity as an act of charity. The payment may not be made to the birth mother contingent upon placement of the child for adoption, consent to the adoption, or cooperation in the completion of the adoption.
Consent is not required if the birth parent has abandoned the child, failed to respond to notice of a pending adoption, had his/her parental rights terminated, been found to be incompetent, or relinquished the child to a child-placing agency.	Consent can be withdrawn for any reason within five (5) days of the birth of the child or the signing of consent, or within fourteen (14) days if the court finds it consistent with the child's best interest. Consent can be withdrawn any time prior to the final adoption decree for fraud, duress, undue influence, or mistake.	
Ala. Code §§ 26-10A-7, 26-10A-9, 26-10A-10 (2006).	Ala. Code §§26-10A-13, 26-10A-14 (2006).	Ala. Code § 26-10A-34 (2006).

Who may/must consent?	When can consent be obtained/ withdrawn?	What birth parent expenses are permissible?

Alaska

Written consent is required from the birth parents, and if the birth parents are minors, then consent must also be obtained from the birth parents' parent or other legal guardian. Consent must also be obtained from the husband of the birth mother, if the husband was married to the birth mother at the time the baby was conceived or at any time after conception. Consent must also be obtained from any person lawfully entitled to custody of the child. Consent is not required when a parent has abandoned the child, failed to communicate or otherwise support the child, has had his/her parental rights terminated, or has been declared incompetent. Alaska Stat. §§ 25.23.040, 25.23.050, 25.23.060 (Michie 2006).	Consent can be obtained any time after the birth of the child. Consent may be withdrawn before the entry of a decree of adoption, within ten (10) days after the consent is given, or after the ten (10) day period has expired if the court finds that the withdrawal is in the best interest of the child. Consent cannot be withdrawn after entry of a final decree of adoption. Alaska Stat. § 25.23.070 (Michie 2006).	Adoptive parents may pay for expenses incurred in connection with the birth and placement of the child, medical or hospital care received by the birth mother, and services related to the adoption. Alaska Stat. § 25.23.090 (2006).

Who may/must consent?	When can consent be obtained/ withdrawn?	What birth parent expenses are permissible?

Arizona

Consent must be obtained from the birth mother and the birth father if he was married to the birth mother at the time of conception or has otherwise established paternity. Any legal guardian of the child and/or the Department of Health or other child-placement agency must also consent. Consent is not required if the court has terminated the birth parents' rights upon a determination that the child was neglected. Ariz. Rev. Stat. § 8-106 (2006).	Consent cannot be given before seventy-two (72) hours after the birth of the child. Consent is irrevocable unless obtained by fraud, duress, or undue influence. Ariz. Rev. Stat. §§ 8-106, 8-107 (2006).	Adoptive parents can pay any reasonable and necessary expenses, including costs for medical and hospital care for the birth mother and child, counseling fees, legal fees, agency fees, living expenses, and any other costs the court determines are reasonable and necessary. Payments exceeding $1,000 must be approved by the court. Ariz. Rev. Stat. § 8-114 (2006).

Who may/must consent?	When can consent be obtained/ withdrawn?	What birth parent expenses are permissible?

Arkansas

Written consent must be obtained from the birth mother and birth father, the birth mother's husband (if any), or any person lawfully entitled to custody of the child.

Consent is not required when a birth parent has deserted the child, failed to communicate or provide for the care of the child for a period of not less than one (1) year, relinquished or had parental rights terminated, or been declared incompetent.

Ark. Code. Ann. §§ 9-9-206, 9-207 (2006). | Consent can be obtained any time after the birth of the child.

Consent may be withdrawn within ten (10) days after it is signed or the child is born, whichever is later. Consent cannot be withdrawn after the entry of a decree of adoption.

Ark. Code. Ann. § 9-9-209 (2006). | Adoptive parents may pay for expenses incurred in connection with the birth of the child, fees related to the adoption or placement of the child, medical or hospital care received by the birth mother, and legal fees to attorneys.

Ark. Code. Ann. § 9-9-211 (2006). |

Who may/must consent?	When can consent be obtained/ withdrawn?	What birth parent expenses are permissible?

California

Consent is required from the birth parents.	In a direct placement consent may only take place after the discharge of the birth mother from the hospital. If the birth mother is required to be hospitalized longer than the child, consent may be given with verification of her competency to relinquish parental rights in writing from her physician.	Adoptive parents may pay for birth mother expenses related to the adoption, the birth mother's or child's medical or hospital care, attorney's fees, counseling fees and living expenses.
Consent is not required when a birth parent has relinquished parental rights, had parental rights terminated, deserted the child, or willfully failed to contact or support the child for a period of not less than one (1) year.		Any request for payment for expenses by a birth parent(s) must be made in writing.
Cal. Fam. Code §§ 8603, 8604, 8606 (West 2006).	Relinquishment to an agency can take place any time after the birth of the child.	Cal. Fam. Code § 8812 (West 2006).
	In an agency adoption relinquishment is binding.	
	In an independent adoption the birth parents can withdraw consent any time prior to thirty (30) days from execution of the consent.	
	Cal. Fam. Code §§ 8700, 8801.3, 8814.5 (West 2006).	

Who may/must consent?	When can consent be obtained/ withdrawn?	What birth parent expenses are permissible?

Colorado

| Consent must be obtained from the birth parents or any legal guardian of the child.

Consent is not required when the birth parents' rights have been terminated due to their unfitness (as provided by Colorado law), or the birth parents have failed to provide support or have abandoned the child for a period of not less than one (1) year.

Col. Rev. Stat. §§ 19-5-203, 19-3-604 (2006). | Consent may be executed any time after the birth of the child.

Consent may be revoked only if within ninety (90) days of entry of the order if it is established by clear and convincing evidence that the consent was obtained by fraud or duress.

Col. Rev. Stat. §§ 19-5-104, 19-5-203 (2006). | Adoptive parents may only pay a birth mother's attorney fees and such other charges and fees as may be approved by the court.

Col. Rev. Stat. § 19-5-213 (2006). |

Who may/must consent?	When can consent be obtained/ withdrawn?	What birth parent expenses are permissible?

Connecticut

Consent can be obtained from any statutory parent; a surviving parent when one parent has died; an unwed birth mother, provided that the putative father has received notice or had his parental rights terminated; or the child's guardian. Consent is not required if parental rights have been terminated; the birth parent has abandoned the child, caused the child intentional injury, failed to maintain a relationship with the child for a period of not less than one (1) year; or was convicted of a sexual assault that resulted in the birth of the child. Conn. Gen. Stat. §§ 45a-724, 45a-717 (2004).	Consent may be obtained from the birth mother anytime after forty-eight (48) hours after the child's birth and must be approved by the court. Consent may be withdrawn at any time prior to entry of the final decree of adoption. The court will consider the child's best interests when entertaining a petition to set aside the relinquishment of parental rights. Conn. Gen. Stat. §§ 45a-715, 719 (2004).	Adoptive parents may pay for the living expenses of the birth mother in an amount not to exceed one thousand five hundred ($1,500) dollars or such amount as may be approved in unusual circumstances by the court. Adoptive parents may also pay reasonable telephone and maternity-clothing expenses of the birth mother. Conn. Gen. Stat. §45a-728c (2004).

Who may/must consent?	When can consent be obtained/ withdrawn?	What birth parent expenses are permissible?

Delaware

Consent must be granted by both birth parents and the department or agency to which rights are vested. Consent is not required when the child has been abandoned, the birth parent is legally incompetent, the birth parent has been convicted of a felony child abuse count involving harm to the child, or there is a history of neglect or chronic abuse. Del. Code Ann. tit. 13 §§ 904, 908, 1103 (2006).	Consent by the birth mother may be executed any time after the child is born. Consent by the birth father or presumed birth father may be obtained before or after the child's birth. Consent may withdrawn within sixty (60) days of filing of the consent. Del. Code Ann. tit. 13 §§ 1103, 909 (2006).	Only court costs and legal fees may be paid by adoptive parents to an agency. Del. Code Ann. tit. 13 § 928 (2006).

Who may/must consent?	When can consent be obtained/ withdrawn?	What birth parent expenses are permissible?

District of Columbia

Consent must be obtained from the birth parents, or from the court-appointed guardian or from a licensed child-placing agency, if parental rights have been terminated.

Consent is not required when a parent cannot be located, has abandoned the child, has failed to support the child for at least six (6) months, or has relinquished parental rights to an agency.

D.C. Code Ann. § 16-304 (2006).

Consent may not be obtained until seventy-two (72) hours after the child's birth. The birth parent must first undergo counseling.

Consent to a voluntary relinquishment may be automatically revoked by a verified writing submitted to the agency within ten (10) calendar days.

D.C. Code Ann. § 4-1406 (2006).

District of Columbia statutes do not address birth mother expenses.

Who may/must consent?	When can consent be obtained/ withdrawn?	What birth parent expenses are permissible?

Florida

Consent must be obtained from the birth mother; the birth father, if he has acknowledged he is the biological father; the birth mother's husband if they were married when the child was conceived or born, or he supported the child; any person lawfully entitled to custody of the child; or the court under certain circumstances as provided by statute.

Consent is not required when the parent has abandoned the child or has made "marginal" efforts to assume parental responsibility, when parental rights have been terminated, or when the parent is incompetent.

Fla. Stat. Ann. §§ 63.062, 63.089 (West 2006). | Consent may be obtained from the birth mother anytime after forty-eight (48) hours after the birth of the child, or upon her release from the hospital, whichever is earlier. Consent may be obtained from the birth father any time after the birth of the child. Consent from a birth father who cannot be located or is not known may be implied, provided that he has been served with notice as provided by the statute.

Consent is irrevocable for children less than six (6) months of age, unless obtained by fraud or duress. Consent may be revoked in adoptions for children older than six (6) months within three (3) days, or anytime up until placement, whichever is later.

Fla. Stat. Ann. § 63.082 (West 2006). | Adoptive parents may pay birth parent expenses, including reasonable living expenses that the birth mother is unable to pay due to unemployment, underemployment, or disability; reasonable and necessary medical expenses (during the pregnancy and for a period of up to six (6) weeks postpartum); court expenses and professional fees; costs for other services related to the adoption.

Fla. Stat. Ann. § 63.097 (West 2006). |

Who may/must consent?	When can consent be obtained/ withdrawn?	What birth parent expenses are permissible?

Georgia

Consent must be obtained from any birth parent or legal guardian. Consent is not required if the child has been abandoned and the parent cannot be located after a diligent search, the parent is insane or incompetent, or the parent has failed to exercise proper parental care. Ga. Code Ann. §§ 19-8-4, 19-8-10 (2005).	Consent may be obtained any time after the birth of the child. Consent may be withdrawn within (ten) 10 days of its execution. Ga. Code Ann. §§ 19-8-9, 19-8-26 (2005).	Adoptive parents may only pay a birth mother's expenses for medical or hospital care during the birth mother's prenatal care and confinement and for other expenses related to the birth, placement, and adoption. Ga. Code Ann. § 19-8-13 (2005).

Who may/must consent?	When can consent be obtained/ withdrawn?	What birth parent expenses are permissible?

Hawaii

Consent must be obtained from the birth mother and the birth father, or an adjudicated or presumed father; any person or agency having legal custody; or the court, if the legal guardian is not empowered to consent. Consent is not required if the parent deserted the child for a period of not less than ninety (90) days, voluntarily surrendered care and custody of the child to another person for a period of not less than two (2) years, failed to support or contact the child for a period of at least one (1) year, had parental rights termi-nated, or was declared mentally ill or retarded. Haw. Rev. Stat. § 578-2 (2005).	Consent may be obtained at any time following the mother's sixth (6th) month of pregnancy, provided that no judgment may be entered until after the birth of the child, and the birth parent(s) have reaffirmed their desire to relinquish the child after birth. Consent may not be withdrawn after the individual has been placed for adoption without the express approval of the court based upon a written finding that such action will be in the best interest of the child. Haw. Rev. Stat. §§ 571-61, 578-2 (2005).	Hawaii's statutes do not address what birth parent expenses can be paid.

Who may/must consent?	When can consent be obtained/ withdrawn?	What birth parent expenses are permissible?

Idaho

Consent must be obtained from both birth parents if conceived during a marriage, or if conceived outside of marriage by the birth mother and adjudicated biological father, any legally appointed custodian or guardian or agency that is authorized to place the child for adoption.

Consent is not required when parental rights have been terminated; the parent(s) has abused, neglected or abandoned the child; has caused the child to be conceived as a result of rape or incest; has killed the child's other parent; has been jailed with no possibility of parole; is not the biological parent; or is unable to discharge parental responsibilities.

Idaho Code §§ 16-1504, 16-2005 (2005).

Idaho statutes do not explicitly provide when consent may be obtained. It is customary practice for consent to be obtained any time after the birth of the child.

The statute does not give a time period in which consent can be revoked. However, if consent is revoked, the birth parents must reimburse the adoptive parents for all paid expenses.

Idaho Code § 16-1515 (2005).

Adoptive parents may pay a birth mother's legal and medical costs, reasonable maternity and living expenses during the pregnancy and for a period not to exceed six (6) weeks postpartum based upon demonstrated financial need.

Idaho Code § 18-1511 (2005).

Who may/must consent?	When can consent be obtained/ withdrawn?	What birth parent expenses are permissible?

Illinois

Consent must be obtained from the birth mother; the birth father, if he is married to the mother or has established paternity; a legal guardian; or any person or agency having legal custody of the child.	Consent may be obtained from the birth mother beginning seventy-two (72) hours after the birth of the child.	Adoptive parents may pay a birth mother's expenses related to activities of daily living and basic needs, including, but not limited to, lodging, food, and clothing for the biological parents during the biological mother's pregnancy for a period commencing 120 days prior to the biological mother's expected date of delivery and for no more than sixty (60) days after the birth of the child.
Consent is not required when the parent is found to be unfit, is determined not to be the biological father, has waived his/her parental rights, or has caused the child to be conceived as a result of sexual abuse.	The birth father can consent before or after the birth. Consent is irrevocable unless obtained by fraud or duress. 750 Ill. Comp. Stat. 50/9, 50/11 (2005).	
750 Ill. Comp. Stat. 50/8, 50/12 (2005).		Payment may not be made for lost wages, gifts, educational expenses, or other similar expenses of the biological parents except when need is demonstrated. Reasonable and actual medical and hospital charges; and reasonable attorney's fees may be paid with permission from the court. 720 Ill. Comp. Stat. 525/4.1 (2005).

Who may/must consent?	When can consent be obtained/ withdrawn?	What birth parent expenses are permissible?

Indiana

Written consent is required from each living birth parent of a child born in wedlock; the birth mother of a child born out of wedlock and the father of a child whose paternity has been established; each person, agency, or county office of family and children having lawful custody of the child; or the court, if the legal guardian or custodian is not empowered to consent to the adoption.

Consent is not required when the child has been abandoned for six (6) months, the parent(s) has failed to contact or support the child for a period of not less than one (1) year when the child has been in the custody of another person, has caused the child to be conceived as a result of rape or incest, has not established paternity or has failed to register with the putative

Consent may be executed by the birth mother or birth father any time after birth of the child. The birth father may also consent before the birth of the child, if the consent is in writing, is notarized, and acknowledges that the consent is irrevocable and the father will not receive notice of the adoption proceedings.

Consent may be withdrawn not later than thirty (30) days after consent to adoption is signed if the court finds it is in the best interests of the child.

Ind. Code. Ann. §§ 31-19-9-2, 31-19-10-3 (2005).

Adoptive parents may pay for hospital and medical expenses related to pregnancy and birth; reasonable expenses for counseling for birth parents; reasonable costs of housing, utilities, and phone service for the birth mother during the second or third trimester of pregnancy and not more than six (6) weeks after childbirth; reasonable costs of maternity clothing for birth mother; reasonable costs of travel expenses relating to the pregnancy or adoption.

Ind. Code. Ann. § 35-46-1-9 (2005).

Who may/must consent?	When can consent be obtained/ withdrawn?	What birth parent expenses are permissible?

Indiana, continued

father registry, has had parental rights terminated, has been declared incompetent or insane, or has been convicted of a specified crime involving a member of the child's family. Ind. Code. Ann. §§ 31-19-9-1, 31-19-9-8, 31-19-9-10 (2005).		

Who may/must consent?	When can consent be obtained/ withdrawn?	What birth parent expenses are permissible?

Iowa

Written consent must be obtained from any guardian of the person to be adopted. Consent is not required if the parent refuses to consent or cannot be located to consent; has signed a release of custody or a petition to terminate rights; has abandoned or failed to support the child; is a chronic substance abuser; has committed more than one act of domestic abuse; or has abducted, removed or improperly retained the child. Iowa Code §§ 600.7, 600A.8 (2004).	Parental consent may not be executed until at least seventy-two (72) hours after the child's birth. A request to revoke consent may be made prior to termination of parental rights. If the request is made within ninety-six (96) hours of executing the release, the court shall allow it. If the request is made after ninety-six (96) hours, the court must find by clear and convincing evidence that good cause exists for revocation, such as fraud, coercion, or misrepresentation of fact. Consent may not be withdrawn after the filing of the final adoption decree. However, the adoption shall not be decreed until the child to be adopted has lived with the adoptive parent(s) for a minimum of 180 days. This period may be	Adoptive parents may pay expenses relating to the birth of the child to be adopted, including placement and legal expenses; pregnancy-related medical care received by the biological parents or the child (during pregnancy, delivery or postpartum); living expenses of the birth mother (room and board or rent and food only), and transportation expenses (for medical purposes only) for no longer than thirty (30) days after the birth of the child; counseling costs for the biological parents. Iowa Code § 600.9 (2004).

Who may/must consent?	When can consent be obtained/ withdrawn?	What birth parent expenses are permissible?

Iowa, continued

	shortened by the juvenile court on good cause shown. Iowa Code §§ 600.7, 600.10, 600A.4 (2004).	

Kansas

Written consent to an independent adoption is required from the birth mother and birth father or only one parent if the other parent's relationship has been previously terminated or determined not to exist by a court. Consent is required from a legal guardian of the child if both parents are deceased. Consent to an agency adoption shall be given by the authorized representative of the agency. A minor parent shall have the advice of independent legal counsel as to the consequences of the	Consent may not be given by the birth mother or accepted until twelve (12) hours after birth of the child. Any consent given before that time is voidable prior to the final decree of adoption. A written consent filed in the district court becomes irrevocable, absent proof that the consent was not freely and voluntarily given. In all cases written consent must be executed not more than six (6) months prior to the date the petition for adoption is filed. Kansas Stat. Ann. §§ 59-2114, 59-2116 (2004).	Adoptive parents may pay all reasonable fees for legal and other professional services rendered in connection with the placement or adoption of the child; reasonable fees of a licensed child-placing agency; actual and necessary expenses incidental to placement or to the adoption proceeding; actual medical expenses of the birth mother attributable to pregnancy and birth; actual medical expenses of the child and reasonable living expenses of the mother that are incurred during or as a result of the pregnancy. A detailed

Who may/must consent?	When can consent be obtained/ withdrawn?	What birth parent expenses are permissible?

Kansas, continued

consent or relinquishment prior to its execution.
Consent is not required by the birth father if he has neglected or abandoned the child, has failed to contact or support the child, is unfit or incapable of consent, failed to support the birth mother during pregnancy, abandoned the birth mother, raped the birth mother, or failed to assume parental duties for a period of not less than two (2) years.

Kansas Stat. Ann. §§ 59-2114, 59-2115, 59-2129, 59-2136 (2004).

accounting of all consideration given or to be made shall accompany the petition for adoption for review by the court.

Kansas Stat. § 59-2121 (2004).

Who may/must consent?	When can consent be obtained/ withdrawn?	What birth parent expenses are permissible?

Kentucky

Consent must be obtained from the parent(s) of a child born in wedlock, of the birth mother if born out of wedlock, the birth father if he is married to the mother or has otherwise established his paternity.

Consent is not required if the parent has abandoned or failed to support the child for a period of not less than ninety (90) days, has inflicted serious injury or allowed the child to be sexually abused, has had parental rights terminated to this or another child, or has been adjudicated mentally disabled.

Ky. Rev. Stat. Ann. §§ 199.500, 199.502 (2005).

Consent for adoption must not be given prior to seventy-two (72) hours after the birth of the child. Consent will become final and irrevocable when: (1) if placement approval by the secretary is required, twenty (20) days after the later of the placement approval or execution of the consent, or (2) if placement approval is not required, twenty (20) days after the execution of the consent.

Ky. Stat. §199.500 (2005).

Expenses paid for any fees for legal services, placement services, and expenses of the biological parent by the prospective adoptive parents for any purpose related to the adoption must be submitted to the court for approval.

Ky. Stat. §199.590 (6)(a) (2005).

Who may/must consent?	When can consent be obtained/ withdrawn?	What birth parent expenses are permissible?

Louisiana

Consent is required from the birth mother of the child; the father of the child, regardless of paternity if: (1) the child is born of the marriage, or (2) the father is presumed to be the father; the alleged father who has established his parental rights; the biological father whose paternity has been determined by the court and the custodial agency that placed the child. The statute does not address when consent is not required in an extrafamilial adoption. La. Ch.C. Art. 1193, 1195 (2005).	The birth mother may consent five (5) days after the child's birth. At any time prior to or following the birth of the child, any alleged or adjudicated father may execute a consent to the adoption of the child. Upon acceptance by the court, or after five (5) days after the child's birth, the parent's consent is irrevocable except upon a showing of fraud or duress. La. Ch.C. Art. 1123, 1130, 1147 (2005).	Adoptive parents may pay reasonable medical expenses incurred by the biological mother and child incidental to birth and expenses incurred on behalf of the child prior to the decree of adoption; mental health counseling provided to birth mother for a reasonable time before and after the child's placement; reasonable living expenses incurred by the birth mother; reasonable attorney fees, court costs, travel and other expenses incurred on behalf of the birth mother. La. Ch.C. Art. 1223 (2005).

Who may/must consent?	When can consent be obtained/ withdrawn?	What birth parent expenses are permissible?

Maine

Written consent must be given by the birth parents or the person or agency having legal custody or guardianship of the child. Consent is not required if the parent has abandoned the child, the parent fails to assume parental responsibility, the parent's rights have been terminated, or the putative father fails to respond to notice. Me. Rev. Stat. Ann. tit. 18-A, §§ 9-302, 9-201 (West 2005).	Consent can be executed any time after the child's birth. A petition for adoption must be pending before consent is executed. Consent will not be valid until three (3) days after it has been executed. It then becomes final and irrevocable. Me. Rev. Stat. Ann. tit. 18-A, §§ 9-202, 9-302 (2005).	Adoptive parents may pay the actual cost of legal services related to the consent portion of the adoption process; prenatal and postnatal counseling expenses; medical expenses; necessary transportation expenses; foster-care expenses; necessary living expenses for mother and child; legal and counseling expenses related to the consent portion of the adoption for the biological father; and fees to a child-placing agency. Me. Rev. Stat. Ann. tit. 18-A, § 9-306 (2005).

Who may/must consent?	When can consent be obtained/ withdrawn?	What birth parent expenses are permissible?

Maryland

Consent must be obtained from both parents, if living (unless parent is unable to be located or fails to respond); or the child's guardian; or the director of the local department with custody. Consent is not required if the child has been out of the parent's custody for a period of not less than one (1) year and is in the custody of a child-placing agency or has formed a significant attachment to the petitioner; the child has been abandoned; the parent has failed to have meaningful contact with or to support the child; the parent has been convicted of a crime of child abuse or violence against the child. Md. Code Ann. Family Law §§ 5-388, 5-350 (2006).	Consent may be obtained after the birth of the child. Consent may be revoked thirty (30) days after the parent signs the consent or thirty (30) days after the adoption petition is filed, whichever is later. Consent to an adoption entered into before a judge is irrevocable. Consent by a local department or guardian of the child is revocable any time before the court enters the order of adoption. Md. Code Ann. Family Law §§ 5-339, 5-351, 5-3B-20 (2006).	Adoptive parents can pay customary and reasonable charges or fees for hospital, legal, or medical services. Md. Code Ann. Family Law §§ 5-362, 5-3A-45, 5-3B-32 (2006).

Who may/must consent?	When can consent be obtained/ withdrawn?	What birth parent expenses are permissible?

Massachusetts

Consent is required from the birth mother only if the child is born out of wedlock, or both parents if born to a valid marriage. Consent is not required if the court determines a waiver of consent is in the child's best interest; the child has been abandoned, abused or neglected; the child has been in foster care for fifteen (15) of the latest twenty-two (22) months; or the parent has been convicted of murder or manslaughter and the victim was a parent or sibling of the child. Mass. Gen L. ch. 210, §§ 2, 3 (2005).	Consent can be obtained at any time commencing four (4) days after the birth of the child. Properly executed consent is irrevocable. Mass. Gen. L. ch. 210, § 2 (2005).	Massachusetts statutes do not address birth parent expenses.

Who may/must consent?	When can consent be obtained/ withdrawn?	What birth parent expenses are permissible?

Michigan

Consent is necessary from each living parent; the department or child-placing agency to which the child has been permanently committed; the court or tribal court with permanent custody; or the guardian of the child or parent, if one has been appointed and if that guardian has the authority to consent.

Consent is not required if the putative father denies paternity or interest in custody of the child or he fails to respond to the notice of a pending adoption, the putative father or his whereabouts are unknown, the putative father fails to file notice of intent to claim paternity prior to birth, the parent fails to provide support, parental rights have been terminated or relinquished or the noncustodial parent has failed for two (2) years or more to provide

Consent cannot be executed until after an investigation.

A person granting consent can request a hearing to have the consent revoked. A release of custody cannot be revoked if the child has been placed for adoption unless the child was placed with an adoptive parent while the court order terminating parental rights was pending.

Mich. Comp. Laws §§ 710.29, 710.41 (2005).

An adoptive parent may pay reasonable and actual charges for the services of a child-placing agency; the medical, hospital, nursing, or pharmaceutical expenses incurred by the birth mother or the child, if not covered by the birth parent's private health-care payment or benefits plan or by Medicaid; counseling services related to the adoption for a parent or a guardian; living expenses of a mother before the birth of the child and for no more than six (6) weeks after the birth; expenses incurred in ascertaining the information required under this chapter about the child's biological family; legal fees, including legal services performed for a biological parent or a guardian and necessary court costs in an adoption proceeding; travel expenses

Who may/must consent?	When can consent be obtained/ withdrawn?	What birth parent expenses are permissible?

Michigan, continued

support to or commun- icate with the child. Mich. Comp. Laws §§ 710.43, 710.37, 710.51 (2005).		necessitated by the adoption. Mich. Comp. Laws § 710.54 (2005).

Minnesota

Both birth parents must consent unless they are under the age of eighteen (18), in which case the consent of the minor's parent or guardian is required. Minn. Stat. § 259.24 (2006).	Parental consent may be executed seventy-two (72) hours after birth and no later than sixty (60) days after the child has been placed in an adoptive home. Consent may be withdrawn for any reason within ten (10) days after it is executed. Minn. Stat. Ann. §§ 259.24 (6)(a), 259.47 (7) (2006).	Payments for counseling, medical expenses, legal fees, transportation, meals, board/lodging, adoption services provided by an adoption agency, reasonable living expenses (not to extend more than six (6) weeks past the child's birth). There can be no payment for lost wages or educational expenses. Minn. Stat. § 259.55 (1) (2006).

Who may/must consent?	When can consent be obtained/ withdrawn?	What birth parent expenses are permissible?

Mississippi

Both birth parents must consent, if living. Otherwise a guardian for the child or agency must consent. The birth father is not required to consent if he has abandoned or abused the child, failed to assume parental responsibilities, suffers a medical or emotional illness or a chemical dependency, has had parental rights termi-nated, or is a father to a child born out of wedlock who has not shown a commitment to parent the child within thirty (30) days of the child's birth. Miss. Code. Ann. §§ 93-17-5, 93-17-7 (2005).	Consent may be executed seventy-two (72) hours after the child's birth and (according to cases from the state of Mississippi) likely is irrevocable absent a showing by clear and convincing evidence of fraud, duress, or undue influence. Miss. Code Ann. § 93-17-5 (2005).	Mississippi statutes do not address birth parent expenses.

Who may/must consent?	When can consent be obtained/ withdrawn?	What birth parent expenses are permissible?

Missouri

The birth mother; the putative birth father, if he has acted to establish his paternity within fifteen (15) days of the child's birth or has filed with the state's putative father registry; any other legally recognized parent of the child must consent. Consent is not required of any person whose parental rights have been terminated, whose identity is not known, who is incompetent, or who has abandoned or failed to support or care for the child. Mo. Rev. Stat. §§ 453.030, 453.040 (2005).	Consent may be executed before a judge or notary public forty-eight (48) hours after the birth of the child, either before or after the petition of adoption has been filed in court. Consent may be withdrawn at any time until it has been reviewed and accepted by a judge, at which point it is irrevocable, absent evidence of fraud, duress, or coercion. Mo. Rev. Stat. § 453.030 (2005).	The adoptive parents may pay hospital and other medical costs, including counseling services, legal expenses and court costs, travel and living expenses, and any other expenses the court finds reasonable and necessary. Mo. Rev. Stat. § 453.075 (1) & (2) (2005).

Who may/must consent?	When can consent be obtained/ withdrawn?	What birth parent expenses are permissible?

Montana

The birth mother and her husband (if married) if he is the putative father, any other person whose parental rights have been established, or an agency or legal guardian with custody of the child.

Consent is not needed from any person whose parental rights have been terminated for unfitness or who has waived rights, who has been declared incompetent, or who has not been married to the mother and denies paternity.

Mont. Code. Ann. §§ 42-2-301, 42-2-302 (2005).

Consent may be taken seventy-two (72) hours after the birth of the child and after the birth mother has received counseling.

Once an order terminating parental rights has been issued, a relinquishment cannot be revoked.

Consent by a minor parent is not valid unless the minor received independent legal counsel.

Mont. Code Ann. §§ 42-2-408 & 42-2-410 (2005).

The adoptive parents may pay for medical and prenatal care, foster care, counseling for the birth mother, travel and temporary living expenses, legal fees, and any other expense approved by the court.

The adoptive parents may not pay for education, vehicles, salary, wages or vacation, permanent housing, or counseling for the birth mother beyond a maximum of ten (10) hours.

Mont. Code Ann. §§ 42-7-101, 42-7-102 (2006).

Who may/must consent?	When can consent be obtained/ withdrawn?	What birth parent expenses are permissible?

Nebraska

Consent must be obtained from any court having jurisdiction over the custody of the child, both parents if married, the birth mother if unmarried, the birth father if not married to the birth mother and he has filed with the state's biological father registry, the department or adoption agency, or any guardian of the child. Consent is not needed if a parent has relinquished the child for adoption in writing, has abandoned the child for a period of not less than six (6) months, has had his or her parental rights terminated, or is incapable of giving consent. Neb. Rev. Stat. §§ 43-104, 43-105 (2005).	Consent may be made forty-eight (48) hours after birth. Nebraska cases indicate that consent is irrevocable once signed, except upon a showing that the consent was not in the child's best interest or that there was fraud, duress, or undue influence. Neb. Rev. Stat. § 43-104 (2005).	Nebraska statutes do not address birth parent expenses.

Who may/must consent?	When can consent be obtained/ withdrawn?	What birth parent expenses are permissible?

Nevada

Consent is required from both parents, if living, or from the guardian of the child.

Parental consent is not needed if parental rights have been terminated by a court order or the parent has been determined to be insane for two (2) years and the insanity is incurable.

Nev. Rev. Stat. §§ 127.040, 127-090 (2006).

Consent may be executed by the birth mother before the child's birth or within seventy-two (72) hours thereafter. The birth father may consent before birth if he is not married to the birth mother.

Consent must be executed in front of two (2) witnesses, identifying the child and adoptive parents, and a copy must be delivered within forty-eight (48) hours to the welfare department with jurisdiction. A child cannot be placed in an adoptive home until the birth mother has executed her consent.

Consent by the birth mother to a specific adoptive placement is irrevocable except when the adoptive parents are deemed unsuitable.

Consent by the birth father is invalid if the birth father marries the

Adoptive parents may pay for all reasonable medical and other necessary living expenses as long as payment is not contingent upon the adoption.

Nev. Rev. Stat. § 127.287(3) (2006).

Who may/must consent?	When can consent be obtained/ withdrawn?	What birth parent expenses are permissible?

Nevada, continued

	birth mother before the child is born, the birth mother does not consent to the adoption within six (6) months of the child's birth, or no petition for adoption has been filed within two (2) years of the child's birth.	
	Nev. Rev. Stat. §§ 127.053, 127.043, 127.057, 127.070, 127.080 (2006).	

Who may/must consent?	When can consent be obtained/ withdrawn?	What birth parent expenses are permissible?

New Hampshire

The birth mother. If she is a minor, the court may require the consent of her parent or guardian. The legal or biological father. If he is a minor, the court may require the consent of his parents or guardian. If both birth parents are deceased or have had their parental rights terminated, the guardian of the child or the agency or department having custody of the child must consent to the adoption.

Consent from a birth father not married to the birth mother is not needed if he has failed to establish his paternity. Consent is not required from any parent who has voluntarily or involuntarily had his or her parental rights terminated.

N.H. Rev. Stat. Ann. §§ 170-B:5, 170-B:7 (2005).

Consent is not valid until seventy-two (72) hours after the birth of the child.

Consent may be withdrawn in writing at any time prior to entry of the final decree. Consent cannot be withdrawn absent a finding by the court that the parent withdrawing his or her consent has proven by a preponderance of evidence that the consent was obtained by fraud or duress, or that the withdrawal of the consent is in the best interest of the child. Consent may not be withdrawn for any reason after entry of a final decree by the court.

N.H. Rev. Stat. Ann. § 170-B:12 (2005).

Adoptive parents may pay a birth mother's expenses related to counseling, medical care, legal fees, transporta- tion, board/lodging, clothing and meals, and reasonable living expenses.

Adoptive parents may not pay for education expenses or living expenses beyond six (6) weeks after the child's birth, or any other monetary payment providing financial gain to the birth parent.

N.H. Rev. Stat. Ann. § 170-B:10(a) (2005).

Who may/must consent?	When can consent be obtained/ withdrawn?	What birth parent expenses are permissible?

New Jersey

The parent, guardian or agency with custody of the child must consent to the adoption.

Parental consent is not required when a biological parent has executed a valid surrender, parental rights have been terminated, there has been a failure to contact or support the child, the birth father has not acknowledged paternity, the birth father's whereabouts are unknown, or the birth father does not file a written objection to a notice of a pending adoption within twenty (20) days of service of the notice.

N.J. Stat. Ann. §§ 9:3-41, 9:3-45-46 (West 2005).

Consent by the birth mother may be executed seventy-two (72) hours after the birth of a child.

A birth father may execute a consent at any time, including prior to the child's birth.

If executed in accordance with the requirements of the law as to form and content, a consent made to an approved agency is irrevocable and constitutes a termination of parental rights unless, at the discretion of the agency, there is a determination that the consent was executed as a result of fraud, duress, or misrepresentation.

N.J. Stat. Ann. §§ 9:3-41(a)-(e) (West 2005); see also N.J. Stat. Ann. § 9:3-45(b)(4) (providing for how consent must be executed) (West 2005).

Adoptive parents may pay a birth mother's medical and/or hospital expenses, counseling fees, or other expenses incurred in connection with the birth. Adoptive parents may also pay for reasonable living expenses and legal fees or costs.

Payments to a birth mother cannot extend beyond four (4) weeks after the birth or termination of pregnancy.

N.J. Stat. Ann. §§ 9:3-39.1 (West 2005).

Who may/must consent?	When can consent be obtained/ withdrawn?	What birth parent expenses are permissible?

New Mexico

The birth mother and the putative birth father must consent. The department or adoption agency or other guardian to whom custody of the child has been given must also consent.

Parental consent is not required when a birth parent's rights have been terminated or relinquished by an adoption agency, a person is the biological father of a child conceived by rape or incest, a person has failed to respond to a notice of a pending adoption, or a birth father has failed to register with the putative father registry within ten (10) days of the child's birth.

N.M. Stat. Ann. §§ 32A-5-17, 32A-5-18 (Michie 2005).

Consent may be made forty-eight (48) hours after birth.

Consent may not be withdrawn prior to entry of a final judgment unless the consent was obtained by fraud.

Once a final judgment has been entered, the consent is irrevocable.

N.M. Stat. Ann. §§ 32A-5-21 (G) & (I) (Michie 2005).

Adoptive parents may pay a birth mother's medical, hospital, pharmaceutical, and nursing expenses. They may also pay for travel expenses and counseling for the birth mother, living expenses, legal and court-related fees, and any other court-approved expense.

Adoptive parents may not pay a birth mother's living expenses beyond six (6) weeks after the child's birth.

N.M. Stat. Ann. §§ 32A-5-34 (B) & (C) (Michie 2005).

Who may/must consent?	When can consent be obtained/ withdrawn?	What birth parent expenses are permissible?

New York

Consent must be obtained from both birth parents, provided that if a child is born out of wedlock, the birth father has shown an interest in the child. Any person or agency having custody or guardianship of the child must also consent.

Consent is not required when a parent has failed to visit or contact the child for six (6) months, has surrendered the child to an agency for purposes of adoption, shows an intent to forgo parental rights, whose child has a legally appointed guardian, is unable to care for the child due to mental illness, or has executed a legal instrument denying paternity of the child.

N.Y. Dom. Rel. Law §§ 111, 113 (McKinney 2006).

New York statutes do not address when consent may be given. A review of cases reveals that consent likely may be given at any time after the child's birth.

In a private adoption consent given in court is irrevocable except upon a showing of fraud, duress or coercion. A consent taken outside of court (in a hospital or at an agency or other office) is revocable for forty-five (45) days.

N.Y. Dom. Rel. Law § 115-b (McKinney 2006).

Adoptive parents may pay for a birth mother's actual medical and hospital costs, other necessary expenses related to the pregnancy, and her legal fees. Payment of a birth parent's expenses may not exceed thirty (30) days after birth or consent unless a court determines otherwise.

N.Y. Soc. Serv. Law § 374(6) (McKinney 2006).

Who may/must consent?	When can consent be obtained/withdrawn?	What birth parent expenses are permissible?

North Carolina

The birth mother must consent to the adoption, and any man who was married to the mother or has claimed or attempted to claim paternity for the child. The agency that is placing the child for adoption must consent to the adoption as must any birth parent who has not yet reliquished the child for adoption. In the event that a birth parent has been declared incompetent, the guardian ad litem of the incompetent parent must consent to the adoption.

Parental consent is not required if a parent fails to respond to a notice of a pending adoption within thirty (30) days of service of the notice, from a putative father who denies paternity or is declared by a court not to be the biological father, from an individual whose parental rights have been terminated or from a

A birth father may consent at any time, including prior to the child's birth. A birth mother may consent at any time after the child's birth. An agency must consent no later than thirty (30) days after being served with notice of a proceeding for adoption.

Consent is generally considered final and irrevocable on signing.

N.C. Gen. Stat. §§ 48-3-604, 48-3-607, 48-3-608, 48-3-609 (2005).

Adoptive parents may pay a birth mother's medical, hospital, pharmaceutical, and nursing costs; travel expenses; counseling fees; ordinary living expense; and legal and court costs. Living expenses may not be paid beyond six (6) weeks after the child's birth.

N.C. Gen. Stat. § 48-10-103 (2005).

Who may/must consent?	When can consent be obtained/ withdrawn?	What birth parent expenses are permissible?

North Carolina, continued

putative father who is convicted of rape. N.C. Gen. Stat. §§ 48-3-601, 48-3-602, 48-3-603 (2005).		

North Dakota

The birth mother must consent to the adoption, as must the birth father or putative birth father, any individual entitled to custody of the child, a court having jurisdiction to determine custody, and the spouse of the birth mother, whether he is the birth father or not. Consent is not required when the child has been abandoned, the parent fails to communicate with or support the child for a period of at least one (1) year, parental rights have been terminated or relinquished, or the parent is incompetent. N.D. Cent. Code §§ 14-15-10, 14-15.1-06 (2005).	The birth mother and father may execute consent at any time after the child's birth. Consent may be withdrawn before entry of the final adoption order but only in the event that the court determines it to be in the best interest of the child. Consent cannot be withdrawn after entry of a final judgment of adoption. N.D. Cent. Code §§ 14-15-07, 14-15-08 (2005).	Adoptive parents may pay a birth mother's medical or hospital expenses and, for services rendered in connection with the adoption, including legal fees, counseling, and or living expenses. Payments may not continue past six (6) weeks after the child is born without court approval. Adoptive parents may not pay for wages, gifts, educational expenses, or vacations. N.D. Cent. Code §§ 14-15-05, 14-15-06 (2005).

Who may/must consent?	When can consent be obtained/withdrawn?	What birth parent expenses are permissible?

Ohio

The birth mother must consent to the adoption. The birth father must consent if the child was conceived during the course of his marriage to the birth mother, if he has established paternity, or if he is the putative birth father. An agency must consent to the adoption if it has permanent custody of the child. A court having jurisdiction to determine custody must consent.

Consent is not required when a parent has failed to contact or provide for the child for a period of not less than one (1) year, the putative father has failed to register with the putative father registry within thirty (30) days of the child's

Consent cannot be executed until seventy-two (72) hours after the baby's birth.

Consent is irrevocable upon execution, except if it is withdrawn prior to entry of the inter-locutory order or entry of the final decree when no other order has been entered and the court determines it is in the best interest of the child.

A final decree of adoption shall not be issued and an interlocutory order of adoption does not become final until six (6) months after the child has been placed in the adoptive home.

Adoptive parents may pay for a birth mother's physician and hospital expenses, attorney's fees, and court costs. The court retains the power to determine an expense to be unreasonable.

Ohio Rev. Code Ann. § 3107.10 (Anderson 2005).

Who may/must consent?	When can consent be obtained/ withdrawn?	What birth parent expenses are permissible?

Ohio, continued

birth, the putative father is not the biological father, the parent(s) has relinquished parental rights or they have been terminated, or the birth father or putative birth father is convicted of rape.

Ohio Rev. Code Ann. §§ 3107.06, 3107.7 (Anderson 2005).

Ohio Rev. Code Ann. §§ 3107.08, 3107.084, 3107.13 (Anderson 2005).

Who may/must consent?	When can consent be obtained/ withdrawn?	What birth parent expenses are permissible?

Oklahoma

Consent must be obtained from both birth parents, a legal guardian, any person having legal custody of the child, or the head of an adoption agency to whom the child has been relinquished.

In the event that one or both birth parents are minors (under the age of sixteen (16) years), consent must be obtained from their parents or guardians.

Consent does not need to be obtained when parental rights have been terminated, when a parent has failed to support the child for a period of not less than twelve (12) months, a parent has been convicted of physical or sexual abuse or is in jail, a putative father fails to acknowledge paternity, or a parent has a mental illness or deficiency.

Okla. Stat. tit. 10 §§ 7503-2.1, 7505-4.2 (2005).

The birth mother cannot execute her consent to the adoption until after the child's birth. A putative birth father may consent before or after the child's birth.

A permanent relinquishment may be executed at any time after the birth upon court authorization and providing it is in writing and contains a statement of irrevocability.

An extrajudicial consent (one made outside of court) is revocable for any reason for fifteen (15) days after it is made.

Consent is otherwise irrevocable except if it was obtained by fraud or duress or a court determines it to be in the best interest of the child and there has been no adoptive placement for nine (9) months.

Okla. Stat. tit. 10 §§ 7503-2.3, 7503-2.6, 7503-2.7 (2005).

Adoptive parents may pay a birth mother's medical and counseling expenses, attorney's fees and court costs, and other necessities incurred as a result of the pregnancy and only in extraordinary circumstances. Payments to the birth mother may not extend past two (2) months after the placement of the child. Payments for counseling may not extend past six (6) months after placement of the child.

Okla. Stat. tit. 10 § 7505-3.2 (2005).

Who may/must consent?	When can consent be obtained/ withdrawn?	What birth parent expenses are permissible?

Oregon

Consent must be obtained from the birth parents, a guardian, or the state office or agency to which the child has been surrendered.	Oregon statutes do not address when consent may be executed.	Adoptive parents may pay a birth mother's medical and legal expenses and any living or travel expenses.
Consent does not need to be obtained when a parent does not retain custody of the child, is mentally ill or deficient, has been in jail for more than three (3) years, has deserted or neglected the child, or when the birth mother's husband is found not to be the biological father of the child.	Consent may not be revoked unless the court determines there to have been fraud or duress with respect to any material fact surrounding the adoption procedure. Or. Rev. Stat § 109.312 (2003).	Or. Rev. Stat. § 109.311 (2003).
Or. Rev. Stat. §§ 109.312, 109.316, 109.314, 109.322, 109.324, 109.326 (2003).		

Who may/must consent?	When can consent be obtained/ withdrawn?	What birth parent expenses are permissible?

Pennsylvania

Consent must be obtained from the birth parents and/or the husband of the birth mother unless it is proven that he is not the biological father of the child. Consent is not required when the parent does not maintain contact with the child for a period of four (4) months, the child was conceived as the result of rape or incest, parental rights have been terminated, or the birth mother's husband is not the biological father. 23 Pa. Cons. Stat. §§ 2711, 2713, 2714 (2005).	Consent may not be executed until seventy-two (72) hours after the birth of the child. A putative birth father may execute his consent at any time. The birth or putative father's consent may be withdrawn within thirty (30) days after the child's birth or execution of the consent, whichever occurs later. After the thirty (30) day period has elapsed, the consent is irrevocable. The birth mother's consent is irrevocable thirty (30) days after it is executed. The validity of a consent may be challenged only by a petition alleging fraud or duress within sixty (60) days after the birth of the child or execution of the consent, whichever is later. 23 Pa. Cons. Stat. § 2711 (2005).	Adoptive parents may pay a birth mother's medical, hospital, and counseling fees; and for any training services. 23 Pa. Cons. Stat. § 2533 (2005).

Who may/must consent?	When can consent be obtained/withdrawn?	What birth parent expenses are permissible?

Rhode Island

Consent must be obtained from the birth parents; a legal guardian of the child; or, when the birth parent is a minor, the birth parent's parent or guardian. Consent does not need to be obtained if parental rights have been terminated, the parent has neglected or abused the child, the parent is deemed unfit due to mental or emotional illness or excessive drug or alcohol use, or the parent has voluntarily placed the child in the care of a licensed agency. R.I. Gen. Laws §§ 15-7-5, 15-7-10, 15-7-7 (2005).	Consent may be executed fifteen (15) days after the child's birth. Consent may only be revoked by a petition filed within 180 days and after a finding by the court that the adoption is not in the best interest of the child. R.I. Gen. Laws §§ 15-7-6, 15-7-21.1 (2005).	Rhode Island statutes do not address allowable birth-related expenses. R.I. Gen. Laws § 15-7 (2005).

Who may/must consent?	When can consent be obtained/ withdrawn?	What birth parent expenses are permissible?

South Carolina

Consent must be obtained from the birth parents, the birth father if he is not married to the birth mother, a legal guardian of the child, and the child-placing agency.

Consent is not required when parental rights have been terminated, the parent has executed a relinquishment, or the parent has been determined to be mentally incompetent.

S.C. Code. Ann. §§ 20-7-1690, 20-7-1695 (Laws, Co-op 2005).

Consent may be given at any time after the child's birth.

Revocation of consent is not permissible absent a finding that it was executed involuntarily or under duress and that it is in the child's best interest. The consent is irrevocable once the final decree of adoption is entered.

S.C. Code Ann. §§ 20-7-1700, 20-7-1720 (Laws, Co-op 2005).

Adoptive parents may pay a birth mother's actual and necessary medical costs and reasonable living expenses. All expenses must be verified by receipt.

The court may determine that an expense is unreasonable.

S.C. Code Ann. §§ 20-7-1690, 20-7-1775 (Laws, Co-op 2005).

Who may/must consent?	When can consent be obtained/ withdrawn?	What birth parent expenses are permissible?

South Dakota

The birth parents must consent to the adoption. Consent is not required if the parent or putative father is incarcerated for a critical period of time, has abandoned the child, is unfit due to habitual drug or alcohol use, has neglected or failed to provide for the child, or has otherwise been deprived of custody. S.D. Codified Laws § 25-6-4 (Michie 2005).	Consent or petition to terminate parental rights cannot be filed until five (5) days after the child's birth. Consent may be revoked for up to two (2) years, except in any case involving fraud. S.D. Codified Laws §§ 25-5A-4, 25-6-21 (Michie 2005).	Adoptive parents may pay for any of the birth mother's expenses that are approved by the court. S.D. Codified Laws § 25-6-4.2 (Michie 2005).

Who may/must consent?	When can consent be obtained/ withdrawn?	What birth parent expenses are permissible?

Tennessee

The birth parents must consent to the adoption. If the birth parent is under the age of eighteen (18), s/he has the capacity to consent, but the court may appoint a guardian ad litem and may require the birth parent's parent(s) to consent.

Consent is not required if the birth parent has abandoned the child; has shown noncompliance with a permanency plan; has placed the child outside his/her home for six (6) months; has committed severe child abuse; has been imprisoned for two (2) years for conduct against a child; or failed to support, contact, or visit the child.

Tenn. Code Ann. §§ 36-1-110, 26-1-111, 36-1-113 (2005).

Consent may not be executed until three (3) days after the child's birth, counting from the first full day after birth. The court may, for good cause, waive the three (3) day waiting period.

A consent may be revoked within ten (10) days if such revocation is made in the presence of a judge. After ten (10) days a surrender cannot be set aside except when there is clear and convincing evidence of fraud, misrepresentation or duress.

Tenn. Code Ann. §§ 36-1-112, 26-1-118 (2005).

Adoptive parents may pay a birth mother's usual and customary legal fees, medical fees incurred in connection with pregnancy and delivery, counseling for both birth parents, housing, clothing, and transportation.

Payment may not be made past ninety (90) days prior to or thirty (30) days after the birth or surrender, absent court approval.

Tenn. Code. Ann. § 36-1-109 (2005).

Who may/must consent?	When can consent be obtained/ withdrawn?	What birth parent expenses are permissible?

Texas

The managing conservator to the adoption must consent. Parental consent is not required if the parent is unable to care for the child due to mental illness; has voluntarily terminated his/her parental rights; was convicted of a crime resulting in the birth of the child; or his/her parental rights have been terminated on the grounds of abandonment, nonsupport, endangerment, abuse, or neglect. Texas Fam. Code Ann. §§ 162.010, 161.003, 161.005, 161.006, 161.007 (West 2005).	A birth mother may consent any time after forty-eight (48) hours after the child's birth. The affidavit of relinquishment must state that it is irrevocable. A putative birth father may sign an affidavit disclaiming any interest in parenting at any time before or after the child's birth. An affidavit of relinquishment that does not provide that it is irrevocable can be revoked before the eleventh (11th) day after signing. On the 11th day the consent becomes irrevocable. Any time before an order granting an adoption is filed, consent may be revoked by filing a signed revocation. Texas Fam. Code Ann. §§ 161.103, 161.106 (West 2005).	Adoptive parents may pay for legal and medical expenses incurred in connection with the pregnancy and birth and any counseling services utilized by the birth mother. Texas Penal Code Ann. § 25.08 (West 2005).

Who may/must consent?	When can consent be obtained/ withdrawn?	What birth parent expenses are permissible?

Utah

The birth parents or the child-placing agency to which the child has been relinquished must consent to the adoption. A birth parent who is a minor has the legal power to consent. Consent is not required when parental rights have been terminated by a court. The biological father is not entitled to notice if the child was conceived as the result of any sexual offense. Utah Code Ann. §§ 78-30-4.14, 78-30-4.21, 78-30-4.17, 78-30-4.23 (2005).	The birth mother may execute consent commencing twenty-four (24) hours after the child's birth. The consent of any other person other than the birth mother may be made at any time, including prior to the child's birth. Consent is effective and irrevocable when signed. A review of Utah cases reveals that consent may be revoked in cases of fraud, duress, undue influence, or deception. Utah Code Ann. § 78-30-4.20 (2005).	Adoptive parents may pay a birth mother's actual and reasonable legal expenses; medical and hospital costs associated with pregnancy and birth; maternity expenses; and necessary living expenses. Utah Code Ann. § 78-7-203 (2005).

Who may/must consent?	When can consent be obtained/ withdrawn?	What birth parent expenses are permissible?

Vermont

The birth parents, the husband of the birth mother, if he was married to her at the time of conception or who has acknowledged paternity, and the agency that placed the child for adoption must consent. Consent is not required from a person who has relinquished parental rights to an agency, whose rights have been terminated by a court, or a man who denied paternity or fails to appear at proceedings. Vt. Stat. Ann. tit. 15A §§ 2-401, 2-402 (2005).	A birth mother may execute her consent thirty-six (36) hours after the birth. Consent by a guardian may be made at any time after being authorized by a court. Consent by an agency may be made at any time before or during the hearing on adoption. Consent is irrevocable after twenty-one (21) days or if the adoptive and birth parents mutually agree to revoke the consent. Consent may be set aside for fraud, duress, or other statutory conditions permitting revocation. Vt. Stat. Ann. tit. 15A §§ 2-404, 2-407, 2-408, 2-409 (2005).	Adoptive parents may pay a birth mother's medical, hospital, pharmaceutical, and nursing costs; counseling and living expenses; legal fees and court costs; and transportation and other expenses as approved by the court. Payment for living expenses may not continue for more than six (6) weeks after the birth of the child. Vt. Stat. Ann. tit. 15A § 7-103 (2005).

Who may/must consent?	When can consent be obtained/ withdrawn?	What birth parent expenses are permissible?

Virginia

The birth parents must consent to the adoption. An agency or other authorized person may also file a petition for adoption.

Consent is not required if parental rights have been terminated due to the failure of the parents to assume parental responsibilities, the child has been abandoned, there is continuing parental disability, the child has been abused by the parent, the parent relinquished custody when the child was seventy-two (72) hours old or younger, the parent caused the child to be conceived as the result of incest or sexual assault, the parent has been convicted of homicide or solicitation to commit homicide of the child's other parent.

Va. Code Ann. §§ 48.41, 48.42, 48.415 (Michie 2005).

A hearing may be held within thirty (30) days of the filing of a petition for voluntary termination of parental rights but not prior to the birth of the child.

Consent is generally irrevocable except that within one (1) year on petition, a consent may be revoked on the grounds of mistake, newly discovered evidence, fraud, misrepresentation, or misconduct.

Va. Stat. Ann. §§ 48.46, 806.07, 48.42 (2005).

Adoptive parents may pay a birth mother's expenses for pre- and postadoption counseling; maternity clothes; local transportation; medical, hospital, and legal fees; living expenses up to $1,000 when necessary to protect the health and welfare of mother and fetus; and birthing classes.

Adoptive parents may not pay for lost wages or living expenses while receiving medical care or any payments other than those specifically outlined by the statute.

Va. Stat. Ann. § 48.913 (2005).

Who may/must consent?	When can consent be obtained/ withdrawn?	What birth parent expenses are permissible?

Washington

The birth mother and any man she alleges is the birth father must consent to the adoption. The agency to which a child has been relinquished or a legal guardian of the child must consent to the adoption. Consent is not required when a parent's rights have been terminated in the child's best interest and due to failure to perform parental duties or when a parent is withholding consent contrary to the best interests of the child. Wash. Rev. Code §§ 26.33.080, 26.33.160, 26.33.120 (2005).	The parents' consent and petition may be filed prior to the child's birth, but the hearing cannot be held until forty-eight (48) hours after signing or the birth of the child and is approved of by a judge. Consent is revocable until approved by a judge. For one (1) year after consent has been approved, it may be revoked for fraud, duress, or lack of mental capacity. Wash. Rev. Code §§ 26.33.080, 26.33.090, 26.33.160 (2005).	Adoptive parents may pay a birth mother's prenatal, hospital, or medical expenses along with attorney's fees and court costs. Wash. Rev. Code § 9A.64.030 (2005).

Who may/must consent?	When can consent be obtained/ withdrawn?	What birth parent expenses are permissible?

West Virginia

The birth parents or agency having legal custody of the child must consent to the adoption. Consent is not required when parental rights have been terminated, a child was abandoned or permanently relinquished, or the parent is disabled or incurably insane. W. Va. Code §§ 48-22-301, 49-3-1, 48-22-301 (2006).	Consent may not be executed until seventy-two (72) hours after the baby is born. Consent is generally irrevocable unless it provides for conditional revocation if other required consents are not executed or by a showing that the consent was obtained by fraud or duress. The court will award custody based on the child's best interest. W. Va. Code §§ 48-22-303, 48-22-305 (2006).	Adoptive parents may pay a birth mother's reasonable and customary legal fees, medical and hospital expenses and expenses related to the pregnancy and adoption. W. Va. Code § 48-22-803 (2006).

Who may/must consent?	When can consent be obtained/ withdrawn?	What birth parent expenses are permissible?

Wisconsin

The birth parents or an agency or other authorized person must consent to the adoption. Consent is not required when parental rights have been terminated due to a failure by the birth parents to assume responsibility, the parent abandoned the child, the parent abused the child, the parent relinquished custody when the child was less than seventy-two (72) hours old, the parent caused the child to be conceived as a result of incest or sexual assault, the parent has been convicted of homicide or solicitation to commit homicide of the child's other parent. Wis. Stat. Ann. §§ 48.41, 48.42, 48.415 (2005).	A hearing is held within thirty (30) days of the filing of a petition for voluntary termination, but not prior to the birth of the child. Generally, consent is irrevocable. However, within one (1) year a petition to revoke the consent may be filed on the grounds of mistake, newly discovered evidence, fraud, misrepresentation, misconduct, or other grounds enumerated in § 806.07 of the statute. Wis. Stat. Ann. § 48.46 (2005).	Adoptive parents may pay a birth mother's expenses for pre- and postadoption counseling; maternity clothes; local transportation; medical, hospital, and legal fees; living expenses up to $1,000 when necessary to protect the health and welfare of mother and fetus; and birthing classes. Adoptive parents may not pay for lost wages or living expenses while receiving medical care or any payments other than those specifically outlined by the statute. Wis. Stat. Ann. § 48.913 (2005).

Who may/must consent?	When can consent be obtained/ withdrawn?	What birth parent expenses are permissible?

Wyoming

The birth parents or the head of the agency to which the child has been relinquished must consent to the adoption. Consent is not required if the parent fails to respond to notice; parental rights have been terminated; the parent has abandoned, abused or neglected the child; the child was conceived as the result of rape or incest for which the father was convicted; the parent fails to meet support obligations; or a putative father fails to acknowledge paternity. Wyo. Stat. Ann. §§ 1-22-109, 1-22-110 (2005).	Consent may be executed any time after the child's birth. Consent is irrevocable unless obtained under fraud or duress. Wyo. Stat. Ann. § 122-109 (2005).	Wyoming statutes do not address the issue of birth parent expenses.

GLOSSARY

I've put together this glossary in an effort to create order out of chaos (different terms are thrown around by different people in the adoption industry) and give you some sense of what *I* mean when *I* use particular words or phrases.

Agency-assisted adoption

A domestic adoption that is completely conducted by a licensed adoption agency (whether it be for-profit, nonprofit, or a state agency). The agency does everything, including locating the birth family, assisting in making the match between the birth and adoptive parents, providing all counseling and other support services (including providing whatever monetary assistance the agency may legally give) to the birth mother, and completing all legal services necessary to finalize the adoption.

Apostil

A seal from the secretary of state in the state in which you reside verifying that the seal of a notary public is valid and authentic.

Closed adoption

A domestic adoption in which the birth and forever families never meet or share any identifying information about each other. Often there is never any contact of any kind between the birth and forever parents. This type of adoption is becoming increasingly rare; twenty-five years ago this was the norm in adoptive relationships.

Completing an adoption versus finalizing an adoption

The difference between completing all the necessary and legal paperwork to receive placement of a baby in your home (like passing your home study and the birth family signing the necessary legal papers to relinquish its parental rights to the baby) and the state process by which a court of law determines that the baby who has been placed in your home is legally and forever yours. Finalization means just that; your adoption is final, and you can get a social security number for your baby. (Yes, you read that right—you cannot get a social security number for your child until your adoption has been finalized.) State law varies on relinquishment and consent laws (the Appendix outlines these state laws; your agency or attorney can help you navigate the more complicated areas or help answer any specific questions you may have) and how much time must pass before finalization can take place.

For example, in some states your birth mother may sign her relinquishment papers forty-eight hours after birth, but your adoption may not be finalized for another ten days. In others it may take as long as six months before it is finalized. In some states your adoption may be finalized as soon as the birth mother appears in court to relinquish her parental rights after the child's birth.

Consent to adoption versus revocation of consent

Every state in the United States has its own laws that pertain to who may consent to an adoption, when they can consent, and when they can revoke, or take back, that consent. The laws are overly complicated (in my humble legal opinion) and extremely varied. To super-oversimplify things, a birth mother/father can usually consent to an adoption within a period of hours or days after birth. A birth parent consents to the adoption by signing a legal document that relinquishes or surrenders (terms vary based on state law, but they both mean the same thing) his or her parental rights.

Sometimes a birth mother has to appear before a judge to relinquish her parental rights in person, but once the form has been filed or the birth mother has appeared in court, she cannot revoke, or take back, her consent to the adoption unless there is evidence of fraud or coercion.

If your birth mother is very young, her parents may also have to consent to the adoption. The birth father—if he is known—must also consent to the adoption, although many states permit him to consent before the baby is born. If he is known but cannot be located, there are ways that states require that he be given time to claim paternity and parental rights. Sometimes the birth mother will refuse to identify the birth father; state law varies on what you have to do when this happens, but in some states she may have to go before a judge and explain why she is refusing to identify the birth father.

Let me give you an example to help you wrap your brain around this incredibly complicated and über-important aspect of your adoption process. In an agency-assisted adoption in Texas, a birth mother may relinquish her parental rights forty-eight to seventy-two hours after the birth of the baby (depending on whether she received anesthesia during delivery). Once she has signed her relinquishment papers and they have been filed in court, she cannot revoke or take back her consent to the adoption unless she can prove that it was obtained through fraud, duress or undue influence.

Under Texas law the birth father may consent prior to the baby's birth by signing a form relinquishing his parental rights. If he refuses to sign the form, he is given thirty days after being served with the relinquishment/consent forms to contest the adoption. Once those thirty days have passed, if he has not taken steps to contest the adoption, his parental rights may be terminated by a judge.

Dossier

The papers that are put together and notarized, certified and/or apostilled in connection with an international adoption. These papers—your dossier—are sent to the country from which you seek to adopt to help it determine your fitness as a parent and help it make a match with a child for you.

Facilitators or adoption consultants

People who are not attorneys or employees of an adoption agency (although your facilitator might be a social worker and/or might be licensed by the state in which he or she works to act as a facilitator) who will help you locate a birth mother and will help you write your adoptive-parent profile and talk to birth mothers. These people are paid by you for their services.

Many states do not permit people to work with facilitators; you can find a breakdown of states that permit facilitators and those that do not in the Appendix. Please note that a clergy member, physician or other intermediary who helps you locate a birth mother without you paying him or her money is not a facilitator.

Home study

This is the annoying but necessary process by which you become licensed by the state in which you live to become a parent. A social worker comes to your home and interviews you about why you are choosing adoption, how you intend to parent and discipline (as if you could possibly understand how to discipline a tantruming three-year-old before you even have a baby!), how you intend to pay for everything, when and if you intend to return to work, what child-care plans you have made or are making (yes, they expect you to have a plan), and whether your family is supportive of your decision to adopt. This is just a brief summary—the highlights, so to speak—of what your social worker will be interested in (see chapter 3 for an in-depth discussion of the home study process).

The social worker will also look for fire extinguishers and smoke detectors, your effort to begin to baby-proof your home or knowledge of what you will need to do to baby-proof, and information regarding your mental and physical health. You also will be fingerprinted, and a criminal background check will be performed. (You might want to consider disclosing any arrests before someone is calling you at your agency's or attorney's office asking about that arrest for disorderly conduct when you were eighteen.) We talk about what might come up on a home study that might cause hiccups in your adoption process, or even completely stop it, in chapter 3.

Identified adoption

An adoption in which the adoptive parents and the birth family approach an adoption agency or attorney together to finalize the adoption. The adoptive parents have located the birth family using their own resources without the help of an agency, attorney or facilitator. In essence, the adoptive parents are bringing an *identified* birth mother/family to the agency or attorney for placement and/or finalization.

Independent adoption

An adoption in which you use an attorney to assist you with all aspects of the process, including assisting or advising you in how to locate a birth family, managing the process after you've located one and placing the baby in your home.

Indian Child Welfare Act (ICWA)

A federal statute that essentially provides that when a child of Native American heritage is being placed for adoption, that the tribe is to be given an opportunity to independently assess the adoption situation and determine whether the child can be adopted outside the tribe. Most states have comparable laws on adoptions of babies and children of Native American heritage that must be complied with as well.

If you are adopting a child who may be subject to ICWA, please consider consulting with an attorney specializing in this area of the law, as ICWA and all state laws pertaining to this type of adoption are extremely precise, often vary in requirement based on the tribe involved, and don't always mandate tribe approval.

Intermediary

A person who assists you with your adoption in a paid or unpaid capacity. Depending on state law this may be permissible or prohibited depending on the nature of the services provided, to whom they are provided, and the amount of money you pay. This term is often used interchangeably by adoption professionals with "facilitator."

I prefer to refer to use the term "intermediary" when discussing clergy or medical professionals who help you find a baby *without* requiring or asking for compensation. I use the term "facilitator" to describe licensed or unlicensed adoption professionals who charge money to help you find a baby. See chapter 4 for more discussion on facilitators.

Irrevocable

Consent to an adoption cannot ever be taken back (except under some states' laws upon a showing of fraud, duress or undue influence) once it has been deemed by the state to be binding. Some states provide that consent to an adoption becomes irrevocable immediately upon signing; others provide a waiting period of a few days or weeks during which time a birth mother may withdraw her consent for any reason.

Legal guardian

A person who can make legal and/or parental decisions for the baby or child being placed for adoption.

Match/matching

The stage at which you agree to work exclusively with one birth mother/family.

Notary public/notary/notarized

A notary public is an individual licensed by the state in which you reside to attest to the validity of a signature on a document. If you need to get a document notarized, you may take it to a notary at your local post office (or look in your phone book under "notary"; sometimes you can find one at a Federal Express office that is open late or a UPS store or even a local business like a real estate office) to have him or her witness your signature (you and your partner must sign the document in the presence of the notary), and then they will stamp the document, sign, and date it. *Please note that for certain documents in an international adoption, you may need to verify that the notary's license is good for one year past the date your document is notarized.*

Open adoption

One of the most confusing terms in domestic adoption, an open adoption involves the birth and adoptive parents meeting (usually before the baby's birth) and sharing personal information, including last names, phone numbers, addresses, and a desire and commitment to maintain an ongoing relationship.

The form that relationship takes varies widely. On one end of the spectrum there are adoptive and birth families that will visit frequently or at least regularly. At the other end of the spectrum are families that stay in close contact but perhaps don't visit as often, if at all.

The defining characteristic of an open adoption is that there is no secrecy; the birth families and adoptive families know where the other lives, and they can contact each other independent of an adoption agency or attorney by calling, writing or sending e-mail.

There is a commitment to be a part of one another's lives. One point I'd like to make about open adoption, as many people are absolutely terrified of open adoption when they don't know enough about it to really form an educated opinion—it is *not* coparenting. The adoptive parents are the legal, moral, everything, everyday, forever parents of the child! You can read more about open adoption in chapter 5.

Putative birth father

The man believed to be the child's biological father, but who, absent genetic evidence, cannot conclusively be determined to be the child's biological parent.

Putative birth father registry

A state database of the names and last known addresses of men believed to be specific children's birth fathers or men who believe they conceived children out of wedlock. Failure to register with such a registry after notice of a pending adoption can, in some states, result in the termination of parental rights.

Relinquishment or surrender

The term most often used to refer to the forms (paperwork) or process by which a birth parent gives up his or her parental rights. Each state has a different rule regarding when a birth mother and/or birth father may relinquish or surrender his or her parental rights.

Semi-open adoption

This is one of the most common forms of domestic adoption. In this type of adoption the birth and adoptive parents probably meet at some point, and at the very least they speak on the phone. They share first names and perhaps the state where they each live, but they do not share more information about themselves or commit to have an ongoing personal relationship.

Most often in a semi-open adoption, the adoptive parents agree to send, via a third party (the attorney or agency with whom they worked), cards and letters on a regular basis to keep the birth family aware of how the child is doing as he or she grows. The birth family may also send cards and letters. The attorney or agency takes care of forwarding the cards and letters to the appropriate parties, thereby maintaining privacy and anonymity.

Special-needs adoption

An adoption of a child who is facing either correctable or uncorrectable physical defects (for example, cleft palate, clubfoot, or deformed limbs), developmental delays from minor to severe, physical challenges (blindness, deafness or paralysis), or an older child who is deemed "difficult to place."

Transracial adoption

Either a domestic or an international adoption in which the adoptive parents adopt a child of a different ethnicity. If you're Caucasian and adopt a child of Hispanic or African heritage, you're entering into a transracial adoption (across racial lines). If you're Chinese American and adopt a child of Hispanic heritage from Guatemala, you're entering into a transracial adoption.

U.S. Citizenship and Immigration Services (USCIS)

Formerly Immigration and Naturalization Service (INS). This is the federal agency responsible for approving your initial application to become an international adoptive parent.

Waiting children

Children legally available for adoption through public agencies and the foster-care system.

INDEX

Elizabeth Swire Falker is a graduate of Wellesley College and the Benjamin N. Cardozo School of Law. She maintains a private law and consulting practice in the areas of infertility, reproductive, and adoption law (www.StorkLawyer.com). She is a professional member of RESOLVE, the AFA, and the prestigious American Society for Reproductive Medicine. She lives in Westchester County, New York, with her husband and their two children.

Sept. 5/07